NORFOLK IN THE
FIRST WORLD WAR

Bomb damage in King's Lynn, January 1915

NORFOLK IN THE FIRST WORLD WAR

Frank Meeres

 Phillimore

2004

Published by
PHILLIMORE & CO. LTD
Shopwyke Manor Barn, Chichester, West Sussex, England

ISBN 1 86077 290 0

Printed and bound in Great Britain by
MPG BOOKS
Bodmin, Cornwall

Contents

List of Illustrations

Frontispiece: Bomb damage in King's Lynn, January 1915

Acknowledgements

Many of the documents and illustrations used in this book are held at the Norfolk Record Office (NRO). I am grateful to the County Archivist, Dr John Alban, for permission to use documents in his care.

I am also grateful to those who have helped me in the preparation of this book. Irene Maclaughlin assisted with the illustrations; Katherine Adcock, Victoria Horth, Dylan Read and Hannah Verge offered suggestions on the text.

I have been privileged to be shown round battlefield sites on the Western Front by two experts. Paul Reed took me to some of the key sites of the Battle of the Somme and Jonathan Nicholls brought alive the Battle of Arras. Both men were inspiring teachers: thank you.

Frontispiece: Norfolk County Library and Information Service
1. NRO, Y/TC 90/47
2. NRO, MOT 111
4. NRO, MOT 111
5. NRO, SO 153/81
7. NRO, TD 2003/4
8. NRO, MC 365/104
9. NRO MC 2149/1
10. NRO, MC 2043/2/89
11. NRO, MC 2043/2/92
12. NRO, MC 2254/183
13. NRO, MC 1623/1
14. NRO, BR 209/13
15. NRO, MOT 111
16. NRO, MC 578/10
17. NRO, MC 578/10
18. NRO MC 2149/1
19. NRO, MC 497/6
20. NRO, MC 634/85
22. NRO, MC 634/86
23. NRO MC 2149/1
24. NRO MC 2149/1
25. NRO, MOT 111
26. Author's photograph
28. NRO, MC2043/37/1
29. NRO, MC 2043/37/1
30. NRO, SAH 340
31. NRO, MC 2254/183
32. NRO, MC 2254/183
33. NRO, MC 2254/183
34. NRO, MC 2254/183
35. NRO, MC 2149/1
36. NRO, MOT 111
37. NRO, MC 117/3
38. NRO, MC 2254/184
39. NRO, SO 153/81
40. NRO, MC 2254/93
41. NRO, PD 192/104
42. NRO, MC 578/8
43. NRO, TD 2003/4
44. NRO, MC 2254/97
45. NRO, MC 2254/183
46. NRO, MC 2254/183
47. NRO, MC 2254/38
48. NRO, NNH 64/15
49. NRO, NNH 64/15
50. NRO, PD 300/41
51. NRO, BR 209/13
52. NRO, MC 817/5
53. Author's photograph
56. NRO, BR 209/13
57. NRO, BR 209/13
58. NRO, MC 84/206/1
59. NRO, MC 84/206/30
60. NRO, MC 84/206
61. NRO, MC 84/206/46B
62. NRO, PD 300/41
63. NRO, PD 300/41
64. NRO, SAH 340
65. NRO, BUL 16/94
66. NRO, BUL 16/94
67. NRO, MC 2043/38/1
68. NRO, GUN 174
69. NRO, MC 1252/1
70. Author's photo
71. NRO, SO 153/81
72. NRO, MC 299/1
73. NRO, MC 2149/1
74. NRO, MC 634/68
75. NRO, PD 44/54
76. NRO, MC 1237
77. NRO, MC 1237
78. NRO, PD 445/35
79. NRO, MOT 111
80. NRO, MC 497/3
81. NRO, MC 497/3
82. NRO, MC 630/186/34
83. NRO, BR 209/13
84. NRO, FC 10/18
85. NRO, MC 2254/183
86. NRO, SAH 340
87. NRO, SAH 340
88. PD 207/52
89. NRO, MC 497/7
90. NRO, MC 2043/38/1
92. NRO, MC 630/15
93. NRO, MC 630/15
94. NRO, MC 31/45
95. NRO, MC 84/206/77
99. NRO, BUL 16/94/2/53
100. Norfolk County Library and Information Service
101. Norfolk County Library and Information Service
102. Author's photograph
103. NRO, BR 209/13
104. NRO, MC 947/1
105. NRO, MC 947/1
106. NRO, MC 643/7/4
107. NRO, MC 655/44
108. NRO, MC 655/44
109. NRO, MC 655/29
110. NRO, PD 199/33
111. NRO, N/LM 2/1
112. NRO, MC 304/22
113. NRO, MC 304/24
114. NRO, MC 1623/1/12/8
115. NRO, MC 1623/1/12/12
116. NRO, BR 209/13
117. NRO, MC 2019/27
118. NRO, MC 497/6
119. NRO, N/LM 2/7
120. NRO, MC 123
121. NRO, HMN 7/320
122. NRO, HMN 7/320
123. NRO, MC 166/165
124. Author's photograph
125. Author's photograph
126. NRO, PD 207/54
127. NRO, MC31/45
128. NRO, MC 31/14/21
129. NRO, PD 514/53
130. NRO, PD 553/34
131. NRO, DN/CON 187
132. NRO, PD 523/156
133. NRO, Y/TC 90/47
134. NRO, Y/TC 90/47
135. NRO, N/LM 2/2
136. Author's photograph
137. NRO, MC 578/10
138. NRO, MOT 111

One

To Go for a Soldier — or not?

Recruitment

The outbreak of the First World War on 4 August 1914 took most people by surprise. For all it was a dramatic event, for a few a supreme moment in life.

On 6 August, Colonel Alfred Robson hanged himself at his Gorleston home. He was 69 years old and had served in India. He left a note for the coroner – 'the strain of this terrible crisis is too much for me and I feel that I am too old in my 70th year to do anything for my country, and only make an additional mouth to feed. Therefore I had better go at once'.[1]

A much more typical response was that of Canon William Hay Aitken who was staying in Essex on 4 August 1914. He recorded in his diary – 'War! has begun today, a long line of destroyers left Harwich this morning, before night it was reported they had all been in action. I walked to Felixstowe in the afternoon but was stopped by a soldier at the bridge, tried the road but was stopped again. On returning we found that 10 men had been billeted upon us'.[2]

It is difficult to look back on the First World War without being influenced by the events of the Second. Everything that was so organised in 1939-45 was being tried out for the first time in 1914-18. The Government was much more reluctant to *force* people to do things than it was to be a generation later. It preferred to try to persuade people to make sacrifices in their lives, rather than compel them to do so. This applies especially to two key areas – conscription

1 *Supplement to* The War Illustrated, *showing relative strength of the combatants: note the small size of the British army at the outbreak of the war.*

2   *Men in civvies queuing to enlist.*

and rationing – where voluntary schemes were tried at first, before compulsion was eventually introduced.

Most countries had a conscript army, with all men serving their term as soldiers. In Britain the army was entirely voluntary. As soon as war broke out it was obvious that there needed to be a much larger army and advertisements were placed in the press and on billboards, such as the famous 'KITCHENER NEEDS YOU!' poster. Advertisements soon began appearing in the *Eastern Daily Press*:

Your King and Country Need You

A CALL TO ARMS

An addition of 100,000 men to his Majesty's Regular Army is immediately necessary in the present grave National Emergency.

Lord Kitchener is confident that this appeal will be at once responded to by all those who have the safety of our Empire at heart.

TERMS OF SERVICE

General service for a period of three years or until the war is concluded.

Age of Enlistment between 19 and 30.

HOW TO JOIN

Full information can be obtained at any Post Office in the Kingdom or at any Military depot.

GOD SAVE THE KING!

On 31 August another announcement said that a further 100,000 men were needed. The age of enlistment was now raised to 35, or 45 for ex-soldiers and up to 50 for ex-NCOs.[3]

Recruitment meetings were also held, attracting large crowds. A local newspaper described one such meeting, held in Norwich at the end of August:

> The Fiery Cross has been raised with a vengeance in East Anglia. Last night it was held aloft at St Andrew's Hall amid a scene of unparalleled enthusiasm. St Andrew's Hall! What more appropriate place in all England wherein to preach a crusade of righteous war? One cannot think of the noble chancel of the Blackfriars nearby without calling to mind the terrors of a bygone desolation in the Low Countries, whence a stricken people fled, even as some are fleeing now, to a shelter beneath the flag of English liberty.

About 4,000 people crammed the Hall to hear Ian Malcolm MP who had been sent by Kitchener to recruit men in East Anglia. The crowd spilled over into St Andrew's Plain, Princes Street, St Andrew's Hill and St George's Street.[4]

Although many thousands of men joined up in the first couple of months, still more men were needed and the advertising campaign continued. *The Eastern Daily Press* for 13 February 1915 included the following 'Public Notices':

Recruits Urgently Required
FOR THE UNDERMENTIONED REGIMENTS:
ROYAL WEST SURREY
ROYAL LANCASHIRE REGIMENT
NORTHUMBERLAND FUSILIERS
LIVERPOOL REGIMENT
WEST YORKSHIRE REGIMENT
LINCOLN REGIMENT
SOUTH WALES BORDERERS
EAST LANCASHIRE
WEST RIDING
ROYAL SUSSEX
SOUTH LANCASHIRE
SOUTH STAFFORDSHIRE
WELSH
LOYAL NORTH LANCASHIRE
MIDDLESEX
WILTSHIRE

The minimum height for which is reduced to five feet one inch, with standard of chest measurement not less than 33½ inches.
Applicants should apply to the undermentioned Recruiting Officers:-
BRITANNIA BARRACKS, NORWICH
ROYAL ARTILLERY BARRACKS, GREAT YARMOUTH
And Wroxham, Attleborough, King's Lynn, Cromer and all other important towns.

King's Own Royal Regiment
NORFOLK YEOMANRY
Recruits Wanted
OF GOOD CLASS WHO ARE
Willing to Serve Abroad

GOOD HORSEMEN PREFERRED
APPLY in Person or by Letter to -
Major C F GURNEY, Headquarters,
Cattle Market Street, Norwich

5th Batt. Norfolk Regiment
RECRUITS
Wanted for this Battalion
Intending recruits must be for FOREIGN SERVICE, height 5ft 4in., chest 34 in,
age 19 to 35 years.

For particulars apply
OFFICER COMMANDING DEPOT
5th Battalion Norfolk Regiment
East Dereham

Many young men volunteered in search of adventure and in the belief that the war would be a short one – 'all over by Christmas'. One concern was whether a man who volunteered would have a job to come back to. Local firms offered guarantees. As early as 12 August it was announced:

> It has been decided to keep open the places of all tramway operatives who have been called up for service, and pay 10s. a week in every case where a man has a wife and family, and in all other cases where a man may be considered the supper of the household.[5]

Colman's the mustard makers, a major employer in Norwich announced that they would pay five shillings a week to any married man who joined, with an extra shilling a week for each child. This, of course, was in addition to the pay the man would receive in the army and the separation allowance that the Government paid to the wives of soldiers. (The separation allowance is discussed in chapter five of this book). In addition the firm offered to pay the pension contributions of those who joined up, and also to find them jobs when they returned.[6]

One group of people who it was hoped would set an example were professional footballers. Here, too, the employers were supportive:

> Potter and Macdonald of the Norwich City Football Club have joined the Footballers' Battalion of the new Army. The players on Monday presented themselves at the Britannia Barracks and passed the medical examination, and are now awaiting their papers from the commanding officer. Their example is expected to be followed by other players. Members of the Football Battalion are guaranteed the necessary leave from military training to enable them to play for their club each Saturday. The Norwich City directors have promised to continue the wages of their players joining the new Army.[7]

The two men mentioned were to have very different futures. George MacDonald was born in Inverness in 1890. He played for Inverness Thistle and Tottenham before joining Norwich City in 1913. He was described as 'a quiet man, a strict teetotaller and non smoker'. It is not known if he survived the war: he never returned to professional football. Cecil Potter, the son of a Congregationalist Minister, played for Norwich City from 1911 to 1915. He worked in munitions during the war and later became manager of Norwich City. Other City players who contributed to the war effort included Harold Woods who did munitions work and then went to France with the Tank Corps, and John Allen, a local boy (born in King's Lynn), who worked in munitions. Frank Hill returned to his home town of Middlesbrough in order to enlist.

Professional football is a good example of how gradual was the drift into total war. In August 1914, the 1914-1915 season had just begun, and league and cup fixtures continued throughout the winter of 1914 and the spring of 1915. The last game played by Norwich

3   *Recruiting at Carrow gates.*

City was on 3 March 1915, in the FA Cup. After draws at Norwich and Bradford, the second replay was held at a neutral ground, at Lincoln. The official attendance was nil! This was because the FA did not want factory workers to stop doing war work in order to go to the match. They ordered that it should be played behind closed doors. However, a crowd gathered outside the gates and they were eventually let in for the second half: there were about a thousand of them. The game was 0-0 with 10 minutes left, but two late goals saw Bradford go through. This was to be the last formal game that City were to play for four years, although they did play friendly matches during the war. Because so many of the professional players were on war duties, these games gave several local men an opportunity they would never normally have had to play for Norwich City![8]

Signing Up

The first essential was to have a medical. There might be an element of laxity in this, especially later in the war when the army was increasingly desperate for men. Bill Carr gives an amusing description of his medical, admittedly in late 1918, but probably typical of many earlier experiences:

> it was very exciting in the medical: my hight[*sic*] was 5ft 8½ but ones chest mesurment has to be 35½ inches for boys of 5ft 8½. So when the doctor saw my chest was rather small he altared my hight to 5ft 7in so that my chest mesurment need only be 34½ in, but when he came to measure it he found it 34 however he put 34½ and passed me. But the Colonel saw him cheeting and mesared me himself and found it to be 34. Then a lot of other doctors crowded up and asked him to mesure it again and one of them pulled out the measure behind so that my chest seemed to be 34½. But the Colonel saw this man doing it too and got very angry with them all and swore that he would fail me. But he never saw that they had altered my hight, however they seem to have persuaded them to pass me after all.[9]

Malcolm Castle described how he joined the Royal Field Artillery the day after war was declared:

August 5: Wednesday. 9 am At Office as usual. Only stayed half an hour and then went to the Artillery Drill Hall to see Major Percy Wiltshire about taking a commission in the East Anglian Field Artillery. He gave me a note for Lieut-Col Le Mottee of Norwich. Home to get father's permission to go.

10 am. Leonard motored me to Norwich. Had to stop at Acle owing to a breakdown. After some trouble I found the colonel, who accepted me subject to the approval of the War Office. Examined by Dr R J Mills, who is just back from Germany.

1.50 pm. Lunch with Leonard at the Bell – near the Hill.

2.30 pm. Reported myself again at the Barracks, and then on to the Capital Counties Bank with Capt Harvey, the Adjutant, to see Sir Kenneth Kemp who handed me £600 in gold for Major Wiltshire. Called at Stones, Prince of Wales Road, to order my kit. Thunder and rain storm nearly all the way home. Delivered money to Maj Wiltshire & home to tea. To see Dr Ryley who signed my Magistrate's certificate – posted my application for commission. To Britannia Pier afterwards where I met Glad (she rang me up during the day & again at the time when I made this appointment) & stayed with her till 9 o'clock. She was awfully sweet – we made everything up again. Reported myself at Drill Hall and received note for fodder to Shreeve. Met Glad near the Pier and she walked down with me to deliver the note; & then on to Shipley's. Fortunately we had to wait there some time before the others turned up – had a lovely time. Got my bicycle & cycled down the road beside the trap. Glad was ripping & everything is perfect. Fine in morning, wet in afternoon & damp in evening. Joined 1st Norfolk Battery.[10]

Not everyone was so enthusiastic. K. Aston signed up as a private in the 8th Norfolks. He recalled: 'this Regiment seems to be composed of the riff-raff of England, mind you keen men as they show by their drilling, but they smell horribly some of them'.[11]

Records kept by a recruiting agent for the North Walsham area list the men coming him to volunteer – together with their subsequent fate. Typical entries read:

Date	Name and address	Regiment Height/Age	Result	Later career
Sept 4	William George Douglas, Dog Yard, Hall Lane	4th Norfolks 5ft 6½ 19.2	Accepted 6th Norfolks	Discharge under age Aug 1916. Called up June 1917 *Retd*
6th	William Sayer, Hall Lane	4th Norfolks 5ft 4½ 22.5	Accepted 4th Norfolks	*Killed*
6th	Raymond William Barker, Market Street	4th Norfolks 5ft 6 21.5	Accepted 4th Norfolks	Died of wounds Oct 1917
8th	Charles Arthur Catchpole, The Street, Knapton	EAFA 5ft 9½ 22.10	Accepted East Anglian Field Ambulance	Discharged 1917 M U [medically unfit]
8th	Frederick Charles Waterfield, Nelson Street	4th Norfolks 5ft 3 19.1	Only 16.1	

The 'age' shown in the third column is that claimed by the men themselves. A good many people lied. Fred Waterfield had claimed to be 19 years old: later examination showed that actually he was only just sixteen! William Douglas also claimed to be 19, and was enrolled as such, only to be discharged later when his real age was discovered.[12]

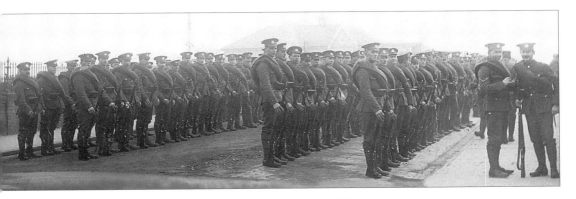

4   *4th Norfolks at Lowestoft, 1915.*

Many men who were too old to join the regular army formed a 'Dad's Army' force in Norfolk. The Volunteer Training Corps was established in Norwich in November 1914. By December there were almost 600 volunteers, all men over 38 years old. Other groups were established elsewhere in the county and they were soon amalgamated as the Norfolk Volunteers. 'In December 1915 the Volunteers were engaged in the 'Battle of Caistor'. They were divided into two 'armies', one of which tried to force the passage of the river Tas at Markshall while the other tried to defend it. It was a great fight, but the only casualty was a rabbit, which one of the attackers accidentally fell on and killed while coming through a plantation.'[13]

Training

Of course, all the new volunteers could not go over to France at once. First they had to be trained. Malcolm Castle describes his artillery training:

> August 8 Saturday. Up at 4.30 – to the Drill Hall and Stables. Home to breakfast – Glad called and left me some field glasses, she came into the study & we had a few minutes together. She was so sweet, the Darling. Back to Drill Hall & afterwards to Southtown station where we entrained the Battery. Father, Mother, Muriel & Iris came to see us off. Glad did not know what time we were going as I did not know till the middle of the morning. Ruddock, Miles & I went on the first train – left about 2. Reached Brentwood about 6.30. As we left the station a horse in one of the wagon teams went down and broke his leg. I galloped for a vet (Capt Tagg) who ordered the horse to be killed. Ruddock and I waited till this was done & then rode on to Cows Farm Doddinghurst, where A & B subsections are billeted. I rode on with some of the chargers – mine are a bay thoroughbred mare & an old chestnut mare both good – & found our Battery Headquarters – Park Barn. I got there at about 11 – & Wiltshire, Ruddock, Miles & Martin did not get there till about 1.30. It was a most awful place. Miles & Martin had to sleep on the floor as there were only two beds, both of which swarmed with fleas.

The Battery moved to Spixworth on 17 August:

> September 11 The Brigade began a period of six months training, doing about 12½ hours work a day – Gun Drill, Foot Drill etc.

5   *Ready for Anything: Boy Scouts in camp at Crown Point, outside Norwich, in the summer of 1914.*

October 9 To the Drayton-Attlebridge Road in the morning & came into action. The colonel turned up and, using the Battery Staff as a group of cavalry, charged the guns. Back about 3, and then to a Court Martial at St Faiths.

November 27. At St Faiths all day. In the afternoon Glad, Norah & Mr & Mrs Bellamy called on their way back from Cromer; they had a look round the horse lines although they only stayed a few minutes.

Turned out at about 10.30 and took part in a Brigade Night March to Drayton where we dug in over the Attlebridge Road, arriving there at about midnight. Had a little sleep on the box of a G S Wagon. Saturday: I acted as battery captain as usual. Fired a dozen rounds of blank at dawn, and returned to St Faith's about 10 o'clock. Slept most of the day.

Dec 25: Christmas Day: Kempson and I took Horse Exercise in the morning – went to Stratton Strawless and back. Went round the men's dinners and had lunch rather late. Very cold and frosty all day.[14]

6   *Royal Field Artillery in training at Carrow: the spire of Norwich cathedral can be seen in the distance.*

By November 1914 there were 20,000 men in training camps in Norfolk. They were housed in tents, but huts were about to be built. This was their first experience of the mud that was to be so characteristic of the Western Front:

The rains of the last few weeks have badly affected the long avenues between the tents and the approaches to the kitchens and stores, where the traffic is necessarily tremendous, but the recruits have become used to their underfoot conditions. The men in parts of the camp where the ground is really bad have adopted a skating movement for walking.[15]

A great concentration of troops in one area upset the routine of everyone in the locality. Aitken wrote of a preaching visit to Exeter in 1915 – 'there is no doubt that the presence of a large number of soldiers in the city is a great obstacle to such an effort – the elder women are kept busy by their billets and the younger by their flirtations'.[16]

The 7th Norfolks were in training at Shorncliffe in Kent. Lance-Corporal G. Morrison wrote to his friend William Carr:

> I thought you might like to know how the Norfolk lads are getting on here, so I am sending you a few lines.
> The 7th Service Battalion are training here, and we shall be the first lot to go to the front. There are a tremendous lot of soldiers training here – Norfolks, Suffolks, Kent, Northants & others, several thousand in all. The work is very hard, but we have all come into it with a good heart. The drill and

7   *A Family Man: Andrew Campbell, of the Royal Flying Corps, with his wife and children.*

> company training is very interesting, and it is amazing the amount the men have learned in such a short time. We expect to go abroad about the end of December.
> I myself have been trusted to the delicate task of training raw recruits, and I am doing my best to train them quickly, & make their work interesting … The company is composed of several intelligent young men, & they are all 'good fellows' & very anxious to help in the firing line.
> If I can see my way, I think I shall apply for a Commission. I have done well in my present rank, & I think I could get one. Our captain is Captain Otter from Norfolk, I suppose you don't know him?[17]

Aston was also at Shorncliffe. He wrote home: 'they are working us like the Devil and a lot of chaps are cracking up owing I think chiefly to rations not being of the best'. He then described the daily routine:

> Reveille goes at 3.30 am, then we have squad drill until about 5.30, then we have a ten minute break. After that we march three miles down to the sea and bathe, come back and have about half an hour for breakfast, and then parade again until 12.30, then one hour for lunch and drill again until 4.30 when we stop for the day and clean up … We are allowed out from 7 to 9.30 when all lights have to be put out.[18]

8 *Troops in Blackfriars Hall, Norwich in the early days of the Great War.*

Arthur Neville-Rolfe was in India when the war broke out. He and his Indian troops arrived in France in the winter of 1914, and they were quickly introduced to the techniques of the new way of war:

On arrival I was appointed battalion bombing officer and together with six Gurkhas was sent to learn the tricks. The only bombs then in use were the 'jampot' and 'hair-brush' varieties'. The first was a tin jampot filled with slugs and high explosive, the second an enlarged lady's hair-brush with a slab of gun-cotton in place of the bristles. Both were detonated by a length of fuse which the thrower could cut to any length required. If he cut it too short the bomb exploded before it reached the German trench and if too long it was returned pretty quickly. All very tricky but after an hour's instructions we were all considered to be bomb experts.

By the autumn of 1915 work in trench conditions had become part of the training process in England: a soldier in training at Sustead Camp wrote to a friend on 15 October 1915: 'I am sorry to hear your cold is no better. I can really sympathise, having one myself. Guess how I caught mine, I got dreadfully hot yesterday – trenching – & then lying about.'[19]

As in all wars, many accidents, some of them fatal, inevitably occurred during training. In July 1916, John Meadows, a 17-year-old driver in the Army Service Corps, was drowned at Wroxham Bridge. He was trying to water the two horses in his care when the current carried them away: a crowd watched in horror from the bridge as both horses and the man were drowned. Meadows' parents lived at Carlton Colville: he is buried in Lowestoft cemetery. In the following summer Private Cecil Boast was training with the Middlesex in Suffolk, using grenades in mock trenches. There was an accident – Boast was killed and four other men seriously injured. Boast was a married man, aged 29, and lived at Swansea Road in Norwich.[20]

Not all men were heroes, of course. The local newspapers quite often contain references to men who have deserted, much easier to do while in England rather than on active service in France. In 1916 William Hold (27) and Thomas Watson (23) were charged with breaking into houses in Hainford and Coltishall and stealing

9 *Norfolks at 'big gun practice', Mesopotamia.*

clothes and money. They were deserters from the Royal Field Artillery, being held under open arrest in Norwich. They broke out of barracks and fled, still in army clothes. They reached Hainford where they broke in to the house of George Moore and swapped their military clothes for civilian ones. They went on to Coltishall where they broke in to the vicarage, 'ransacking room after room'. They appear to have been back at the barracks when they were arrested: they were each sentenced to six months' imprisonment with hard labour.[21]

Many of the volunteers were very young and most were going abroad for the first time. They were given a booklet of advice, *The Health Memoranda for Soldiers.* The advice given included the following:

Cleanliness

In old times the teaching of cleanliness was a part of religion, and this is still the case among Eastern peoples. The daily bath is a luxury enjoyed by the well-to-do class.

Dirt does not exist in nature; matter only becomes dirt when it is in the wrong place. Sand on the shore is clean and in its proper place, but the sand in the mechanism of your rifle becomes dirt, and must be removed.

The refuse and waste that accumulate about men and their dwellings is the most dangerous form of dirt, and is the main cause of preventable disease.

What shall we drink

All alcoholic drinks are likely, when taken in excess, to do harm to both body and mind. The safest and best within your reach are light ale and porter. In strict moderation, and if you take hard out-of-door exercise, they will not hurt you. It is wise to take them with, or after, meals.

10 *In Training: Holt Park Camp, 1915. Note the enormous number of horses: although cavalry was not a key factor in the war, horses still played a vital role.*

Spirits of any kind are without doubt harmful, and are better avoided altogether. In conclusion, it is a common error to suppose that intoxicating drinks are necessary for healthy men; in most cases men are better without them, and in all cases they ought to be used with caution and never abused.

The Question of Chastity
For your own sakes be chaste, in order to avoid the risks of disease spread by infected persons.
Self-control in this respect may seem to you out of harmony with nature, but for all that it must be practised.

On Active Service
On active service the health and comfort of troops are even more important than during times of peace.
The chief danger is not from the enemy, but from disease bred in one's own camp.
The great danger to an army in the field is bad sanitary arrangements.
The most serious diseases that arise from sanitary neglect are entiritic fever and dysentery, these spread from infected water and neglected dirty latrines.

Water – Soldiers should train themselves to drink in great moderation when undergoing exertion. Drinking requires thought. Men rush at water and drink more than is necessary. Great restraint should be taught and practised even in drinking good water; it should be remembered that very little is required during a march, especially early in the day, just enough to moisten the mouth and a little to swallow will be sufficient. The more you drink, the fuller you feel, the more you will want, and the more you will sweat. Your bottleful of good water or of cold

11   *The Cookhouse at Holt Park Camp.*

tea should carry you through your day's march. A trainer or sportsman will tell you the same.

Only use water that has been passed as good.

If you must use bad water boil it before using, or still better, make it into weak tea, without milk: it can then be drunk hot or cold.

Remember that enteritic fever, cholera, and other diseases are spread by drinking water infected by the germs of the disease.

Latrines – These are the factories where the poisons of enteritic fever and dysentery are manufactured. The infection soaks into, or is washed into the water supply, or dries and is blown about as dust, or it may be conveyed by flies. [This was known in very early times, and rules were framed to prevent disease from spreading in camps. Moses, an able leader sanitary officer, who received his training in Egypt, ordered that each man should carry a small spade on the hilt of his spear, so as to dig and cover up when he went abroad to relieve himself, and this is still the best way of managing: everything passed should be covered up *at once.*][22]

Conscription – and Conscientious Objection

More than five million men served in the British Army at some time in the war. Half of them volunteered, but the other half were forced to join up – they were *conscripts*.

It soon became apparent that the British Army was too small to play its full part in the war, despite the many thousands of volunteers who joined it. As early as 5 January 1915, Leigh Barratt of Brundall had a letter published in the *Eastern Daily*

Press: 'it is becoming every day more increasingly apparent that numbers and numbers far in excess of anything previously imagined will be required to crush the German military power'. B. Knyvett Wilson replied on the following day: 'Lord Kitchener's last word in the House was that he was satisfied with the way in which recruits were coming in, and we may well all wait until he expresses a contrary feeling. It is absolutely no use having a quantity of recruits without arms, ammunition and equipment ready for them, and *officers to drill them*'.

As the slaughter at the front continued through 1915, it was obvious that the number of men volunteering to join the army was not enough to replace the losses, and people thought more and more about introducing conscription, as in the countries on the Continent. This had never been done in Britain before and a curious compromise – 'attestation' – was tried first. It was decided that single men ought to join up before married men were called upon. Both groups were invited to attest to their willingness to serve. In practice about half the men in each group did so, and the failure of so many single men to attest was used as a reason to introduce conscription.

The Military Service Act of January 1916 conscripted all *single* men and childless widows who were between the ages of 18 and 41. A second Act, which was passed in May 1916,

12   *Testing parachute harness, Pulham.*

extended conscription to *all* men between 18 and 41. A further Act in 1918 extended the upper age limit to 50, with the power to raise it to 56 if the need arose.

This was not as straightforward as it sounds. Men had the right to appeal against being called up, and their cases were heard by local Military Service Tribunals. The Norwich Tribunal was made up of ten men, chosen by the City Council. In November 1915, the Council had been asked to set up a Committee to act as a local tribunal relative to the *starring* of men for enlistment, that is, deciding which men were in essential civilian occupations. They were recommended to choose five people, but in fact they chose eight:

Alderman Ernest Blyth, a solicitor.
Alderman George Henry Morse, beer-brewer.
Alderman James Porter, a timber merchant.
Councillor Richard Winsor Bishop, a jeweller.
Councillor Frederick Bassingthwaite, baker and grocer.

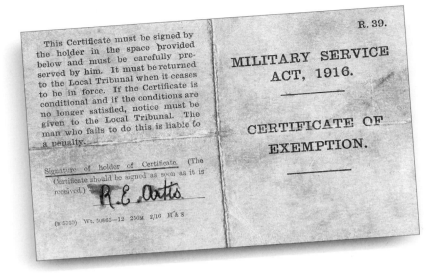

This Certificate must be signed by the holder in the space provided below and must be carefully preserved by him. It must be returned to the Local Tribunal when it ceases to be in force. If the Certificate is conditional and if the conditions are no longer satisfied, notice must be given to the Local Tribunal. The man who fails to do this is liable to a penalty.

Signature of holder of Certificate. (The Certificate should be signed as soon as it is received.) R. E. Artis

(B 5759)   Wt. 50865—12 250M 2/16 H & S

R. 39.

MILITARY SERVICE ACT, 1916.

CERTIFICATE OF EXEMPTION.

13 Certificate of Exemption. The treatment of conscientious objectors during the war is still a topic of much controversy.

Dr John Gordon-Munn, doctor of medicine, and working at Heigham Hall Asylum.
Edmund Reeve, a solicitor.
Alfred Walker, a printer and President of the local branch of the Typographical Association.

Two councillors, Mr Howes and Mr Crotch, wanted Herbert Witard on the Committee either as an extra member or instead of Walker, but they received no support and the eight men were decided upon by a vote of 36-2. This is interesting, as we shall see that Witard was the leading opponent of the war in Norwich!

On 1 February 1916 the Council met to appoint a local Tribunal under the Military Service Act of 1916. The Tribunal was to include 'representatives of labour', who could best decide whether men could be spared for the Army. The Council decided to appoint the same men and add two names:

James Mason, secretary to the Sick Benefit Branch of the Boot and Shoe Operatives Union (local branch).
Frederick Crotch, councillor and managing director of Crotch and Norwich Bill Posting Company.

Walker, Mason and Crotch were chosen as 'representatives of Labour within the district'. Some councillors wanted to delay choosing these representatives until local labour bodies had been consulted, but this proposal was defeated by 22 votes to eight. Similar Tribunals were set up throughout the county at the beginning of 1916.[23]

A very large number of Norfolk men came before these tribunals appealing against their call up into the Army. The hearings often fill a whole page of the local newspaper. Here we consider, as an example, the cases held on 8 March 1916 at the various Tribunals around the county.

At **Yarmouth**, an argument among the Tribunal members revealed the ambiguities involved in their function. One member, Mr Stanford, said that it should be understood that the Tribunal was not a recruiting agent. He had heard a member say to a man 'You are just the man we want'. Another member, Mr Ward, said that he had made the remark about a man who had come before the Tribunal wanting to go into the Red Cross: he was a 'powerful man' and Ward had thought he would be ideal for the job.

Another Tribunal member, Mr Goode, said that the Tribunal sat in the national interest to see that only those who had a right should be exempted. They were not there to help people escape military service unless they proved their right and title to exemption. The Tribunal had not to assist men to get exemption, but to assist the nation to get such men as were necessary. The Mayor of Yarmouth acted as President of the Tribunal. He pointed out that they were a judicial body, which had certain instructions from the Government as to the lines on which they should act. They must judge on the facts before them whether applicants were entitled to exemption or not. They must consider the national point of view. There was a great need for every man who could be spared unless they were absolutely satisfied upon the facts a man was entitled to exemption.

Having sorted our their principles, the Tribunal went on to deal with particular cases: the *EDP* reported five cases heard on that day. A seed and corn merchant aged 23 had his enlistment postponed for two months but a fish-curer, aged 24, who worked as a curer and a cooper had his claim disallowed. The Tribunal said that an older man could do the work.

A carter who had joined the Yeomanry for home service, and had since left, asked to be exempted for three months to help his father in the herring trade. Major Thornhill, for the Army, said that he could not go back to his regiment after three months' absence. The father said that he needed his son to help him as he himself 'could not now lift a pail of water'. However, Mr Ward had personal knowledge of the family, and thought the father was not so sick as he claimed — he had 'seen him raising the whip'.

One 20-year-old man said that 'as a consecrated follower of Jesus Christ he could only do His will; His thinking was contrary to warfare; His word was that a servant of the Lord must not strike, but be gentle to all men; he must obey God rather than man, and he had purposed in his heart, with God's help to stand out regardless of consequences'. His father also applied to the court, saying that his son was indispensable, and he also said that he supplied fish to the military. Asked when he had cured fish last the claimant said on the previous night. In reply to a question from Mr Ward, he said that he belonged to the Society of Friends Non-Conscription Fellowship.

For how long?
  Since January.
After you found you had got a conscience?
  No. I have been engaged in evangelistic work for four years.

The claim was disallowed, but this was not the end of the case. We shall return to this man's story.

At the same Tribunal, a Yarmouth Corporation tram conductor, aged 38, said that he was the only son of his widowed mother, who was dependent upon him for support, and for company and advice. He had been to Norwich and was passed for home service. Last April, when he offered to enlist, he was rejected, the muscles of one arm being wasted, and his vision below normal. The officer at the barracks told him he did not think he could do any good by appealing. Mr Ward said to him: 'you came to the Tribunal for your answer. Everyone has a right to appeal. Thank God this is not a conscript country yet, not quite'. The man was exempted for six months.

At the **Norwich** Tribunal, nine cases were reported in the press, including one man who said that he was a conscientious objector. However he had already attested and therefore received short thrift. He was a Post Office worker and said that he objected on religious grounds. He produced a letter that he had received from his Member of Parliament. The Chairman retorted: 'we are not here to read letters and cannot deal with your objection, as you are an already attested man'. Exemption was refused.

A more frivolous claimant was an export packer who said that he had only been married three weeks and wanted more time with his wife. He did not appear in court and his claim was refused. A fruit and vegetable merchant said that his man was a worker in an essential trade, and that it would be impossible to find an honest man to replace him. It was suggested that he find an honest woman instead, but it was agreed that for the present the man should be regarded as in an essential occupation. A mother who already had one son in France said that if her second son had to go too 'it would mean breaking up the home as she could not keep going on the separation allowance'. The Chairman responded: 'we recognise it is a hard case but you must blame the Kaiser not us'.

At the same Tribunal 'a considerable number of claims were made by men already serving in the Army. These were men who had joined up as Territorials before the war, but to do home service only. Some of them were exempted from foreign service, but the majority were refused.'

There were about 30 claims for exemption at the **North Walsham** Tribunal held on the same day. They included a threshing-drum feeder who said he was the sole supporter of his widowed mother, and also that he was in a certified occupation. He was unmarried. His employer said that the man was indispensable, but Captain Blofeld for the Army retorted: 'are you going to help that man when men are going out leaving three or four little children? It is a question of single men. Are you going to make widows and orphans?' Exemption was granted for two months.

A barman and cellarman aged 40 asked for exemption as he was looking after his crippled mother. He had three brothers, all serving. Blofeld suggested that he be exempted for two months: he would then be over age. The Tribunal agreed.

A farmer applied for exemption for his farmhands. They included a man and his two unmarried sons and another man with an unmarried son. Blofeld returned to his theme: 'here was a man with three single sons, not one of whom was fighting for his country. People who had lost their only sons naturally grumbled, and the authorities looked to farmers to help them out by sparing men'. Four weeks' exemption was granted so that it could be sorted out which of the unmarried men should go.

At the **East Dereham** Tribunal, the cases included that of a young man who said that he supported his widowed mother and that he had three brothers: one had been missing from the Norfolks in France since last August, the second had been discharged from the navy with wrecked nerves. The third brother was a married man in Yorkshire.

Mr Bradley said that this seemed to be one of the cases in which Mr Long had suggested that exemption should be granted. (Walter Long was President of the Local Government Board.) However, the Clerk said that Mr Long's suggestion only dealt with the case of a widow with just one surviving son. The Chairman told the applicant that it was a hard case, but that he could not be exempt. However a woman claiming exemption for her 18-year-old son was allowed her claim: she had lost her husband in an accident in 1912 and she had five other children to look after, all under 14 years of age.

Cases at the **Wayland** Tribunal on the same day included one brought by a master baker. He claimed that his man was in an essential occupation. The reporter here had none of the scruples we saw at the Yarmouth Tribunal: he describes the Army representative simply as 'the recruiting officer'. This officer said that the man was a roundsman rather than a baker, and that the master baker employed other men in another

14   *'Exemption', drawn by a patient at Sheringham Hospital.*

business of his: they could do the deliveries. The Tribunal agreed: the man must join up.

Also at the Wayland Tribunal, a farmer claimed exemption for his son who he said was the farm milkman, and did other farm work. The 'recruiting officer' said that the farmer had other employees who could do the work, and that a milkman could do the milking. Postponement was granted to 30 April, with no further appeal.

As we can see from this sample day, most cases involved claims that the individual should be exempted as he was needed at home, either because he was in essential work, or because he was looking after dependants who would become a burden on the state if he was called up. However, there were also several *conscientious objectors* — a new term in the Act, describing those whose conscience would not allow them to serve in the Army.

The Tribunal at Norwich in April 1916 heard a whole raft of cases involving such conscientious objectors. One case, that of a Norwich school teacher, gave rise to a classic confrontation of opinions:

Lieut Costello (for the Army): Do you suggest that if the Germans came here
    they ought not to be opposed?
Appellant: I suggest that the alternative is that peace should be made and then
    there would be no prospect of their coming.

Costello: Suppose the Germans land tonight, before peace can be made, are they to be allowed to march to Norwich and do as they please?

Appellant: From my point of view, yes.

Costello: Whatever they do? No one is to defend the women and children?

Appellant: I suggest you can oppose them best by not opposing them.

Costello: You suggest that if we all sat down with folded arms they would not interfere with the women and children?

Appellant: I do.

Another man took an even more extreme view. He was an International Socialist and said he had no patriotic feelings whatever: 'he believed the country would be just as well under the Germans as now'.

Almost all these men were told they had to do non-combatant service. (One man's appeal was disallowed as it was felt he was being frivolous.) Presumably most of them accepted this decision, as we hear no more of them. However two brothers, John and Ernest Cornwell, of Spencer Street, Norwich would not agree to do this. They came before the bench on 3 June. John, a cabinet maker, had been arrested at his place of work in Peacock Street by PC John Alcock. He had been told to report to Britannia Barracks by 30 May: asked by Alcock why he had not done so, John said 'as a conscientious objector I am not liable to military service. I did not take the oath'. The court said that he would be fined 40 shillings, or do 13 days in gaol before being handed over to the authorities. He refused to pay, but was not in fact sent to prison, being instead handed straight over to the military.

Ernest, a silk weaver, followed him in court. The case was the same but Ernest was more aggressive saying, 'I am not going to be dictated to by a gang of capitalists'. He, too, was fined 40 shillings and handed over to the military.

Their later treatment led to a question being raised in Parliament by the anti-war Labour MP, Philip Snowden. He said that the military authorities had sent them to Falmer Camp. They were attached to the 9th Royal West Surrey Regiment and sentenced to 28 days in Lewes Gaol. This being found illegal, they were sentenced to 12 months' hard labour, later reduced to 112 days. Meanwhile the Norwich Tribunal heard their cases on 7 July. They granted them exemption, but did not send off the certificates of exemption until 18 July. By then, they had now been in prison for six weeks.[24]

The Cornwells were not the only Norwich brothers ready to suffer imprisonment rather than serve in even a non-combatant role. Two brothers, one a tailor, one a compositor, failed to answer to their names at the Norwich Tribunal in June 1916. A friend explained that they had been convicted by court-martial and were undergoing four months' imprisonment with hard labour. Their names were not given but in fact they were Archie Hobart, aged 21, and his 19-year-old brother Cecil, both of Romany Road. On 9 June both men, together with a 20-year-old schoolteacher, Arthur Magg of Knowsley Road, had come before Norwich magistrates charged with failing to report to Britannia Barracks after they had been called up. All three said that they were Conscientious Objectors, and were handed over to the military authorities. Three days later, seven more Conscientious Objectors met the same fate.[25]

Another man, an 18-year-old, appeared before the Tribunal in June 1916. He said that he objected to military service: 'I believe in the brotherhood of man and I think we ought to get the best out of the world instead of taking one another's lives.' The tribunal suggested he join the Royal Army Medical Corps, but he declined, saying that they carried guns. The Tribunal said that this was not the case, but suggested the Non Combatant Corps instead. The man said that he was already trying for this and he was formally relegated to non-combatant service.

At the Yarmouth Tribunal held on 14 July, six people claimed that they had grounds of conscience for exemption from military service. The first man refused to do military service but declared his willingness to do non-combatant work – 'I don't want to leave the [church] work I am doing in Yarmouth, but, if I am wanted, send me to the front as a stretcher-bearer. I don't want to be kept in England peeling potatoes or work of that sort if I can really be of any use'. The Tribunal was pleased – 'That is the right spirit. We will see to that' – however, it was pointed out that the man's health was so poor he would not actually have been called up in any case.[26]

The other five men were all members of 'a religious sect meeting in Fish Street'. They asserted that military service was contrary to the teaching of Christ as they understood it. The Tribunal allowed the claim in the case of four of the men, but disallowed the claim of the fifth man – a ships' smith named Tidman, as they did not accept that his claim was sincere; Tidman was a former Territorial who had had a previous claim dismissed.

It is clear from these examples that conscientious objectors were not shot, or even imprisoned, as a general rule. If they agreed to serve in a non-fighting role, their claim was allowed. The Non Combatant Corps was set up in March 1916 specifically for them. The men in this corps were equipped and trained just like other members of the infantry, but never armed. They were also trained in field engineering. They could be – and were – sent abroad, but were not sent into the front line. They were thus less likely to be killed in action than other troops, but some did die, either from shellfire, in accidents, or from illness. Private Herbert Laight, of the Eastern Counties Non-Combatant Corps is one example: he died at Etaples Army Hospital on 27 November 1918. He is commemorated on war memorials at both Acle and Norwich: he was the son of the Acle postmaster and was working in the Norwich Post Office when he was called up.

The number of cases heard by the various Norfolk Tribunals must have run into many thousands in the three years after conscription was introduced. The Norwich Tribunal alone met 154 times between January 1916 and November 1918. They made a total of 9,090 decisions, issuing certificates of exemption to 5,028 men. In 790 cases, there was an appeal to the Norfolk Appeals Tribunal. Of these appeals, 133 were by the Military authorities claiming that the Tribunal had exempted men they thought should join up, the other 657 were by men, or their employees, resisting the Tribunal's decision that they should be called up.[27]

There was, in fact, a three-stage system. If either side was not satisfied with the decision of the local tribunal, there was the possibility of an appeal to the Norfolk Tribunal, and beyond that to the Central Tribunal. The process can be seen in the case of a 27-year-old market gardener. The local tribunal said he must serve, so he appealed to the Norfolk Tribunal. They granted him conditional exemption. The Military authorities insisted that the case be re-considered. He came up before the Tribunal once more: he was told he would have to serve in four weeks' time. Mr Daynes, who appeared on the man's behalf, said that he would appeal to the Central Tribunal.[28]

The Norfolk Appeals Tribunal was held at Shire Hall in Norwich: part of this building is now the Norfolk Regimental Museum. George Edwards, the Norfolk leader of the farm workers' union, was the labour representative on the Tribunal. At one session he became embroiled in a row with the authorities. Lieutenant Costello, the army representative, told a 20-year-old man who said that he was a conscientious objector: 'you have not done anything for your country' and the Chairman, Lord Kimberley, accused him of being 'simply a coward'. Edwards leapt to the man's defence: 'conscientious objectors are not here to be bullied, Lieutenant Costello, and I do not think you are respectful. I am not going to sit here and see this man bullied, and [I] protest straight away. If I cannot do that I'll resign from this Board (Applause).' Kimberley denied that the man was being bullied and ordered him to do non-combatant service.[29]

Newspaper reports of Tribunal cases do not name the individuals involved. However we do know the name of the 20-year-old conscientious objector who had come before the Yarmouth tribunal in March. He was Robert Artis and his family papers give details of the Tribunal process, and also of the Appeals process that could follow it. Artis lived at England's Lane in Gorleston. In February 1916 he received a *Notice of Hearing*, a standard printed letter which reads:

> Notice is hereby given that the case of which particulars are stated below will be considered at the place and on the date indicated. You may appear in person or may submit a written statement provided that it is received by the Tribunal at least two days before that on which the case is to be presented.

Artis was summoned to appear at Yarmouth Town Hall at 3.30 pm on Wednesday 8 March. As we have seen, the Yarmouth Tribunal rejected his claim. Artis then appealed to higher authority, the Norfolk Appeals Tribunal. They issued a *Notice of Decision* on 19 April 1916. This states that the appeal had been considered by the Tribunal: they had decided that Artis was to be exempted from the provisions of the Military Service Act of 1916. 'The exemption is for Combatant Service only.' So Artis was still to be called up, but would not actually have to fight.

The next document shows that Artis, or his father, tried to appeal further, but was not able to do so. Dated 18 May 1916, it read simply

> Sir, re Robert Edmund Artis
> I have to inform you that the Norfolk Appeal Tribunal have REFUSED leave to appeal to the Central Tribunal in this matter.

Even before this second appeal, Artis had been issued with his Certificate of Exemption. This was dated 4 May 1916 and reads:

> This is to certify that:-
> Name (in full)   *Robert Edmund Artis*
> Address (in full)   *5, England's Lane, Gorleston*
> Age   *20*
> Occupation, profession or business   *Fish Smoker and Curer*
> Is exempted from the provisions of the Military Service Act, 1916

> This exemption is (state whether the exemption is absolute, conditional (in which case the conditions should be stated) or temporary (in which case the period of time should be stated).

If the exemption is granted on conscientious grounds and is from combatant service only this should be stated

From Combatant Service only

The ground on which the exemption is granted is

By Order of Court of Appeal [30]

By the summer of 1916 the authorities were more tolerant of conscientious objectors, provided they were prepared to do *something*. Men were no longer handed over to the military authorities, but dealt with by the police. They were not to be kept in military custody but handed over to civilian prisons. Prison life was tough in the early twentieth century, however: a number of the conscientious objectors held in prison actually died from their treatment.

In the summer of 1916, the Pelham Committee was set up: this could find work of national importance for men unwilling to serve under any form of military discipline. One Norfolk example is that of a piano teacher who came before a Tribunal in June. He said that 'he was ready to do work of national importance under civil control. His objection to warfare was based upon religious and moral grounds. He could not accept any work under military control and he was fully prepared to accept the consequences of taking up this attitude'. He was placed under the Pelham Committee.

Other people came under the Brace Committee scheme which created work camps for the conscientious objector – there was one near Thetford, whose inhabitants were sent out to cut down trees in Thetford Forest.[31]

Faced with call-up, the usual response was either to accept and go to the Barracks, or to appeal to a Tribunal for temporary or permanent exemption. Another possible response was simply to do nothing, to carry on working and hope that the authorities did not catch up with you. However, they almost always did. George Forster (22), a single man living in Wroxham Road, Sprowston, was charged in July 1916 with failing to report himself under the Military Services Act. Forster claimed that he was a conscientious objector, willing to do work of national importance but not military service. He had applied for a variation of a provisional certificate granting him non-combatant service, but had not yet had a reply. However Captain Blofeld produced legal proof that the army had the power to call up anyone allocated to non-combatant service while their appeal for variation was pending. In view of this the magistrate fined Forster £2 and ordered him to be handed over to the military authorities.[32]

Two similar cases came before the Cromer Tribunal on 8 May. Samuel Grout had been arrested that morning at his home in Plumstead. He had appealed to the local Tribunal for an exemption, but this had been turned down. So he had just carried on at work, even though the local police called on him twice and told him he had to report to the Barracks. In court, Grout said simply that he had his work to attend to. Geoffrey Gotts, a farm labourer of Trimingham, had also been called upon twice by the police and told to go to the Barracks. He just said 'I consider I am doing what I can for my country'. Unlike Grout he had not even tried to get an exemption. When asked in court why not, he said 'I have been hard at work'. The men were each fined £3 and handed over to the military authorities.[33]

A further, drastic, response to the threat of being called up was self-mutilation. William Copsey, a 36-year-old labourer from Holme Hale, was charged in July 1917 with deliberately maiming himself in order to avoid being called up. Captain Willoughby said that the accused was a member of the Reserve forces. He produced the military papers relating to his attestation. Notice was sent to Copsey to join up on 31 May. On that date, Willoughby received a letter from Copsey saying that he was sorry to say that he had met with an accident, and would not be well enough to attend at Attleborough as required. A certificate was also received from Dr Poole stating that a portion of the index finger of accused's right hand had been severed, and he would be under surgical treatment for some weeks.

Dr Poole said that Copsey had come to his surgery on 30 May and said that he had cut the top off one of his fingers. He added, 'I suppose this will keep me from joining the Army'. Poole asked what he meant, and Copsey said 'I am called up tomorrow'. Poole then examined the finger, and found the arteries exposed and the finger severed at the middle joint. There was another wound in the stump.

Copsey claimed that he had had an accident while he was chopping wood. However he was found guilty, and sentenced to three months' imprisonment with hard labour. After his sentence he would be handed over to the military authorities – Willoughby said he would still be useful to the Army as he could use his second finger to pull a rifle trigger.[34]

Men who did not serve for reasons of conscience, even if they avoided imprisonment, were subject to popular harassment and to the risk of losing their employment. Teachers were especially unpopular as they might 'corrupt' their pupils. Several councils including Leeds and Liverpool dismissed such teachers. At Bideford in Devon the pupils took the initiative. In a bizarre reversal of the Burston School Strike discussed in chapter five, they refused to go to school because they could not accept their teacher: he was a conscientious objector.[35]

In June 1917 the Norfolk Education Committee discussed the position of H. Birks, a teacher at Diss secondary school and a conscientious objector. Many committee members thought he should be sacked. One, Mr Davison, said 'if Mr Birks were dealing with inanimate objects which could not in the least be affected by his influence it would be a different thing, but he is dealing with animate beings who will grow up to be the citizens of this country. In a time of national peril like the present they must seek to inculcate the national sentiment'.

Other members took the opposite view, including Mr Waters:

> His idea of conscience was a man's inward sense of what was right and what was wrong. Some of them came to the conclusion that this was a righteous war. Some of them did not reach that conclusion at a heap, and they foresaw some of the tragedy and the terrible costs in lives and property it would involve … having passed through a conflict of that kind some of them could better understand the position of certain persons, even if they were only few in number, who said that their conscience protested against this war, or even went further and said they were against all war. Any man who took that line conscientiously was entitled to some respect and to his civil rights.

He also pointed out that Lloyd George himself 'idolised as he was today, was not so many years ago a conscientious objector where the Boer War was concerned'.

The committee decided against sacking Birks by 11 votes to eight.[36]

The Labour Party

The outbreak of the war was a crisis of conscience for local politicians as well as the individuals already discussed. The Conservative and Liberal parties supported the war, but the Labour party was split. Local Labour Party leaders almost all supported the war, including George Roberts, Labour MP for Norwich, whose career is described in chapter seven.

George Edwards also came down firmly in favour of the war, perhaps surprisingly as he was a Primitive Methodist. When Edwards died in 1933 William Hansell wrote to the *Eastern Daily Press*:

> I cannot imagine anyone hating the idea of war than he must have done. I was recruiting officer in these parts throughout the war; and sometimes received from him the greatest help at village meetings on greens and in halls. It was the help of such men that resulted in victory, the fruits of which may be a warning against future warfare, but even so all survivors and the present generation ... must realise what a different position we should occupy had we lost.[37]

Before the war Edwards was associated with the Liberal Party, but he had drifted away from them: he became a Labour MP after the war. At a victory celebration in Edwards' home town of Fakenham, a Mr Watson said: 'the majority represented the will of the workers in South Norfolk. England is becoming sane. They had been too long insane, insane enough to follow the lead and dictatorship of the militarists and capitalists'. Edwards' reply is not recorded.

Fred Henderson, the Socialist writer, also firmly supported the war. The *Norwich Mercury* wrote of him in 1919:

> It is in regard to his literary support of the Government policy in the war that Henderson is most remarkable. It is no exaggeration to say that he did far more than any other man to hold down East Anglia to an unswerving war policy, and his services to the Government are greater than those of many other men who for theirs received honours and titles. The former Perfervid Labourite, eighteen months ago was the most confirmed Neverendian of them all'.

However Henderson was opposed to the harsh treatment of Germany after the war. In later life, he became a Quaker.[38]

It was left to a lesser-known man, Herbert Witard, to lead the anti-war movement locally. Paradoxically he was the only one who had seen military service, having joined the militia at the age of 16 – his experience there led to him becoming an uncompromising opponent of militarism. As he put it himself, in a speech made in 1938, 'strangely enough he left the Barracks a convinced Pacifist'. (Laughter.)

Witard was a speaker when the Independent Labour Party held its annual convention in Norwich at Easter 1915. They had difficulty finding a Hall that would accept them but eventually met in a Primitive Methodist schoolroom on Queen's Road. The 'founder' of the Labour party, Keir Hardie was there: this was to be his last public appearance. He said that there were 20 million men engaged in an endeavour to murder each other; 'when the working class got sufficient courage the war would stop. The war could not be carried on without them'.

To be an opponent of the war was not a fatal handicap to a career in local politics in the long term. The conscientious objector John Cornwell was elected to Norwich

City Council in 1931 and served until his death in 1956 – his brother Ernest was present at his funeral. Dorothy Jewson, who became the first woman MP for Norwich in 1923, was a pacifist in the war: however her work in improving conditions for female munitions workers was no doubt remembered with pride. Herbert Witard was heavily defeated by pro-war candidates when he stood for Parliament in 1918. However he remained a city councillor, and he became the first Labour Party mayor of Norwich in 1927-8.[39]

Witard, like Edwards, was a Methodist. After his death in 1954, the Rev. Percy Carden, who had been his minister at the Scott Memorial Methodist Church Thorpe Road, wrote:

> He hated war because he loved humanity. He hated poverty because he knew the world might be rich and beautiful. He hated injustice because he knew that the basic law of the universe was justice. He scorned idleness because he believed in a Creator whose work of creation was ever proceeding.

Two

The Face of Battle

About 100,000 Norfolk men served in the forces, of a total male population of half a million. What this experience like for these men, most of whom had probably never before left the country of their birth?

The 1st and 2nd Battalions of the Norfolk Regiment were the professional or regular soldiers, already serving when the war started. The 1st Norfolks were in Ireland: they were sent to France within a few days and took part in the retreat of the British Army. In fact on 24 August it was one of two battalions detailed to cover this retreat: it suffered heavy losses. The battalion was at Ypres in 1915, and was one of the first battalions to suffer severely from gas attacks by the Germans. The 1st Norfolks fought in the Battle of the Somme, and they remained on the Western Front for the rest of the war, apart from a two-month spell in Italy at the end of 1917, to help the Italian army defend itself against the invaders from the north. They were back in France to take part in the desperate defence against the German attacks in the spring of 1918, and in the Allied counter-attacks of the summer which led to the breaking of the trench lines, and the eventual German surrender.

The 2nd Battalion was in India in August 1914; in November it was sent to Mesopotamia to fight against the Turks. The 2nd Norfolks took part in major battles at Shaibba and Ctesiphon in 1915. They were part of the British Army that was besieged at Kut in the winter of 1915, and with the rest of that army became prisoners of war on the surrender of Kut on 29 April 1916. A new 2nd Battalion was created in the summer, with surviving wounded men and many new men, both volunteers and conscripts. These men took part in General Allenby's campaign against the Turks. They were in Beirut when the war ended.

The 4th and 5th Battalions, more correctly 1/4th and 1/5th, were *territorials*, part-time soldiers who had been training before the war for just such an emergency. They were sent to the Dardanelles, landing at Suvla Bay on 10 August 1915. They were later evacuated to Egypt. They, too, took part in Allenby's campaign in the Near East. The two battalions were so badly mauled at the Battle of Gaza on 19 April 1917 that the survivors were merged into one battalion with the few survivors of the even worse-hit 8th Hampshires.

The men who rushed to volunteer after the war broke out, and those conscripted into the army after 1916, were formed into the 7th, 8th and 9th Battalions. The 7th crossed the Channel on 30 May 1915, the 8th and 9th following in August. The 9th took part in the Battle of Loos on 26 September 1915. All three battalions were

NOTHING is to be written on this side except the date and signature of the sender. Sentences not required may be erased. If anything else is added the post card will be destroyed.

I am quite well.

I have been admitted into hospital
{ *sick* } *and am going on well.*
{ *wounded* } *and hope to be discharged soon.*

I am being sent down to the base.

I have received your { *letter dated* _____
{ *telegram „* _____
{ *parcel „* _____

Letter follows at first opportunity.

I have received no letter from you
{ *lately.*
{ *for a long time.*

Signature
only. }

Date _____

[Postage must be prepaid on any letter or post card addressed to the sender of this card.]

(25343) Wt.W3497-293 1,760m. 4/15 M.R.Co.,Ltd.

15 *Field Service Post Card: these cards were of great benefit to those soldiers who found writing home difficult. Most of the soldiers had left school by their thirteenth birthday.*

involved in the Battle of the Somme, which began on 1 July 1916 and lasted well into the autumn. They continued to serve on the Western Front for the rest of the war. The 8th had suffered 770 dead by 1918, and it was disbanded, its 400 surviving men being sent to fill up the gaps in the 7th and 9th Battalions.

The 12th Battalion was made up of Yeomanry, amateurs who were expert horsemen. However there was little place for cavalry warfare in the First World War: the men served as infantry in the Dardanelles and in Palestine. They were sent to France for the final weeks of the war.

The reader will notice some omissions in the numerical sequence of battalions in the Norfolk Regiment. The 3rd (Special Reserve) Battalion was for training. Almost 19,000 men were trained in it during the war, up to 2,500 at any one time: they then went on to one of the active battalions. The 6th (Cyclist) Battalion was made up of territorials but did not fight as a unit, its men being transferred to other regiments. No 10th or 11th Battalions were ever formed.[1]

These were the battalions of the Norfolk Regiment, which so many local men joined. However many joined other units; when the war memorials are examined later in this book we will see what a wide range of units Norfolk men served in. Many may have simply found it easier to go to recruiting centres in other counties, others will have had family connections with other regiments, or been attracted by the glamour of their names. Others preferred the artillery: the power of the heavy gun is perhaps the single most dominant memory many have of the war. Many Norfolk men joined the navy, natural in a county with such a long coastline and so many professional seafarers. A few brave souls joined the Royal Flying Corps, perhaps the most hazardous choice of all.

In Swaffham church there is a stained glass window that gives a good impression of the wide range of situations in which Norfolk people might find themselves in the war. It contains images of artillery at Mons, General Allenby entering Jerusalem, and HMS *Invincible* blockading the channel at Zeebrugge. A fourth image is of Red Cross nurses: nursing is discussed in chapter three of this book.

The Western Front

The First World War began as a war of movement, with the German army sweeping through Belgium trying to outflank the French and British forces. They met the

16 *Lens: Chapter House Street.*

British at Mons on 23 August. A Norfolk man told his story of the battle. Lance-Corporal H.G. Roberts of the Northumberland Fusiliers, wounded at Mons, wrote to his wife from Netley Hospital, Hampshire, on 30 August:

> We have had a very bad time these last eight days. We got to Mons last Saturday afternoon. We got on fine with the people. They brought us all the food we could eat. We wanted it, for we had not had any food for two days. The Sisters from the Convent were very good to us. I went to the Convent and had a wash, so they made me have some tea. We started from Mons on Sunday morning. We were driven back from Cambrai on Sunday night, and then we had to be up all night. Soon as daybreak on Monday the Germans started. They got the first shell home. It came about 25 to 30 yards away from us. There were not many of us there. We were on sentry. Later on the main body came up and got into trenches. Those who were on outpost duty had to get behind a wall. I was one of them. I think we lay there two hours with artillery firing on us. The shells were dropping a foot behind us, some behind us, some in front, and all around us, but, thank God, none of our outposts got hurt there. Then they dropped firing a bit, so we had to run across the open about 100 yards and get into a lot of trees and lie behind a hedge. As soon as we got there one of our artillery guns came behind us and started firing, and what was more it gave the Germans a place to fire at, for they could see the smoke from the guns. Well, we got shell and rifle fire. It came like pepper out of a box. We were in that about three hours. I put my face into the ground and shut my eyes and said my prayers ... Thank God, I came out of that all right. That was Monday morning. After dinner we started on the March. We finished marching Tuesday night about 8 o'clock in the rain. We had marched from 40 to 45 miles, so you can see how we were when we got there. We got a few hours sleep. In the morning we went to Le Cateau and began digging trenches. That was where the big battle started.[2]

Roberts was wounded as the British retreated. Hearing the buzz of a shell he threw himself on the ground with his left hand over his head: the shell exploded two or

17   *Arras: ruins of the Hotel de Ville.*

three yards from him and a piece struck his hand.

After Mons the British slowly retreated, pursued by the advancing German army. On 9 September battle was joined once more, this time along the line of the river Marne. This time the Germans were forced to retreat, but only for a few miles to the river Aisne.

Sergeant W.E. Walker of 1st Battalion Rifle Brigade was there. He was from Yarmouth and his sister ran the *Feathers Hotel* in North Walsham. Walker was wounded soon after crossing the river Aisne near Soissons:

No sooner had the Germans seen our guns come into position than they let us have it, and it was here that I got hit. I was just getting up and turning round to take my platoon to the left when smack went my leg, and didn't I jump! It did not blow my leg clean off, it was hanging on with a thick piece of flesh, sinews and skin, so I hopped a few yards down the hill under cover, and sat behind some straw sheath and cut my leg off with a penknife.

The shells were still flying round, and one came pretty close to me. I thought my time was come. I lay there for over an hour until I was carried to safety by a sergeant of artillery, and I came across some of my men, who carried me to a cave and put me on a shelter: I might mention I had a piece of string round my leg to stop it from bleeding, which saved my life. In the evening I was taken to a village near by, where they put me in a bed and I lay there all the next morning. I had my leg dressed. I was placed under chloroform and on Tuesday all the wounded were sent down the line. Those who were unfit to travel and the worst cases were taken to the hospital, and I was not sorry when I arrived and saw the nice white sheets. It was like coming out of hell into heaven.

One of the nurses gave me a nice hot bath and then I was put in bed and given a sleeping draught, and slept till next morning. Then I had my leg dressed, and well I know it. I might mention that I had been without food since Saturday (five days without food!).[3]

This was to be the end of the war of movement. Both sides dug themselves in, and trench warfare began. It was to last for well over three years.

December 25, 1914 saw the legendary 'Christmas Truce', when men from both sides stopped firing, and even fraternised over impromptu games of football. The story received local confirmation. On 6 January 1915 the *Eastern Daily Press* published a letter 'received by a Norfolk resident from an officer friend at the front'. He described the incident:

That night (Christmas Eve) it froze hard, and Christmas day dawned on an appropriately sparkling landscape. A truce had been arranged for the few hours of daylight for the burial of the dead on both sides who had been lying out in the open since the fierce night fighting of a week earlier. When I got out I found a large crowd of officers and men, English and German, gathered round the bodies, which had already been gathered together and laid out in rows. I went along those dreadful ranks and scanned the faces, fearing at every step to recognise one I knew. It was a ghastly sight. They lay stiffly in contorted attitudes, dirty with frozen mud and powdered with rime. The digging parties were already busy on the two common graves, but the ground was very hard and the work slow and laborious.

In the intervals of superintending it we chatted with the Germans, most of whom were quite affable, if one could not call them exactly friendly, which indeed was neither to be expected or desired. We exchanged confidences about the weather … one charming lieutenant of artillery was anxious to know just where my dug-out 'the Cormorants' was situated … no doubt he wanted to shoot his card, attached to a 'Whistling Willie'. A tiny spruce lieutenant … attached himself to me and sent his bursche back for a bottle of Cognac and we solemnly drank Gesundheiten.

The burial truce continued on Boxing Day, as many of the dead were not yet buried:

They [German officers] distributed cigars and cigarettes freely among our digging party. The digging concluded the shallow graves were filled in, and the German officers remained to pay their tributes of respect while our chaplain read a short service. It was one of the most impressive things I have ever witnessed. Friend and foe stood side by side bare-headed, watching the tall grave figure of the padre outlined against the frosty landscape as he blessed the poor, broken bodies at his feet. Then with more formal salutes we turned and made our way back to our respective ruts.

The football legend had already become established. The letter continues:

Elsewhere along the line I hear our fellows played the Germans at football. Our own pet enemies remarked that they would like a game, but as the ground in our part was all root crops and mud cut up by ditches, and as, moreover, we had no football, we had to call it off.

Another Norfolk witness to the Christmas truce was Private J.H. Dawson of the Queen's Westminsters. He wrote:

On Christmas Day practically the whole of our battalion spent the morning and afternoon in conversing and exchanging souvenirs with those of the enemy on our front … Personally I succeeded in obtaining a 1 pfenning [sic] piece, a tunic button, an autograph postcard and a mouth organ, in exchange for one of our buttons, a signed card and some chocolate.[4]

The year 1915 saw stalemate along the Western front. Trench warfare involving sniping, shell fire and the occasional raid, was punctuated by unsuccessful attempts to break through the German line at Neuve Chapelle in March and Loos in September.

Private E. Oxborough of Ashill, a professional soldier in the Royal Fusiliers, described his experiences at the Western Front in the spring of 1915. He had been

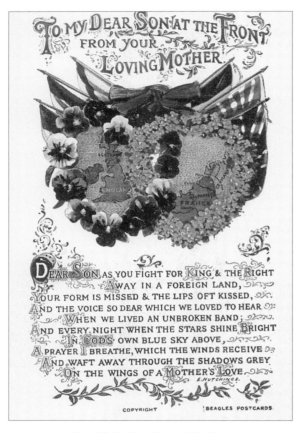

18 *'To My Dear Son At The Front'.*

a soldier for 12 years, including service in India and Ireland, but conditions on the Western Front appalled him:

> At Armentieres the regiment was in the trenches for a few months, within 35 yards of the German trenches. He speaks of the awful condition of the trenches all through the winter, the troops being frequently up to their knees in water and mud. Here they went through five engagements. On the 9th March they received orders to take part in the great battle of Neuve Chapelle, which he states was almost indescribable. Our artillery opened fire at 7 o'clock in the morning, and for three quarters of an hour a terrific hail of shell fire swept the German trenches, doing enormous damage. The awful noise and din caused by the 350 guns he will never forget, it being continuous during this time and nerve cracking in the extreme. The result was awful to look upon, the enemy were mowed down and literally blow[n] to pieces, heads, arms, legs and pieces of bodies were flying about in all directions, and when they got the order to charge the German trenches they found them full of dead and dying mangled corpses horrible to contemplate.

Oxborough was wounded and was convalescing at his parents' home in Ashill when he gave this interview. His report was exceptionally vivid for the time, although it seems now like a factual statement of the horrors of war. However, it appears Oxborough may have been making it up. In July, the *Norwich Mercury* published a refutation by his Commanding Officer. He said that Oxborough had not been wounded, he had reported sick on 26 March, and he was not present at Neuve Chapelle: 'what was purported to have been said by Private Oxborough must have been obtained from accounts in the various newspapers'. The *Mercury* expressed its 'sincere regret' for any 'erroneous statements' in its article.[5]

Sniping was a continual danger at the front. John Gough was General Haig's Chief of Staff. His death, on 22 February 1915, illustrates that the idea of staff officers sitting in chateaux miles from the front line is simplistic: in fact Haig insisted that all his staff officers visit the front line once every day. Jack Keir wrote back home to his family:

> I am indeed fortunate, as so many much more deserving men have not been allowed to reap the reward of their labours. General Gough whose death is

reported to-day is an instance. Young, capable and ambitious, he seemed to have everything before him. Had he been spared he was destined to fill some of the most important posts in our Army. When he was hit he was about 2000 yards from the trenches. A chance shot glanced off a road in front and passed thro his body. A careful examination of his wound was made which tho' serious was not looked on as mortal. He is a brother of General Hubert Gough.[6]

Even in quiet days there were 2,000 casualties a day on average, and the strain on the parents of the men at the front was very great. This was expressed by Charlotte Boyle of Tuddenham Lodge in a letter to a friend in May 1915:

> Thank you for your kind thought about my son. These are terrible days for us all, with the anxiety that must weigh on all who love their country & then the miserable weight at one's heart for all the men one cares for in that awful fighting which goes on & on without end it seems. It takes all one's faith and courage to feel

19   *Captain Boyle of Tuddenham Hall, son of William Boyle MP.*

> there is a chance of any officer coming out alive & even the men one's heart aches with fear for – tho' the Germans pick the former out specially it appears.[7]

Letters home often strike a deliberately cheerful note, such as one from Philip Hewetson:

> A trench is a wonderfully safe place under shellfire, it is so deep & narrow. Though we probably had 100s of shells at us those days none pitched in the trench though some hit the parapet & a shell unless its shrapnel is very local in effect. I lost one poor man in my platoon sniped through the head looking over the parapet, his second day in the trenches, from the last draft. As you know that was my first sight of a man 'Killed in Action' but I'm glad to say I took it quite naturally. I am going to write to his people. 3 July [1915] [8]

Diaries, not being intended to cheer up relatives at home, could tell a darker story. Frank Dunham wrote about his trench at Ypres:

> the losses on both sides had been heavy, and many bodies were still lying in the open unburied, the stench being almost unbearable. Even sticking out of the sides

of our trench were limbs and bodies of the dead, and flies clustered around them. Dunham also records the presence of unwelcome companions in the trench:

> A great nuisance was the louse, as this small fellow was seemingly everywhere about our bodies and clothes, and made one most uncomfortable, and no-one seemed able to find a remedy for their complete extermination. I have spent many evenings on the search, running a lighted candle along the seams of my clothes, even to burning holes in them, and on waking the next morning, find your energies in this direction have been in vain.
>
> I remember one night being awakened by a rat running over my face, and could hear them sniffing away at a parcel of food I had received from home. They would scurry off when disturbed, but would return when everything was quiet again. On many occasions the rats ate parts of the contents of my parcels. It became usual for us all to sleep with our heads under our blankets, after one chap had his nose bitten by a rat.[9]

Letters home naturally varied in literary quality: many soldiers were not accustomed to make use of whatever writing skills they had learned at school. The 'field postcard' with pre-printed statements was helpful to these men. Others did have a go at letter writing: Albert Houghton wrote to his cousin Mr Quantrell of 94, Rupert Street, Norwich on 6 June 1915:

> Just a few line to you & hoping to find you in the best of health as it leave me at present I do not know whether you have had from Sid yet but I should like to know how he getting on and how do you like soldier is it better than working for a living I should keep that side if I was you I have had a letter from Tom and he say getting on all right. so I think I told you all this time with best love to all from your loving cousin Albert roll on a good old pint.[10]

Christmas 1915 produced no 'Xmas Truce' but some officers did manage to make the day special for their men. A letter from Sergeant Potter in the 8th Norfolks to his mother said:

> I thought of you on Christmas day and know you thought of me. We had quite a merry time and were congratulating ourselves all day on being out of the trenches. We have worked hard since we have been in billets, but Christmas Day was quite a holiday. I commenced celebrations by keeping in bed till 10 o'clock, and a ministering warrior was good enough to bring me my breakfast. Captain —— , who was our company commander in the Colchester days, sent us a cheque to help in the festivities, and our present captain and officers did their duty. Every available chicken was done to death. Our captain bought a sheep and plenty of beef. The only vegetable was the 'spud'. Cabbage and cauliflower cost a shilling each. The best cooks in the company prepared dinner and there were plum puddings galore, sent by a society in England. But the most popular item of all was the plentiful supply of good English beer, which was sent up from Amiens. It was drawn straight from the barrel. When the beer was first delivered, and before a barrel was broached, I was instructed to place a man on guard. Now for this post the applications were very numerous and, after careful consideration, I appointed a fisherman who hails from Cromer. He did thorough justice to the job.[11]

Ralph Mottram produced one of the most evocative novels about the First World War, *The Spanish Farm*. His letters and diaries also give a clear picture of life at the front. Here he describes a 'raid' on the enemy trenches in January 1916:

> BOMBING PATROLS SW OF ST ELOI. The main object of these patrols was to secure the identification of the troops opposed to them.
>
> The patrols, which in each case were composed of 2 officers and about fifteen men, left … soon after 6 pm and were back again by 8 pm, this period being selected owing to the brightness of the moon an hour later.
>
> Both patrols succeeded in cutting through the enemy's wire system and reached the parapet unobserved.
>
> The left patrol was discovered at that point and, the trench proving to be strongly held, the patrol was able to do no more than throw bombs, it is believed with considerable effect. Unfortunately both the officers with this patrol were wounded, the first slightly by a stray bullet when still close to our own lines, and the second as soon as the patrol was discovered. The patrol suffered no other casualties, and it is certain that several of the bombs they threw fell into crowded trenches and detonated there.
>
> The right patrol reached the enemy's parapet undiscovered and the two officers and a sergeant crossed the enemy's trench and crawled along behind the parados to a spot where a sentry was keeping watch at the junction of a small sap running out to a bombing post held by two bombers. They climbed into the trench and surprised the sentry but unfortunately the revolver which was held at his head missed fire. Attempts were made to throttle him quietly but he succeeded in raising the alarm and had to be killed. Had the pistol gone off, it is almost certain that the alarm would not have been raised, as there was no one within the immediate vicinity with the exception of the two bombers 30 yards in front of the trench.
>
> As soon as the alarm was raised Germans came up from all sides and the patrol was forced to retreat. Before doing so they bombed the enemy successfully and killed some, including the two bombers at the head of the sap.
>
> The depth of the trench prevented them from getting the dead man out and so no identification was secured. This patrol had one casualty.
>
> At the point where the front trench was penetrated, it was a winding trench with no traverses, 8 feet deep, 6 feet broad at the bottom, the parapet steep and revetted with wood, the parados a bare earth slope and the bottom 3 greasy planks laid parallel to each other lengthwise along the trench.
>
> No signs of any gas apparatus were discernible.
>
> The left patrol discovered a loose bomb hung to a knife rest, presumably as an additional safeguard.
>
> Nearer still to the trench there was a deep ditch full of water and submerged wire.
>
> The right patrol whilst reconnoitring their ground close to the enemy's trench, heard the two bombers previously referred to ring a small bell which was the signal for a Very light to be sent up from the trench behind them.[12]

The year 1916 culminated in the Battle of the Somme, when the British troops went 'over the top' in their thousands to take the German front-line trenches, which they were assured would have been obliterated by artillery bombardment. Unfortunately they had not been obliterated: the Germans rushed from dug-outs to their trenches and mowed down the advancing British forces. Almost 20,000 of them were killed,

Killed in action, our hearts are sore,
As time goes on we miss him more,
His tender smile, his loving face,
No one on earth can fill his place.

——

He bid no one a last farewell,
    He said Good-bye to none,
He took his flight before we knew
    That he from us had gone.
No loved ones stood around him
    To see him give his all,
No words of comfort could he leave
    For those who loved him well.

——

He Died at Duty's Call.

In Affectionate Remembrance of

our dear Son,

Corporal George Hardingham

(8th Battalion Norfolk Regiment),

Killed in Action in France, July 1st, 1916,

Aged 22 Years.

20   *'He died at Duty's Call' – memorial card for a Somme victim.*

the worst day in the history of the British army. Most of these men were the volunteers of Kitchener's Army, many facing battle for the first time. The phases of the first day of the battle are described in the war diary of the 8th Norfolks, quoted in chapter seven. The many men killed in action on that terrible day included 'Bot' Smith and Roy Benson. Bot's father had already lost one son in the war. He wrote to his friend Major Gilbert in Lowestoft:

> I have been a long time answering your very kind letter, but you know at a time like this what a lot of personal letters one has to write. The loss of both my boys is a terrible blow: we were very fond of one another & I was proud of them & intensely interested in all their doings. Poor Bot was a fine soldier, they will miss him in the LRB [London Rifle Brigade]. He led his men at Gommecourt, and was successful up to a point, they reached their objective, but the attack on both sides failed, they were isolated & cut off from their supports: very few got back. Bot was always said to have a charmed life, he was one of three officers left after the second battle of Ypres, & never got a scratch: it seemed like it again on the 1st, they were in the hottest of it all day & he was all right until 4 pm. We have not the exact details of his death, but he was killed in the retreat.
>   My wife is very brave, but the interest of life is gone for both of us.[13]

Second Lieutenant W. 'Roy' Benson had written a cheerful letter from France to Colonel Bulwer (under whom he had formerly served) on 20 December 1915:

> Fortunately we have just finished a long tour of hard work & in a day or two we are having a well earned rest, so my Christmas day will have plenty of time for the usual fun, but of course the frivolity will be rather limited for if we do get nearly everything to make life cheerful, there is just one thing that is wanting – feminine society. I am afraid we cannot hope for a hamper of ladies from even the most generous of our friends, so our holiday will at least be unique in this respect.

When Benson was killed on 1 July 1916, Captain Wansbrough had the task of informing his parents:

> It is with very deep sorrow that I am writing to try to express my great sympathy and that of our officers and men in your sad bereavement. We could hardly believe last night that your gallant son had indeed been taken, and it is a terrible blow to us all, for no one could know him without loving him, and we shall miss him perhaps more than we should anyone else.

21 *'Who fell at the front'. Sergeants Doggett (left), and Clarke, mates who were both to die at the Battle of the Somme, July 1916.*

Our grief helps us to sympathise with yours, immeasurably greater as it is, and his father's; we know what a happy home life he had. There are the only consolations that count to offer you: he died painlessly, and he died as we should all be proud to die, helping a wounded comrade. Another regiment were making a raid last night, and the enemy were shelling our trenches in return. As the bombardment slackened and had nearly ceased, your son left the safety of his dug-out, and with his sergeant went round the front-line trenches to visit his Lewis' guns – to see that all his men were safe. While doing so he came across, in my trench, a wounded sentry, who was half buried through the explosion of a shell, and was also pinned down by a box of ammunition. With one of my officers and his own sergeant your brave son helped to release the man; while he was so engaged a shell burst right above him, a piece entered his back, and he sank down unconscious. His wound was at once dressed, and he was taken to the dressing station, but he expired as he reached it, without regaining consciousness.

Roy's father wrote to Bulwer on 20 July:

(By the special permission of the Proprietors of "Punch.")

COMRADES IN VICTORY

COMBLES, SEPTEMBER 26TH.

POILU. "BRAVO, MON VIEUX!"
TOMMY. "SAME TO YOU, MATE."

" The Lord watch between me and thee, when we are absent one from another."

Christmas, 1916.

To My Dear Bob
From Lily 19. 11. 16 xx

HOME WORDS No 165

22   *'Comrades' – a* Punch *cartoon used as a Christmas card.*   23   *Christmas 1916.*

Your King and Country Thank You.   HOME WORDS No. 168

Christmas Greetings from   Beatie.   to my dear Bob

24   *Your King and Country Thank You.*

With his great abilities, his charming personality, his keen sense of duty and his honourable ambitions, his life appeared to be full of promise & he would have gone far.

To lose such a lad is a great grief, but that grief is tempered by the knowledge that he willingly gave his young life, bravely fighting for the dear old country he loved so well. England is pouring out the blood of her very best, we stay-at-home civilians have a duty to perform – to see that our beautiful lads have not died in vain, and that the politicians shall not give away what the soldiers have won. It is very kind of you to ask that my second son may be posted to your Battalion & I sincerely hope that my dear dead boy's wish may be gratified in this particular. The second son is also a good lad, but as he was severely wounded in the jaw at Gallipoli, I sincerely trust that the war may be over before it again becomes his turn to face the bullets.[14]

What was it like to face the dangers of the front for the very first time? Philip Hewetson's letters in chapter seven of this book give one man's impression of this experience. Bombardier E.G. Hill recorded his feelings on first serving on the Western Front in 1917:

One's first experience under shell fire is not too pleasant. I cannot quite describe the feeling, but it is hardly fear. Doubtless its effects taken in individual cases vary a good deal, but one soon grows accustomed to the whistle and bursting of the various shells, and soon acquires a fairly accurate knowledge as to the distance a shell is likely to burst from you, and, having judged, if you decide it is near at hand, you take the best cover possible, and, what is more, you move to it pretty sharp. Failing cover, down you go, flat as a plaice, mud, slush and water are all the same, it's flat you want to get, you breathe hard, wait for the crash, and take your chance. It is advisable to remain prone for at least ten seconds after the burst, as pieces go a fair height, and while flat your shrapnel helmet protects the head and neck.[15]

The year 1917 saw stalemate continue: the Germans shortened and strengthened their front line by withdrawing to the massive defences of the Hindenburg Line. The devastation cause by the war was the first thing that men new to the Western front noticed. Bombardier Hill wrote home:

The trees in the actual zone of shell-fire are pitiful indeed. In fact, the vast majority of them are nothing but bare splintered poles filled with fragments of iron. You may take it the land is swept clean, full of shell holes, craters, battered trenches, broken debris of war. Weeds and chaos hold the sway, houses there are none, villages are gone, and in most cases the bricks are powdered into dust[16].

Of course men were not always at the front line, and rest periods could even produce an idyll reflected in this poem by Tom Copeman, written in a very different style to the war poetry of people such as Wilfred Owen and Siegfried Sassoon:

A pleasant orchard bounded by hedgerows
Within whose fastnesses you may suppose
The sweet voiced thrush is resting now
And lazy wonder when & why & how
Some village boys will find her cunning nest.

25 *Kemmel – ruins of the Church and the Mount.*

In such a place beneath old apple trees
The scent of whose blossom a wayward breeze
Blows far and wide, I lingering dream
Of England, with other things that hardly seem
Less dear than that sweet Island in the West.

The heady perfume of lilac and may,
A butterfly meand'ring on its way
Gold of buttercups and white of daisies,
Such things as your poet often praises
Remind me of boyhood's short-lived day.

Alas! distant cannon the vision dispel
The passing road leads to the mouth of hell
All may be peace & quietness to the eye
The ear gives to her sister quite the lie
And sings a song of man's furious fray.

Despite the awakening, thoughts still sleep
Within my breast, and still I dream & keep
A tiny spark of hope alive, and wait
Warily the day – magic, mystic date
When war shall cease & men no longer slay

France. 23rd May 1917.[17]

Apart from the big set-piece battle, small attacks were continuous and very dangerous. James Neville's description captures vividly the feeling of coming under shell fire:

Dec 11 1917, Lebucquiere

You seem to be very anxious about me, and I am sorry that I have been unable to put you out of the anxiety.

I will now try and tell you what happened. The 5th Brigade was, luckily for us, in reserve when the enemy attacked the Division. We woke up to the tune of a barrage which we could see plastering our front line. I said to myself 'now we are for it' and at noon the 52nd moved up to support either of the two Brigades in the front line, as help was required.

We stayed at Lock 7 for some time, and then orders were received for the Regiment to counter-attack the Sugar Factory on the Bapaume-Cambrai road. (As a matter of fact, this factory had never been captured by the enemy, though it was being pasted to hell.)

We moved again soon after into Hughes Support Trench, which ran parallel to the Hindenburg Line. Here we remained from 5 pm till 2 am. The trench had been evacuated

26   *Soldier on the Cromer War memorial.*

by some reserve troops of the 47th London Division, who had left their packs stacked high in the bays of the trench. We were packed like sardines, my platoon occupying half a traverse only. Some very heavy stuff was coming over at odd intervals, and one 8 inch shell laid out 20 men. As you know, you can hear these very heavy birds coming from a considerable distance; they seem to take ages to arrive, and there is always a spell during their flight when you know whether they are going to fall near you or far from you. I heard this particular bird from afar, and felt relieved that he was going to plant himself away from us. Then I began to doubt my supposition: a second later it was touch and go: then I realised that it was probably going to blot me out. I lived through one agonising second of uncertainty. There was no way of escape: we could not dodge the brute as we were too cramped for space. With a tearing, rushing mighty roar as of an express train screaming at top speed through an enclosed station, it crashed in the next bay from me, right in the middle of my platoon! I darted round the corner and found a shambles. It had fallen in the centre of the trench, a magnificent shot from the enemy's point of view. Among the killed was Sergeant Archer, Platoon Sergeant of No 7 and a damned good chap. The only man who escaped untouched of all the men in that bay, was sitting on the top of a pile of packs, at the foot of which the shell had landed. The packs were utterly destroyed, and he was lifted off his perch but unhurt!

As soon as it was dark, we collected some bits of men, put them in a sandbag, carried out the recognisable bodies over the top and dumped them in a shell-hole, and Billy Barnard said the Lord's Prayer over their remains. I think it was probably the only prayer he knew for certain!

27   *Entraining of wounded horses from the front.*

It is not always appreciated how the character of war on the Western Front changed totally in the spring of 1918. The Germans suddenly had a massive numerical advantage: Russia had collapsed and they were able to move their troops from the eastern front to confront the Allies in the west. However this advantage was only temporary. America had declared war in 1917 and US troops were beginning to appear on the western front: soon the advantage would be with the allies. Because of this, the Germans made a whole series of attacks, beginning in March 1918 and continuing into the summer. Each one overwhelmed the allied front line and advanced some miles, before grinding to a halt.

Although food could be supplied to the men relatively easily while the line was static, the war of mobility of 1918 meant that supplies could not always keep up. For Neville this had drastic consequences:

> Ellam and I scrounged about and found an old dugout, which had partially collapsed at the bottom. It was damp and cold and musty at the bottom, and smelled of decay, rats, and putrescent vegetation and food. But, here, I found a half-opened tin of bully beef, and picking out the biggest pieces of chalk with my penknife, ate the remainder of the contents. How the tin had got there, or how long it had been there, I never stopped to consider. We had been through strenuous days, marching over shell-torn country on underfed stomachs; never knowing if or when we should see food again, and here, at least, was a form of food! But never shall I forget the taste in my mouth after it! For four days I had a dry stickiness in my mouth, incessant heartburn, and a feeling of overwhelming depression which almost blotted out the instinct of life. Ellam would not touch it, and, therein, he was wiser than I.[18]

By the summer the German attacks had run out of steam. In August it was the Allies' turn to advance, and this time they did it so forcefully that the Germans were

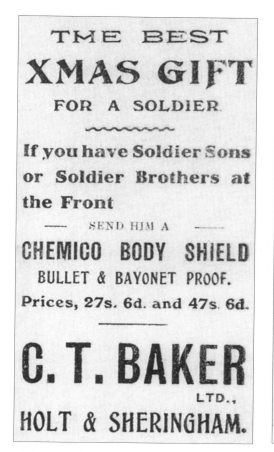

28 *Advertisement for the Chemico body shield.*

29 *Reading material for the Troops.*

not able to hold them up, even on the Hindenburg Line. They were forced slowly back, fighting all the way. In November the Germans realised their position was hopeless – although they were still on French and Belgian soil. The Armistice was concluded on 11 November 1918.

A soldier from Ashill described the Allied advance in a letter home:

We are got a good way forward to what we were when I last wrote to you & hope to keep still on the go, altho one can't expect such good news every day like we have been having lately. I have seen lots of prisoners lately, some of them are mere boys. I have also seen 1 of their big guns which was captured on the line A good prize it was & it used to fire right over the house we were in one place leading to a big town. So we were glad to see it captured. It was a big naval gun mounted on a special carriage in all weighing hundreds of tons & we also had the pleasure of seeing it fired on the Germans from right against where we had a place on the side of the line. I have also seen lots of his other guns that we got & seen lots of villages & a few towns that I know. Also saw the old place where I spent Xmas 1915. Lots of places seemed very familiar, but what was not knocked

"IF I DUCK I GET DROWNED, IF I DON'T I GET SHOT."

30   *'If I Duck …'.*

down then, are now all burnt. Last week we could see big fires in front of us
every night 13 & 14 at a time all scattered about on a large frontage: it was all the
villages & his own huts that he was burning & there's hardly a brick left
untouched in some of the places. We have been living a very rough & ready life
as dug outs are all mined, it not safe to go into them as they are likely to go up
any time, as long as a week or two after, some the moment one enters as there are
all kinds of traps, neat little parcels & books, some times a clock but the moment
its touched up goes the show.

   In most places we have been the stink has been enough to kill anything, men
& horses laying all over the place; as many as 30 or 40 horses within 50 or 60
yards square in places that were killed last March so you can guess the putrid state
of them. They were regular humming birds, some in shell holes some in streets
some on main roads. Our chaps are burning them where they lay all over the
place, but we are now got to an open country where there was not much of a
stand for fighting so it's a little sweeter. Leave seems to be going well again now,
in fact it has all through this advance men have been going every day, & its time
some of us did for 3 years & 9 months & we had of it 3 years & 5 months out
here & only 2 leaves, it looks very nice in the papers to say men are to have leave
every 6 months, but the ones that gets it are the ones at the Base; not the ones
that are always up in the firing line, the ones that deserve it, the ones that are
bombed & shelled day & night besides carting heavy shells ranging from 60 lbs to
1400 each, & at it day & night for weeks at a stretch with very little sleep.[19]

31 *The monitor HMS Terrible at Suvla Bay.*

Other Fronts

As we have seen, Norfolk men fought on other fronts too. Tobacco was valued almost as much as food by the troops in Greece who were trying to break through the 'soft underbelly' of the enemy alliance. Private S.H. Harris wrote back from Salonika:

> Your very welcome present of cigarettes arrived safely a few days ago, and came at a very opportune time. We are very short of both Bacca and Cigs, our canteen does not seem able to get supplies. When yours reached me I was reduced to some terrible French stuff, and the next step was 'Twist'. Rumour says the boat with the Bacca on it has been lost. It seems to me that all the boats with good things on are lost, but we never, never hear of a Bully Beef boat being lost.[20]

Many Norfolk men served at Gallipoli against the Turks. William Roche described his experiences on the peninsula in a letter to a Norwich friend dated 8 September 1915:

> Many thanks for your welcome letter received yesterday. I was forced to pay my debt, now doubled!
>
> The letter enclosed I handed to the Regt Postman as he is down at the Base hospital and I am up at an advanced Dressing Station, two miles distant, the Postman will see that he gets it. I will also give your message to Daniels when I see him. We are very much not at Alexandria! but have been in the thick of things out here on the Peninsula since Aug 16th. Our casualty list so far apart from sick totals 6 namely
>
> Pte Bussey (wounded)
> Driver Brooks (killed)
> Lieut Flynn (wounded seriously)
> Sergt Batch (wounded seriously)
> L Cpl Gumble (wounded)
> Pte Connors (wounded).

32   *Landing craft, Dardanelles.*

33   *Balloon section transport, Dardanelles.*

Considering the experiences we have been through this is a very small list and we have been very fortunate. We were under shell fire within an hour of landing on Aug 16th.

Shrapnel and snipers are the worst thing out here, I think my nearest shave has been from a sniper.

This is a terrible country for RAMC work. We use no ambulance wagons and all transport of wounded has to be done by stretcher bearers. We have often to carry a man by this means four miles along a rough mountain path in the dark. It is very hard and difficult work. Then up at our advance dressing stations we get very badly shelled sometimes. Then again at night the snipers are very busy all over the place. We live in 'dug outs' and live mainly on 'bully beef', jam and biscuits. I have had

34 *Turkish Prisoners of War, Dardanelles.*

one proper wash since we landed, that is to say with soap and clean water. Water is very precious out here. Now I must shut up, very many thanks for your kind offer of cigarettes and novels, either or both! would be very welcome.[21]

The most well-known Norfolk involvement in Gallipoli also occurred in 1915. Sir Ian Hamilton's despatch tells the story:

> The 1/5 Norfolk were on the right of the line, and found themselves less strongly opposed than the rest of the brigade. Against the yielding forces of the enemy Colonel Sir H. Beauchamp, a bold, self-confident officer eagerly pressed forward followed by the best part of the battalion. The fighting grew hotter and the ground more wooded and broken. At this stage many men wounded, or grew exhausted with thirst ... but the Colonel, with 16 officers and 250 men, still kept pushing on, driving the enemy before them. Nothing more was ever seen or heard of any of them. They charged into the forest and were lost to sight and sound. Not one of them ever came back.

The men included Captain Frank Beck, land agent on the estate of King Edward VII at Sandringham, and commander of a company made up of workers on the king's estate. In September 1919, 180 of their bodies were located, a distance of 800 yards behind the Turkish front line. It remains uncertain whether they were killed in battle or whether they were murdered after they had surrendered.

A Norfolk recruiting officer captures an unsung moment of individual gallantry at Gallipoli in an all-too-brief diary entry:

> Regimental Sergt Major Elliott, King's Own Royal Regiment, Norfolk Yeomanry, Late of 5th Dragoon Guards, Killed by a sniper at ANZAC, Dec 6th 1915 whilst attending a wounded comrade, Corpl F W Clarke, Norwich, Buried Dec 7th in Rhondda Valley, Graveyard, ANZAC.

35   *Norfolk Regiment soldiers in Baghdad.*

Cpl F W Clarke KORRNY, Ward 10 Splott Road Hospital, Cardiff, This is the lad Elliott was attending when sniped, Mr Edward Clarke, father of Corpl Clarke, 69 Carrow Road, Thorpe Hamlet, Norwich. [22]

Elliott was 41 and had formerly served in South Africa. He and his wife Florence lived in King's Heath, Birmingham. He is remembered with honour on the Helles memorial, which bears more than 21,000 names.

Norfolk men fought further east too, in what is now Iraq and Israel: many men died, either in action or through disease. The Wilson family of Norwich lost two sons in this campaign: Alfred was killed in Mesopotamia in February 1917 and Albert died of wounds in Palestine in September 1918. Major 'Harry' Jewson died at Gaza on 19 April 1917. Lieutenant Jack Jewson, his nephew, described the circumstances:

At 7.30 am on the morning of the 19th after a preparatory bombardment by our artillery we advanced from our positions to the Turkish trenches about 2,000 yards away. We were met by heavy fire both from artillery and machine guns. Harry with his company was in support and came over just after us. I was not able to see him during the advance, but so far as I can find out he was hit early in the advance but continued to lead his company until mortally wounded by a bullet through the heart. One of the last words he said to the men 'Come on, we will fight to the death'.

Harry Jewson's servant, Private Atkins, was with him when he died. He wrote:

He received four bullet wounds. The first one in the foot, which we managed to get our [*sic*] fairly well, and bound the foot up, but he insisted on going on. We got about another 8 hundred yards and the Major got the second across the back which compelled him to lie down. We had been lying about an hour continually being sniped at when he received the third which went through the fleshy part of the right side of the chest, but that did not make much difference to the Major, he was still in good spirits. Soon after I received mine in the back which rendered my lower limbs almost useless. We layed there about two more hours and circumstances made it impossible to stay any longer and the Major managed to get up and go back. After a while I also managed to get on my feet and followed him. He had gone about 5 hundred yards when I saw him stagger and fall. When I reached him I found he had got his fourth wound, in the chest and he was passed [*sic*] all human aid. He did not recognise me at first. After about 10 minutes he spoke. His words were 'Give my love to my people' he never spoke no more.[23]

The war meant that many Norfolk people went overseas for the first time in their lives. They also came into contact with men from many other countries – Australians, Indians, Americans and many others – fighting in the same cause. Beatrice Gurney, in Namur in 1919, was not impressed by the American soldiers there:

> The men who have been in the canteen are not attractive, far less well mannered than any of our men. In fact they are rather rude & come armed to the teeth with revolvers.

The Indian soldiers made a very different impression on her:

> A glorious pair of Indian soldiers, with long khaki ends to their turbans, arrived yesterday on 2 huge white percheron horses. It was a sight for the gods …. They speak English quite well & told me the other day it was too hot. They did not like it.[24]

36   *Major 'Harry' Jewson, killed in action at Gaza on 19 April 1917.*

This was truly a world war. One former Colman's employee found himself in Mombasa in Africa in 1915. He wrote home:

> Our last camp abounded with white ants, whose industry was more to be commended than admired, as nothing softer than steel seemed to come amiss to them. One instance seemed the height of impudence – to eat the largest portion of a man's socks at night whilst they were on his feet – and this actually happened, much to the disgust of the owner.[25]

37   *Truly a world war – Indian troops at the Western Front, from the diary of Beatrice Gurney.*

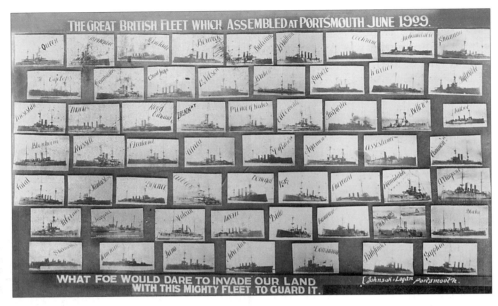

38   *The mighty British fleet. HMS* Formidable *is second from the right in the third row up.*

Lieutenant Geoffrey Johnson wrote from Africa in August 1917:

> The only two things against this place are the mosquitoes and heat … The River
> Shire, which runs into the Lake just here, is full of crocodile, so we cannot get
> any bathing. We live quite comfortably in 'wattle and daub' huts, and can get
> plenty of food in the way of eggs, fowls and fish, all of which are very cheap.[26]

Captain Page of the 4th Norfolk Regiment was made aware of the world-wide nature
of the war when he was at Lemnos Bay in 1915, awaiting his move to Gallipoli:

> The thousands of troops, white men, black men, Indians, Egyptians, and
> apparently every nation save Germans, turning the whole scene into a hive of
> industry, and a picture which will for ever live in the minds of those of us who
> witnessed it.[27]

The Navy

Many Norfolk men fought in the navy, and they were present at all the major nautical
dramas of the war. The great new German menace of the war was the submarine or
U-boat. These did tremendous damage to English naval ships. On New Year's Day
1915 a German submarine in the English Channel torpedoed and sank the battleship
Formidable, the first battleship to fall victim to this weapon. Out of a crew of 781
just 141 were saved: 71 were picked up by a British light cruiser and 70 by a Brixham
trawler. (These are the figures given in the local newspapers at the time, the true
figure seems to be that just 133 men survived: of course some men pulled alive from
the water may have died later.) Photographs of Norfolk men drowned in the disaster
began appearing in the *Eastern Daily Press* on 7 January, beginning with that of Leading

Stoker John Pells of King's Lynn, whose body had been landed at Lyme Regis. Another local victim was Able Seaman Robert Grand, son of George and Alice Grand of 125, Armes Street, Norwich. Robert Grand had had a double reason to look forward to 1 January 1915: not only was it New Year's Day, it was also his 20th birthday. Instead of celebrations he was to meet his death in the icy waters of the English Channel. Pells is buried at Lynn but Grand's body was never found: his name is commemorated on the Chatham Navy Memorial.

The paper went one better on 9 January, with an interview with a survivor, Able Seaman John Harlow, whose parents lived at Leonard Street in Norwich. Harlow was among the last to leave the *Formidable*. He told reporters:

39 *The German submarine menace: the* Deutschland. *Launched in 1916, she was designed to beat the British blockade by carrying cargo between America and Germany. This picture shows her in Great Yarmouth after the war.*

I came off watch at midnight on Old Year night and turned into my hammock. At 2.30 am on New Year morning I was awakened by the noise of the crew hurrying about. Everyone was making for the upper deck. I did not then know what had happened. I thought we had struck a mine. I did not stay to dress, but blew up my swimming collar and tied it round my neck. I then ran to the upper deck. The ship was heavily listing on her starboard side. I saw Captain Loxley standing calmly on the bridge with his terrier beside him. The order had been given to lower the boats, and I lent a hand. They were partly manned, but the sea was so rough that the boats could not stand by near enough for us to get to them.

I felt sure the *Formidable* had been torpedoed. The vessel for a time regained its balance, but continued to gradually sink. The order was then given to throw overboard every piece of wood etc, that would float. This done we all stood by and awaited further orders. There was no sort of panic. Everyone was perfectly calm, though we felt that it was practically all up. Those who hadn't a cigarette had a pull at somebody else's, and we sang 'It's a Long Way to Tipperary' and 'Get Out or Get Under'.

At last the captain gave the order 'Every man for himself'. I jumped over the stern into the water. I had nothing on except a blue guernsey and my swimming collar. One of the ship's boats picked me up, and then we were hailed by a light cruiser. When we got alongside of her, the waves knocked the boat violently against the side of the cruiser and smashed the boat. There were about 40 of us in the boat. We went into the water, but were rescued by ropes thrown from the cruiser. The next thing that I remember was that I found myself in the sick bay, having become unconscious.

40   *Marines at gun drill.*

'It's all in the business of war', added Harlow. 'You can't blame the Germans for torpedoing us if they get the chance. I still like the sailor's life, though I did not expect I should ever have any more of it when I stood on the *Formidable* during those last few minutes.'

It was a common practice for a village or community to 'adopt' a ship and take an especial interest in its activities. The parish of St Giles in Norwich adopted HMS *Hyacinth*. By the beginning of 1915 she was off the coast of East Africa. Her adventures are described in a booklet presented to the parish:

> Calling at Zanzibar for coal we next proceeded to Mafia island, it having been captured from the Germans in January [1915] after a short but sharp resistance. This island is situated conveniently near the Rufiji Delta and figured largely in our programme for the next few months, the headquarters being at Kilindoni, officially known as Tirene, near the south west end.
>
> From now until the middle of July the Rufiji Delta was the scene of attraction for a considerable number of HM Ships with the Konigsberg as centre, for she had been seen to enter the Simba Uranga mouth by the Chatham as far back as October 1914, so it was a matter of much speculation into which branch of the Delta she had worked herself and whether she would hide there for the duration of the war or make a surprise emergence, with a sporting chance of doing considerable damage before being 'strafed'. [British ships eventually found the *Konigsberg* and put her out of action on 11 July.][28]

The white ensign of the *Hyacinth*, together with a photograph of the ship, hung in the church of St Giles until recent years.

41   *HMS* Hyacinth. *This picture formerly hung in St Giles parish church, Norwich, with the ship's flag above it.*

42   *Photograph by Judith Ferrier of two German submarines in Yarmouth after the war. The submarine on the right is British. Note Jewson's timber yard across the river in Southtown: Harry Jewson came from this family.*

43 *Dressed to kill? – Royal Flying Corps pilots at Thetford.*

As with any service, deaths in accidents were common. William Laight of Acle was one of 20 men killed when the gunboat *Spey* was rammed by a Thames dredger in the Thames estuary on 7 March 1917. He was one of 13 men who escaped from the doomed ship on a raft. They drifted for hours in a gale before the raft eventually came to ground on mud flats off the Isle of Grain carrying only corpses: all 13 men had died from exposure. Laight was the brother of Herbert Laight, mentioned in chapter one.[29]

The Air

The First World War saw a new dimension in warfare: the war in the air. Norfolk was in the forefront in the development of both the aeroplane and the airship. They were exciting to watch. Philip Hewetson, on the Western Front, wrote to his father in July 1915: 'Another sight you're always seeing is aeroplanes high up in the sky, with little white puffs of cloud keeping appearing all around & under them. They are too high for the inexperienced to tell whether they're friend or foe but the gunners on each side know & are shelling them!'[30]

Older people were more frightened – Edith Upcher was at Sheringham in 1916 when 'a very swift airplane went over fairly low as I was talking to old Mrs Dawson Gidney who fled indoors in terror. Oh I do hate them things – I don't care if they're ours or not, they scare me'.[31]

44 *Crashed aeroplane in Norfolk.*

Flying aeroplanes was an extraordinarily dangerous pursuit. Many airmen were killed in training, even before getting to France. William Bell-Irving died in a crash at Mousehold aerodrome in October 1915; George Hake and George Sumner were killed after their aeroplane collided with a tree at Hellesdon in May 1916; Joseph Phillips died from injuries after being thrown from an army aeroplane at Harleston in July 1917.[32]

Over in France, the fatalities continued. They included men from the RNAS station at Narborough, which had been set up after Zeppelin raids of 1915. George Devenish and his observer Harold Cotterill died in France on 6 June 1917 when their plane was attacked by enemy aircraft. Bob Egerton, also formerly at Narborough, was killed in France on 23 December when his plane nose-dived into the ground.[33]

Another personal tragedy lies behind a laconic note sent to William Carr at Ditchingham:

> 22 June 1918. My dear Carr, would it be possible to excuse me from going with you tomorrow – Have heard of the death of my boy – he crashed into the sea yesterday while on patrol duty – & it is rather a knock out blow. Yours very truly, Vera Packe.[34]

The high death rate led to broken nerves among a few flying officers. In 1917 Dr James Annesley was consulted about two cases of neurasthenia in Norfolk. (Officers with nerves were considered to be suffering from neurasthenia. Men in the same state were described as 'shell-shocked', like Walter Abigail, whose career is described in chapter seven.) Annesley said that it was very difficult for him to judge the effect of flying upon the nerves until he had had personal experience – he wanted, at the age of 52, to have a go! It was arranged for him to be taken up as a passenger by a Lieutenant Beaumont. The plane was seen to do a right bank and then a spinning nose dive, crashing into the ground and killing both men instantly.[35]

Travellers in South Norfolk will have noticed the striking village sign at Pulham St Mary: an airship, tethered to a mast, floats underneath a large cloud. There was a Royal Naval Airforce Station at Pulham before the war: from 1916 airships were based at the Station. The earliest airships were non-rigid, that is, the shape of the envelope depended on the gas and air inside: they became known as 'Pulham Pigs'. They were used to patrol the North Sea. Rigid airships were introduced in England in April 1917: the first was the HMA 9, based at Pulham.

One of the key men at the Station was Chief Petty Officer Edwards, whose story was told in *Pulham Patrol*:

> Enlisting in the Royal Marines in April 1906, his first connection with airship work was in 1910 on Naval Airship No 1. The untimely end of this airship temporarily brought CPO Edwards' connection with airship work to an end, and in March 1912, we find him afloat again, this time on HMS *Commonwealth*.
>
> In September 1912, he was recalled from the sea and attached to the Royal Flying Corps (Naval Wing) at ――. Here he worked on the following Airships: No 2 or the Willows, No 3 The Astra Torres, No 4 The Parseval (our old friend), the Beta, Gamma 1 and 2, Delta, and Eta
>
> The outbreak of the present war in 1914 marks another episode in CPO Edwards' service, for in October of that year we find him setting for sail for Dunkirk with our late CO and a few others, now on this Station, taking with them

45   *No 1 shed, Pulham, with windscreen.*

a spherical balloon, with which they worked for months in the Nieuport-Dixmude district. Then back to England, this time to Roehampton, where he took over Instructor's duties with the then new Drachan Kite Balloon, which, by the way, was a very different balloon to the one in use at present.

In May 1915, No 3 Kite Balloon Section sailed on board HMS —— for the Dardanelles with CPO Edwards in the party. This was perhaps the most interesting and exciting time in his career up to the present. They were at the memorable Suvla Bay landing, and saw most of the big things which happened at that time, both there and at Smyrna and Salonika, being engaged in spotting for the battleships and land batteries. The ship and balloon were known to one and all as 'Granny' and her 'Canary'. Many exciting times fell to their lot during this period. To mention one only, the —— was at the same time attacked both with torpedoes from enemy ships and with bombs from enemy aircraft.

In April 1916, we find our friend back again once more at Roehampton, this time on the Experimental Staff and as Officers' Rigging Instructor. During this time CPO Edwards was brought into touch with many of the present heads of the Flying Corps KB Section, several of them passing through his hands for instructional purposes. Much of the experimental work in the development of the Kite Balloon was done at this time at Roehampton, and naturally CPO Edwards was connected with this work, so that it will be seen that he has had very considerable and varied experience with both airships and balloons.[36]

A small number of British airships were lost to enemy action in the war. The airship C17 was shot down by a seaplane over the North Sea in April 1917: the crew of five all perished. The C27 was shot down on 11 December, again with the loss of all five of her crew. The C26, sent out from Pulham to look for the C27, ran out of fuel over the North Sea and came down in Holland: the crew were interned. The C25 was lost at sea in July 1918, probably shot down by a crippled German submarine.

The crew of the C27 had strong Norfolk links: *Pulham Patrol* paid tribute to each of them:

46 *Coastal Class C27 at Pulham.*

Flight-Lt J.F. Dixon, DSC, RN

Born February 11 1892, was educated at the Hibernian Marine School, Clontart, Dublin. Before the war he served as second officer in the Merchant Service. He joined the RNAS in September 1915. He was lately awarded the DSC. He has served at several Air Stations in Great Britain.

Flight-Lt Herbert Hall, RN

Second son of Mr J.T. Hall, FCS, MRSI, of Staines. Born February 1892, educated at King's College, London. Gained a clerkship in HM Civil Service. Upon the inauguration of the RNAS, he was transferred to the Admiralty (RNAS branch), being the first Civil Clerk to serve under Commodore Suetor, KCB, RN, first DAS. He received his commission as Flight Sub-Lieutenant in May 1915, and as Flight-Lieutenant on 1 January 1917. He has served at several Air Stations in the United Kingdom, and also with the BEM Squadron at Salonika.

AM J.E. Martin

Recently mentioned in despatches, joined up shortly after the outbreak of war. He received his training on HMS *Impregnable* and after volunteering for the RNAS was drafted to Kingsnorth, where he received Rigger's training. He was coxswain on the CP to which he was attached, and was one of the youngest coxswains on that type of ship. Of a thoroughly genial and manly disposition he was much liked by all, and his lost to us is very keenly felt.

AM E.R. Whyte

The loss of E.R. Whyte, who was first engineer on C—, is very keenly felt by us at Pulham.

At the outbreak of war he attempted to enlist, but owing to lameness in one leg, from which he had suffered since childhood, he was rejected. Shortly afterwards, however, he enlisted in the Armoured Car Section of the RNAS, and soon left for Egypt. Later he volunteered for the Machine Gun Section of the

HE:—I'VE REACHED AN ELEVATED POSITION
IN THE R.A.F.

HIS ELEVATED POSITION.
ON TOP OF A LADDER STICKING ON PATCHES.

47   *'An Elevated Position'.*

Army at Gallipoli, through which campaign he passed unharmed. Shortly afterwards he joined up as engineer rating in the RNAS, and soon found himself promoted to second engineer, and later first engineer on the CP to which he was attached. He was highly respected by his superiors, who speak well of his ability, and was described by his Commanding Officer as a 'brave young man and a most capable engineer'.

'Knocker', for that was his nickname amongst his friends, was a great favourite, and his good-hearted nature endeared him to all with whom he came in contact.

AM Jack Collett

Wireless Operator, hailed from Walthamstow, London. He enlisted in the RNAS about July 1916, as boy mechanic, undergoing wireless training at Cranwell until he reached the age of 18 years. He was then rated to Eastchurch to undergo a course of aerial gunnery and bomb-dropping, and eventually reached Pulham early in June last. During July he was appointed to C— as operator. From his very earliest flight he proved himself to be a capable and excellent operator, and his reliability was vouched for by Flight Commander Barton, with whom he flew for some time, and also by the late Flight-Lieut Dixon.

'Jack', as we all knew him, had qualities unquestionably rare, and was always cheerful, and reliable in every sense. His loss is deeply felt by all his colleagues in the Wireless Section, and by all who knew him.[37]

Although the pilots and crew took the most obvious risks, the back-room boys played their part too and should not be forgotten. Four people died in accidents at Pulham in 1916 and 1917. James Elinor was killed when a screw jack fell onto him, fracturing his skull, in September 1916, Fred Cooper and George Woolnough were killed in a gas explosion in April 1917, and Charles Ventners died in September 1917 after a fall from the staging of the airshed. Ventners was just 18 years old.[38]

The Prisoner of War

It is never easy to have one's surrender accepted in the heat of battle, but as the months passed the number of prisoners of war held on each side gradually increased.

In 1917 George Stephen, the Norwich City librarian, appealed for donations of books, both for soldiers at the front and for prisoners of war in Germany – 'prisoners cannot live by bread alone, they need also food for the mind'. They needed serious books for study; 'standard works on almost any subject will be welcomed provided they are not obsolete'. Stephen made no mention of anything frivolous like fiction![39]

However, in a starving Germany unlikely to treat its prisoners kindly, even bread might not be easy to come by. Providing food for them became a major concern. In 1916, The Reverend R.A. Bignold, the rector of Carlton Colville, wrote to his parishioners: 'it is incumbent upon us to redouble our efforts for provision of food for British prisoners in Germany; that, whereas at the outset we were admittedly sending comforts supplementary to the ration provided by the German government, the nutritive value of the ration has now become so poor, that we must recognise that our prisoners are dependent upon us for saving them from virtual starvation'.[40]

In the following year, Frances Burton, secretary of an organisation for helping Norfolk Regiment prisoners of war, wrote: 'in Germany all our prisoners would long since have died but for the parcels and bread sent them, and we send each Norfolk Regiment prisoner there three parcels of groceries a fortnight, costs 6s 6d a parcel, and an additional 7lbs of bread a week from Switzerland'. In September it was reported that there were currently 528 Norfolk Regiment prisoners: 129 in Germany, 293 in Turkey, 37 in Bulgaria and 10 in Switzerland. A recently repatriated prisoner, Sergeant B. Fretwell, said that 'but for the parcels from England the prisoners would certainly starve'.[41]

Corporal Ralph Wilson, of Ramnoth Road, Walsoken, served in the Royal Fusiliers. He was captured during the German advance in spring 1918 and spent eight months as a prisoner of war. As a former reporter he was able to pen a vivid account of his life as a prisoner, which appeared in his local paper. He writes:

> The small party that I was captured with was marched, after a night's sleep in the line that the Germans had advanced from, to a prisoners' cage at Esnes, a small French town, where the women secretly and gladly gave us a share of their small food supplies to supplement our first experience of semi-starvation rations, which have been typical all along of what the Germans have regarded as sufficient for human beings – other than themselves. Our next march was to Caudry, where we spent three days in a rather comfortable factory, and when we walked from there to a prisoners' cage at Le Quesnoy, the mounted escort relieved the monotony of the journey by chasing women and children who were trying to give us pieces of bread and biscuits. And in that occupation they were ably assisted by the lances they carried. Our numbers had by this time been considerably augmented.
>
> At Le Quesnoy we were left in open cages for two days and nights, and before we entrained from there we had become saturated with rain. It was a frightfully uncomfortable journey in locked-up cattle trucks, with exceedingly limited food supplies, to Munster, in Westphalia, where is a very large camp. For about eighteen

days we lingered there, on rations that were very scanty in quantity and very unsatisfying in quality. In addition, we suffered severely through loss of sleep, for a bath and the fumigation of our clothing were of course non-effectual against the hordes of fleas that infested the wood-shaving mattresses and blankets that constituted our bed. Before we left this camp we were scarcely able to walk, and when we departed to another place we merely tottered to the station as a result of our weakness. We were removed to Limburg (on the river Lahn), a promising looking camp which fed us better as regards quantity, though the food itself was extremely poor. Again we were troubled with fleas in the dirty barracks that we were unable to clean because the means were not provided to sweep them out.

By this time we had been informed of something that we had no knowledge of while we were at the Front: that our public and other authorities at home, through the Red Cross Society, kept us supplied with rations weekly from England, and we began to look for them. Already we had had two small issues of what were known as 'emergency rations' – food from England sent in bulk – but we knew that our own people were doing their very best to fortify us against the inadequate feeding of our enemies. So we had to await as patiently as possible for our own parcels of food to arrive. At Limburg, all information concerning us was again taken, as a form of registration, and once more when we arrived at Parehim, on May 3rd, after over two days railway journey. In Springhirsch lager we seemed to be miles from anywhere. The surrounding country is only partially developed agricultural land, very marshy, and at one time covered by pine forests, thousands of acres of which still remain. The camp stands on the side of the very picturesque and very straight main road running from Hamburg to Neumunster. It consists of two compounds, with the German sentries' quarters (numbering about 160) outside the barbed wire at one end.

Gradually the original number of prisoners (about 300) was increased to just under 1,500, and some idea of the state of overcrowdedness there may be imagined when I mention that our space for exercise was three square yards per man. But our chief objection was not so much to outside overcrowding, as the fearful lack of space inside the barracks. The beds there, in the middle of the room, were constructed after the fashion of ships' bunks, one above the other, three feet high, and there were other bed spaces along the floor on each side. There were insufficient tables, inadequate heating and lighting apparatus, and most of us had to have our meals upon our bunks. All we had to sweep out with were bunches of heather gathered a few times a week from a neighbouring wood. We were free from vermin when we arrived there, but before long we were considerably troubled with lice. On two occasions only did we have our clothing and blankets fumigated, and the fumigation apparatus was only a partial success. It was useless too, for every nook and cranny seemed to contain the irritating parasites, so we could never be free from the filthy vermin. Two hours daily we had compulsory exercise. That, I think now, was for our benefit, though in those days, when we were very hungry, we had scarcely strength to walk around the compound for the period laid down.

This compulsory exercise resulted in many fellows having troubles piled on to them in the way of close confinement. In many instances, being too weary to walk about – more vigorous exercise was demanded of us until the Germans found it useless to urge us – men rested or hid themselves and being caught, were put in cells on reduced rations for periods varying from seven to twenty one days. The German camp comedian was an aggravating toadying interpreter, whose chief occupation seemed to be seeking out exercise-defaulters, threatening them with

'Eine und zwanzig tagen' and then taking their names. Sentence followed without us having any chance whatsoever of defending ourselves or presenting an excuse; and there was no appeal. When I speak of ill-treatment I do not mean actual physical violence, for there was very little of that. I can remember only a few cases where Germans assaulted any of our men, and then not of a serious nature. But ill-treatment was meted out in a rather more subtle fashion – by the issuing of extremely unjust orders, which could not often for human reasons be complied with.

During the very hot weather, the suffocating atmosphere of the huts was intolerable. We could not sleep or rest: yet if we went outside to get fresh air after a certain hour at night, we rendered ourselves liable to imprisonment for being out of barracks after what was, ironically enough, termed 'Lights Out', though in those days we never had lights, for German time was so far advanced that for a long time it was daylight until after ten o'clock at night. Other discomforts were seriously deficient sanitary arrangements, and parades that were totally unnecessary, and were held at inconvenient hours. It is impossible to go into much detail, for detail would fill volumes. But of all the suffering that we had, that of hunger was the worst. Until August and September, the majority of us were dependent on German rations, and here I think you will be particularly interested. I still cannot understand how the country can have held out so long during the war on such rations. Not only was the quantity small, but the quality was extremely low. 'Substitute' was a word stamped across every article of diet. The feeding of prisoners could not have been a very difficult problem. I cannot accuse them of doing their best to keep us alive, but I charge them with doing their very worst to prevent us from starving. I further declare in all seriousness that were it not for the sending of food from our own country, we should gradually have died – and I cannot imagine a more agonising death than that of slow starvation. As it was, some few, to our own knowledge, died through want of nourishment. We should have shared the fate of the unfortunate Russian and Italian prisoners (who, we were told by some Germans, had, through want of food developed consumption and other diseases, and gradually expired to the number of thousands), were it not for the hopes we placed in our sympathetic people back home.

The best food we had would not compare favourably to the worst in England. Under the category of the best come the bread, oats, potatoes, beans and horse meat, all of which were issued in very sparing quantities. The worst, of which we naturally had most, though often not enough, in spite of the fact that it was practically uneatable, were sauerkraut and pickled mangolds and swedes. There were other 'foods', the names for which I know not, because they were a mysterious substitute. The bread, which averaged 250 grammes a day, was a black, heavy, solid, sour substance, but there were times when we regarded it as cake, for often it was all we had for the whole day, the other food being uneatable, hungry as we were. We generally had that for breakfast, with nothing to put on it, unless we were lucky enough to have a little salt. To drink with it, we usually had a hot fluid, which we dignified by the name of coffee, but was nothing of the sort. It was, we believed, a drink made from burnt ground acorns. There was no taste to it, but we drank it because the water supply in the camp was polluted: though often we went days together without taking anything to drink at all. Occasionally we had a distasteful herb tea, sweetened with a little saccharine.

The horse-flesh was rare, but valued because it was meat. Sometimes it was served up like sausages, boiled in with potatoes or oats or sauerkraut. More often than not it was strongly tainted, visibly green, before it was cooked. It had a disagreeable flavour, but we had to eat it or nothing at all. Most of the food was served up as a sort of soup, served up in huge coppers. A mixture of beans, potatoes, meal and meat was accepted as a great luxury, and it was possible for a couple of litres of that to satisfy us for half-an-hour almost. There were occasional small issues of something resembling butter and jam, but as there was never enough to go round, they were used for flavouring the 'soups'. The filthiest of all foods was sliced mangolds, preserved in some kind of acid, and, boiled up as it was, or with a little meal, it was disgusting to smell and extremely difficult to swallow. It was that we existed on mainly and for one period of a month we had it for dinner and tea. Ultimately our stomachs revolted against it, so that we had nothing the whole day long save that 250 grammes of bread.[42]

An inscription in the Rosary Cemetery, Norwich, commemorates William Burrows who died while a prisoner of war in Germany on 9 November 1918, just two days before the Armistice: he was 20 years old. Another Norfolk soldier to become a prisoner of war was Philip Hewetson: his career is described in chapter seven.

Three

The Healing Game:
Nursing Work at the Front

If the war did consist of 20 million men trying to murder each other, behind them were thousands of men and women trying to patch up those who were not killed outright.

No women fought in the British Army in the First World War. They did invaluable service in a more traditional role – as nurses, usually well away from the front line. This, however, was not always by their choice. In May 1915, the *Eastern Daily Press* carried this article:

Women as Stretcher-Bearers

While admitting to the full the generous suggestion made by a number of devoted women that they and their sisters should be allowed to act as stretcher-bearers at the front, we must condemn the proposal, says the *Evening Standard*. The place of women is emphatically not in the firing line, nor will men abrogate their duty so far as to concede this. Further, we cannot support the argument that 'they would be much less likely to be fired on'. We wish we could think so. But the outrageous and appalling savagery now being displayed by the enemy puts such a supposition utterly out of court. [This was written just three days after the *Lusitania* sinking described in chapter four.][1]

By the winter of 1914, the battle line on the Western Front had become fixed, with both sides building a series of trenches, separated by a narrow zone known as No Man's Land. As the line was so fixed, it was relatively easy to organise a system where wounded men could be taken back from the front to hospitals in safer zones, or even back to England.

Most people were wounded either in the front-line trench or out in No Man's Land. To be caught helpless in the latter, with nothing to do but wait hoping for help, was a terrifying experience. Harry Daniels, the Norwich VC whose career is described in chapter five, lay wounded in a shell hole for four hours before he was rescued. He recalled: 'I'm not troubled with nerves as a rule but I tell you I never felt so scared in my life as I did while lying there'.[2]

The people who had the task of rescuing the wounded at the Front were the stretcher-bearers. Frank Dunham of Norwich was one: 'I now discovered that each infantry battalion had four SBs [stretcher-bearers] to each company, who were responsible for the sick and wounded, and had to take them to the Regimental Aid Post.

Many soldiers were too badly wounded at the Front to be evacuated. It was not long before Dunham was meeting death face to face:

'Stretcher Bearers' was shouted and out I had to go, and along the front line for about 100 yards, where I found one of our chaps badly wounded. In trying to dodge one trench mortar, he had run right into another one, and he was literally peppered all over with small pieces of shrapnel, some had even passed through his cheeks. Frankly, I didn't know where to start bandaging him up, and from his appearance, he seemed to be almost past human aid, so I made him as comfortable as I could, and bathed his face wounds. It may be unpleasant to write of death stealing across a person, but I do so here, because this was the first time in my life that I had witnessed such a thing, and it remains embedded in my memory. In a very short time he commenced to twist and twirl himself about the trench, I tried to hold him still but failed, and from inarticulate sounds, his voice turned to groans, which sounded horrible coming through a mouth full of blood. This rather upset some of his pals, who had stood by to help if necessary, and they all went further down the trench out of hearing distance, leaving me alone with him. I should probably have gone with them, had it not been my job to stay. I was indeed relieved when the poor fellow's end came, and we put him on the side of the trench, covered with a ground sheet, for we had to wait until dusk before we took him down for burial, as we could not carry a stretcher along the front line without being seen by Fritz.[3]

Those wounded who could be moved were taken by the stretcher-bearers to staff of the Royal Army Medical Corps. These men, too, were risking death to save lives. A Cromer man, Captain Harold Ackroyd, won both the Victoria Cross and the Military Cross for his courage in this work:

Utterly regardless of danger he worked continuously for many hours up and down and in front of the line, tending the wounded and saving the lives of officers and men. In doing so he had to move across the open under heavy machine gun, rifle and shell fire. On another occasion he went some way in front of our advanced line and brought in a wounded man under continuous sniping and machine gun fire.

Ackroyd was killed in the action. In September 1917, Ackroyd's wife and son travelled to Buckingham Palace where King George V presented the medals. The King handed the Victoria Cross to his widow and the Military Cross to the son – 'the youngster looked wide-eyed at his Majesty and appeared not to understand'.[4]

For the wounded who were able to walk, it could be a lengthy job finding aid. Wounded soldier Edward Kemp told Edith Upcher what happened to him:

He dragged himself about from dressing station to dressing station, always finding that it had been evacuated but another 'half a mile along the road'. A very long half mile & then when at last he reached a station where there were RAMC men, he was begged 'if you can go on to the next half a mile further on'. This went on for days – some of the time being spent waiting in shelters during heavy bombardment. Incidentally one gathered the deeds of heroism done by the wounded. Each one helping a comrade who was a little worse than himself, and cheering them on to keep up courage and to crawl on to a place of safety. After many stages – and changes of trains & ambulances he got into Hospital in England in 8 days time, very nearly worn out.[5]

The Reverend Charles Lanchester, the vicar of Heigham St Barnabas, went to France in August 1915 as an ambulance driver for the Red Cross. His letters home describing his life and work were printed in his parish magazine:

November 1915 – It will make it easier to understand our present work if I explain the various stages by which a wounded man gets from the firing line back to England. First of all he is carried or walks to an 'advanced Dressing Station', from which he is taken by an army ambulance to a building called a 'Field Ambulance', several of which are to be found a few miles behind the trenches. From there as soon as possible he is removed by us to larger hospitals in this town called 'Casualty Clearing Stations', where the first serious operations are attempted, and when he is well enough he is then taken by us again to the hospital train or to a hospital barge on the canal which carries him to the base hospitals, from which, if he is lucky, he gets a free passage in a hospital ship to England and home.

December 1915 – 'Besides our ordinary work, there are occasionally other jobs which are sometimes very interesting. I will try to describe two such expeditions. One was at night, when about fifteen cars started off to pick up some stretcher-bearers and take them up to the lines. After some miles the order was passed down to extinguish all lights, and thence we crawled slowly, one behind the other, many columns of motor lorries, wagons and horses lumbering past. We halted in a village which seemed to be entirely destroyed, with not a whole house standing. Our final destination was a Field Ambulance, near which we stopped for two or three hours. A battery of our own guns close by were firing vigorously, and making a hideous din, just like a violent thunderstorm, and we could hear the crack of rifle fire in the trenches. Some companies of men just out of the trenches marched passed us, some carrying German helmets in triumph. At length our stretcher-bearers were taken off to their dangerous work and we crawled back empty in the early hours of the morning.

The other expedition gave us an idea of the soldier's life 'at the Back of the Front'. A battalion of the Blankshires had come out of the trenches and were billeted in and around some farm buildings. Our cars brought out baths, coppers for heating water, and bales of clean under linen and a portion of the barn was turned into a huge bathroom. Platoon after platoon were marched in and coming out clean and refreshed. … As the bathing operations took some time they provided us with a meal of Maconochie's rations and biscuits (round and hard like puppy biscuits), washed down by tea made in the travelling kitchen, very strong and sweet such as Tommy loves.[6]

Hospitals behind the front lines were staffed by both men and women. These could occasionally be vulnerable to long distance shelling or to air raids. Norfolk novelist Henry Rider Haggard wrote to his friend William Carr: 'Tom has been under heavy fire. His hospital was shelled – direct hits but mercifully they had time to get into the cellars.'[7]

The German advances in the spring of 1918 created many British wounded, and led to a desperate shortage of nurses and helpers. Lady Leicester, the President of the Norfolk Branch of the Red Cross Society, wrote to the local press:

A large number of women orderlies are wanted at once for service in the military hospitals in France. No previous training is necessary for the work that is wanted. I, therefore, earnestly ask every woman who is of average strength and between the age of 20 and 50 years, and who is able to leave England, to volunteer for this service at once. I say at once because it takes a little time to put applications through and to get applicants to France, and until the supply of orderlies is complete there must be unnecessary suffering, if not unnecessary loss, among the wounded. The terms of service are £22 2s. a year with everything found if applicants sign for a year, and £26 a year with everything found if they sign for the duration of the war.[8]

As the war spread, medical staff were needed at the other fronts as well. We have already seen a description by William Roche of RAMC work in Gallipoli. He mentions the death of Driver Brooks. This was Stephen Brooks, who, in civilian life, had worked in the mustard department at Colman's. His mother received a letter from the padre:

> With deep sympathy I tell you of Stephen's sudden end this morning. Last evening he spoke to me so cheerily and slept in his dug-out next to mine. He carried a wounded comrade to the Clearing Hospital, was struck by shrapnel in the heart, and died almost at once … I buried him on the side of a hill today overlooking the bay with the men standing around and the Colonel (who cast a handful of earth).[9]

A colleague of Brooks paid him a heartfelt tribute: 'he was a cheerful and obliging boy and much liked by all his comrades'.

In October 1915 Canon Aitken's daughter left for Egypt to do 'Red Cross Work'. She wrote home: – 'Egypt is a place for cats – such poor starved wretched looking specimens almost all'.[10]

These hospitals had to deal with those suffering from illness as well as the wounded. George Durbidge wrote philosophically to his schoolteacher friend Tom Higdon in 1916:

> Now I must tell you a little about myself here I am at the presant [sic] stuck on an iland [sic] how long for I do not know, was taken Bad at a place called Lichovan up the line and forced to return to Hospital at Salonica and from there to where I am now but I am pleased to tell you that I am quite myself again. I was very sorry to hear such bad news about the boys around us but their it is. It has to be done and some one has got to pay the piper it is an aufull [sic] war I shall be Pleased when it is finished and the boys return home again if it was not done now it would have to come to it later and it might have been worse then we have a stubborn enemy to deal with.[11]

Travelling to these hospitals was in itself not without risk. Nurse Hayward of Hardley had a dramatic tale to tell. She was in Camp in Marseilles when she heard on 2 May 1917 that she was one of the nurses there selected to go to Salonika. Transports arrived for them at 11 am the next day and by 12.30 pm they were on board the *Transylvania* along with 3,500 British soldiers:

> After dinner Matron gives us a private rehearsal of what to do if we are torpedoed. We walk to our life belt. I am to be in charge of our corridor. Life belts always to be worn (some grumble).
>   May 4 was a lovely day: 9 am Up on deck, the sea so blue & just flicked with white foam, here & there, the sun glorious but a good breeze blowing.
>   10.15 A bang which those who heard will never forget. Sister S & I got up & I said the Ship has been struck. There is no panic, everyone goes to two allotted places, what white faces all afraid. A Scotch officer tightens my life belt (I have never seen him since) & we are to get in 'Ladies first' how often I have read but never expected to hear that cry. Pte Francis helps me in I immediately find my

feet wet, but this is a mere detail. Matron & 45 of us all pushed in 3 Tommies & then the boat is lowered. I really think this is the worst moment. The captain gives orders from the bridge. We hear there is no crew. Who will volunteer? Two sailors come down the roap [*sic*]. Jack acts as skipper, we shall never forget him. Only a lad of 17, but how brave & splendid he was throughout. Our boat sets out & the men from the ship give 3 cheers! I cannot look back. The sea seems quite rough. The sisters help with the oars, we are in sight of shore. My rowlock is broken, so I cannot row, I wish could, only to do something one feels better. 'Throw the extra oar overboard, some poor soul may be glad of it', Jack says.

It seems a long way to shore. A second torpedo strikes our ship & an answering shot from the Destroyers. The *Transylvania* seems to be going down on one side. Many boats are now launched all round us. Why don't they pick us up? Our boat is filling with water, we start bailing out, but it seems so fruitless & the waves are so big. We throw all socks, coats, rugs etc overboard. Another bang and HMS *Transylvania* is no more.

Another big wave & the boat is swamped, but somehow is still floating & we are all hanging on. One VAD [Voluntary Aid Detachment] jumped out as she could swim, & is clinging to an oar behind me. I am washed out & find myself clinging to an oar & piece of rope. At first I felt very frightened & believe I was calling out.

After a time I felt calmer, but my arms were aching so I felt I must give in. Will they never come? Jack says 'Hold on Sister, a 2nd boat is coming to pick us up'. The waves seem so big, quite over my head, the salt water makes me feel so sick. I thought of home & all my dear ones. Life is sweet. It seems hours we were in the water, some one tried to get me back in the boat, but I could not. I could see and feel little now. A Cheer! From the distance it seemed & then someone said the Destroyer was alongside. I thought my head was going to be knocked & it was a pity to be killed after all 'the holding on'. Two hands come down & I was pulled up first. My hair seemed caught. The rope ladder was there, & I got one foot on. I felt the ship boards under my feet, & crowds of men all around me. All went black! I knew I was lying down & some one was chafing my hands & face.

Sister Hayward was landed at Savona and eventually taken to a convent with 21 other nurses. Two days later she went to the funeral of the captain and other victims of the disaster. They were taken by train to Marseilles and then to Havre, crossing the Channel overnight: 'None of us slept very well & clung to our life belts, although the steward said they were not necessary!' They arrived at Southampton at 8 am the next day [17 May], and by 11 pm she was back home at Hardley.

Also on the *Transylvania* was another Norfolk-born medical person, William Norman, a sergeant in the RAMC, and pastor of Wardlow Congregational Church in Glasgow: he went down with the ship. He is commemorated in the Rosary Cemetery, Norwich.

The most well-known of the Norfolk nurses at work abroad is, of course, Edith Cavell: her story is told in chapter seven.

The dream of many men at the front was to get a 'blighty', a wound that was not life-threatening but was serious enough for the man to be sent back to England. As soon as the war broke out, hospitals in England made themselves ready to receive wounded from France, and also from expected battles at sea. The Norfolk and Norwich Hospital led the way:

48   *Tented wards at the Norfolk and Norwich Hospital.*

On the day following that on which war was declared, the Board of Management offered 50 beds to the Admiralty, with 50 more to be ready in four days, and offered to erect four marquees in the Hospital grounds to hold 150 more beds. By discharging as many patients as possible, by transferring all the children to the Jenny Lind Infirmary and arranging with that Institution to take all children's cases during the war, and by erecting four tents in the grounds, well over 100 beds were ready for the reception of the sick and wounded in a very short while. As the chances of these beds being utilised by the Admiralty became more remote the Board, in September, transferred their offer to the War Office and on the 7th October 1914, the first convoy of 100 sick and wounded men from the British Expeditionary Force was received. After receiving convoys of 100 men at the rate of about one in ten days for two months i.e. during October and November, it became evident that unless additional beds could be provided, the intervals between the convoys would have to be considerably lengthened, owing to the residuum of bad cases. This fact had only to be mentioned to the Norfolk public by the editor of the *Eastern Daily Press* when a sum of over £2,600 was subscribed through its columns in less than a week for a new temporary building. This 'temporary building' with 60 beds, known as the Eastern Daily Press ward admirably fulfilled its functions during the war and today is used for the accommodation of discharged soldier patients.

For a long period of the war the hospital contained 424 beds, namely 150 for civilians and 274 for military patients, and altogether 97 convoys, with 7,880 men, were

49 *The Eastern Daily Press Ward at the Norfolk and Norwich Hospital.*

admitted from overseas in addition to a large number of patients from among the troops stationed in the district.[12]

By 1915 even this was not enough. Many more beds were needed, and the lunatic asylum at Thorpe St Andrew was taken over for wounded soldiers, the patients being moved to Hellesdon Hospital and other institutions, where they remained throughout the war, probably largely forgotten.

The Hospital was renamed the Norfolk War Hospital. Its house magazine describes 'The First Convoy':

> A telegram OHMS was despatched from Dover on the afternoon of July 9th 1915, with the curt announcement 'You will receive 150 British men etc.' To the officials it meant just another convoy, but to us it meant the birth of a new hospital, and that the NWH was at last a going concern. Short we were of many things, for in spite of months of telegrams, the WO was slow to supply, and when they did the first consignment was 150 pairs of green spectacles!
>
> It is a warm June night for our first convoy. On the platform the senior surgeon is pacing up and down, waiting. Rows of stretchers and ambulance men are waiting also. A shrill whistle is heard, the squads stand at attention, and the green and white lights of the ambulance train come into view. Slowly the long heavy Pullman train comes in and stops gently without jerks, careful of those within. Specially picked men are the engine drivers, who have a gentle touch with

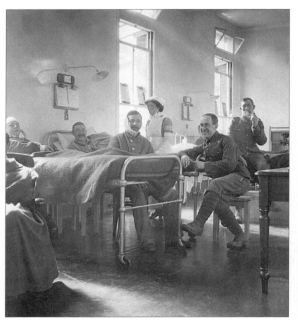

THE BEST TWO MEDICINE TOMMY. LOOK FORWARD TOO.

50 *King Edward Ward, Norfolk and Norwich Hospital.*

51 *'The best two medicines', drawn by a patient at Sheringham Hospital.*

their powerful brakes. The train is motionless, the doors are locked, blinds are drawn, no sound is heard. From the last coach the officer in charge steps down and hands the major the nominal roll of the wounded on the train. A few short words with the ambulance man, and in an instant the unloading is in full swing. Cots to stretchers, and stretchers to ambulance in quick methodical succession. The last ward is cleared, watches are consulted with a short 'Just under the hour, sir. Smart work!' The officers salute and part, the officer-in-charge to his quarters at the end of the train, while the major speeds home in the last ambulance, conscious of a full day's work on the morrow. Safely in hospital, the last stretcher is soon out of the wards, and soon the men are washed, fed, and asleep in bed. The MO [Medical Officer] goes his round amidst profound slumber for the most part, here and there someone in pain, and then he, too, turns in and sleep reigns over the hospital.

Next day various minor arrangements, excellent in theory, had to be altered in practice. For instance, two copies of the front sheet of the patient's case board were supposed to be made through the medium of a carbon paper. It was not foreseen that when the patient wanted to write home he would use his board as a support; and so the second sheet often went down to the office as follows: Private Jones. Fractured tibia, beer, pudding. Dear Mary – I have got here; chicken & fish etc. And so the carbon paper was given up. But sisters, nurses, probationers, and medical-officers pulled together with a will, and now, like Kipling's ship, we might be styled the 'hospital that found itself'.

The magazine also has a light-hearted description of 'A Day in the Life of an MO' at the hospital:

52 *Wounded soldiers on the* Jenny Lind.

AM

5.30 – Roused from slumber by patients in Ward X, just round the corner, singing in unison. They appear to know every comic song written since the Boer War.

6.00 – Consider whether I have sufficient energy to go and stop them.

6.05 – I haven't.

6.30 – Singing stops owing to the superior attractions of breakfast. Drop off to sleep again.

6.45 – Orderly in Ward Y, overhead, drops a scuttle of coals. Hope he has hurt himself severely.

6.50 – Afraid he hasn't, for he starts picking them up one by one, dropping each piece not more than three times.

7.15 – Sleep again.

7.30 – Slight difference of opinion between two members of the nursing staff (also in Ward Y), followed by smashing of crockery.

7.35 – Doze

7.45 – Violent agitation of my door Handles, being polished by Charwoman A.

7.50 – Ditto, ditto Charwoman B.

7.52 – Loud altercation between A and B as to whether A has cleaned it first or not.

8.10 – Point eventually settled by mass meeting of charwomen, assisted by passing orderlies and patients.

9.0 – Rise after nearly a whole hour's unbroken sleep. To breakfast, feeling ill-used and at enmity with the world at large. A coal has dropped into the porridge, all the bacon has been eaten, and the last user of the teapot has omitted to replenish it with water, there being nothing but cold tea leaves in it. Compromise with toast and marmalade and tepid milk and water, realising that, after all, war is war.

10.15 – Enter Ward Z, not feeling particularly bright. Sister appears cross – must have had no breakfast either. Will I see Private Brown 'poor man hardly slept all night – agonies of indigestion'. Elicit from Private Brown that before going to sleep he had consumed two bananas, one orange, and a stick of chocolate. Am not feeling sympathetic so tell him it serves him right, and threaten to knock off his beer if it occurs again. Watch sister do three dressings, giving helpful advice the while. Firmly veto all sister's suggestions; must be master in my own ward.

10.45 – Tiring work; feel I would like a cigarette.

10.50 – *Must* have one.

10.51 – Escape on the plea that I have promised to do an important dressing in Ward Q at a quarter to eleven.

11.20 – On the way to Ward Q meet Sister Z, who eyes me suspiciously. Try to look as if I were returning from an urgent call to someone else's ward.

11.25 – Enter Ward Q, feeling slightly better. Sister remarks that she is afraid all the dressings are done. Rejoicing inwardly I express sorrow. 'Been very busy in Z, could not get away before'. (Hope Sisters Z and Q do not compare notes when off duty. Still, I must take *some* risks). Sister deceived by my expressions of sorrow, offers to take down any dressing I may select. I select Corporal Smith. Corporal Smith objects to being dressed by sister. I overheard him telling his neighbour yesterday that at the last hospital he was in the doctor dressed him every day himself as he was such an important case. I strafe Corporal Smith for five minutes by the clock with a large probe, and ask sister to continue dressing him as before. Corporal Smith heaves a sigh of relief. I feel distinctly better. Satisfactorily settle several knotty points, such as 'May Sergeant Jones lie on his back?'; 'Will I change Private Robinson's medicine as he doesn't like the taste', 'Private Jones feels sure massage would do his toe good, may he have it?' Feel I have done enough for one morning, so compliment sister on the remarkable health of all her patients, and escape hurriedly before she can recover from the shock to play 100 up till lunch. In rather good form. Am twenty ahead of my opponent and getting my eye in nicely, when urgent message comes from Ward Z. Private Buggins (recently operated on) has got out of bed unobserved to chat with a bosom friend at the other end of the ward and has broken his stitches. Feel very annoyed with Private Buggins, and say so (also with sister, but don't say so). Put in fresh stitches there and then. Private Buggins decides he won't get out of bed again, even if a Zeppelin comes. Billiards ruined, of course!

PM
2-4.30 – In the theatre, a somewhat dull afternoon, only enlivened by Private Tonk, who, on coming round from the anaesthetic, attempts to conduct a conversation in French with a lady of his acquaintance 'somewhere in France'. Hope none of the nurses understand French. Wish I understood it better. Must

ask the anaesthetist's help in translating one or two words later on. Gross haul for the afternoon, six pieces of shrapnel, one trouser button, some pieces of bone, and a finger (damaged). Not so bad.

5-7 – A little fresh air as antidote to over-work. On returning am met by an orderly with three notes and two messages from sundry sisters.

7-7.30 – Pacify them with promises and soft words.

10.0 – Night round Ward Z. Five minutes conversation with night nurse.

10.30 – Ditto, ditto ward Q.

11.0 – Bed at last. Night round must have taken longer than I thought: still, work must be done. Zeppelins about, but am consoled by the fact that if a bomb drops on the roof over me the coal-dropping orderly will get the full benefit. Perhaps even the charwoman – but perish the thought!

11.5 – Asleep.[13]

This light-hearted approach covers up the fact that a long term stay in such an institution could be a most depressing experience.

It was too much for Sergeant James Townsend of the Suffolk Regiment. In August 1917, just as the bugle ordering the men to dress at 6 o'clock on Sunday morning died away, a shot was heard: Townsend was found in his bunk with a gunshot wound to his head: it took him several hours to die. He was a London man, and he is buried at Abney Park Cemetery.

Another man to die of self-inflicted wounds at the NWH was Driver James Thomas of the Army Service Corps. He was in billets in Norfolk in June 1916. His landlady heard a gunshot from his room at 5.30 on a Sunday morning. She rushed up to find him badly wounded: he was taken to the Hospital where he died on the following day. He had left a note in his room reading: 'Dear Ma – I am almost mad at the toothache, and am going to do myself in. Goodbye – Jim'.[14]

Some patients inevitably succumbed to their wounds: the graves of several of these can be seen in the Earlham Road Cemetery in Norwich. One was an Australian, Private James Evans, from Wodonga in the state of Victoria. He had served in Gallipoli, where he was wounded, and was wounded again while serving in France. He was one of the convoy of casualties that arrived at the NWH on 2 July 1916. He died at the end of August and was buried in Earlham Cemetery: two dozen wounded men from the Hospital, including several Australians, attended the funeral. Evans' sister was also present: she was a nursing sister in France. Evans' grave can be seen today, close to the Cross of Sacrifice.

There are almost 350 First World War graves in the Earlham cemetery, including that of James Evans. Not all are of men who died of their wounds in hospital: others are

53 *'He gave his life' – grave of Private James Evans of Australia, in the Earlham Road cemetery, Norwich.*

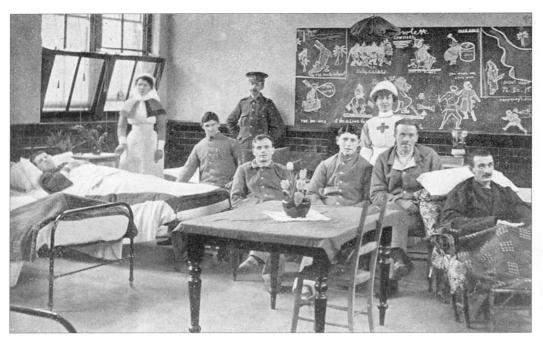

54 *Lakenham Military Hospital, built as a school – note the blackboard.*

those who died of disease or in accidents in training, such as Cecil Boast, mentioned in chapter two. Many of these cases were also sent to the NWH. Edgar Collison of East Bilney had been wounded at Gallipoli. After recovering in England he joined the Royal Flying Corps. He had only just completed his six weeks' training when he was badly hurt in a flying accident on 18 June 1916. He was taken to the Hospital. At first his wounds were not thought to be fatal, but he weakened and died on 26 June: he was 25 years old.

There was a third military hospital in Norwich, at Lakenham in a newly built school hastily comandeered for the war. The girls at Colman's in Carrow were especially interested in this hospital, as it was close to their place of work:

> Not content with sending several parcels of eggs, fruit etc to the Lakenham Military Hospital, the girls of the Carrow Works Starch Packing and paper Box Departments decided that something of a non-perishable nature ought to accompany the comestibles. Having ascertained that a gramophone would be an acceptable present, they at once despatched to the Hospital a very nice instrument, together with a supply of records.[15]

By 1917 even the beds at these three hospitals were insufficient. In May the War Office wrote to the Norwich Board of Guardians asking to be allowed to take over the infirmary of the workhouse for use as a war hospital. This would have involved moving out the 240 inhabitants, and spreading them around about a dozen neighbouring workhouse infirmaries, some a considerable way from Norwich. This provoked lively debate among the Guardians. Mr Crotch said that he did not think

55 *Gramophone presented to Lakenham Hospital by the girls at Colman's.*

anybody could accuse him of lack of sympathy with the sick and poor, but the men who had suffered in defending us should have first consideration. Mr Keeley said they must put sentiment aside: 'were not the poor old people who were sick in the Infirmary as important as the wounded soldiers (Members – 'No')'. It was decided to wait and see if the War Office repeated the request.[16]

In the end the newly-built infirmary belonging to the Wayland Union Workhouse, near Attleborough, was turned into a military hospital in November 1917. Almost a thousand patients were treated there in the final year of the war.

As well as the major institutions, there were a large number of much smaller auxiliary hospitals. They were run by the Red Cross and the St John Ambulance Brigade. There were 62 of these in Norfolk, but some were very small, and not all functioned for the full period of the war. They were really convalescent homes, often in the private houses of the gentry: people were sent on to them from the major war hospitals. A typical newspaper entry for autumn 1914 records:

A party of 15 wounded soldiers arrived at Thorpe station from Colchester Hospital to convalesce at Brundall House, placed at the disposal of the Red Cross Society by Mr ffiske. The house contained 30 beds and was run by Mrs Harker – 'for its size Brundall shares with Woodbastwick in the provision it has made for our wounded soldiers'.[17]

56 *'Just a few of the boys', Red Cross Hospital, Sheringham.*

57 *'Where are they staying?', drawn by a patient at Sheringham Hospital.*

The hospital at Brundall was actually at Brundall Hall: it had 40 beds. The hospital at Woodbastwick was rather larger, with 70 beds. It was in Woodbastwick Hall, which was owned by John Cator. Another grand house to be used as a hospital was Overstrand Hall. 'It was funded by Lady Hillingdon and the costs were supplemented by the War Office.' It was for officers, and was equipped for 15 patients. Lady Hillingdon had a personal interest in the war: her son, Charles Mills, died at Loos on 6 October 1915.[18]

There was a Red Cross hospital of similar size at Attleborough: this was in the Town Hall. It closed down when the nearby Wayland Military Hospital opened: It had treated 656 patients in its three years of existence.[19]

Edith Upcher of Sheringham Hall was doing local hospital work, probably at the hospital in Cliff Road, Sheringham. In her diary she is reticent as to details, although the brief entry for 5 February 1916 – 'good deal of knife in OP [outpatients] ward' – is a telling one. She calculated that between June 1915 and March 1916, they had dealt with 2,600 outpatients from among the troops stationed in North Norfolk. The in-patients included a man called Hargon who had served in the Royal Field Artillery from 1914 until being wounded in January 1916. When he left the Hospital for Norwich at the end of February 1916, Hargon was 'too depressed for words', saying that he was 'going from Heaven to Hell'.[20]

Another soldier at Sheringham, Lance-Corporal Forsyth of the Black Watch, put a similar thought into a young girl's autograph book:

> I am in Sheringham today,
> But where tomorrow? I cannot say!

58   *Nurse Florence Amherst.*

> Perhaps in Hades for all I know,
> 'Praise God from whom all blessings flow'!

Another soldier took a more philosophical view of his situation in hospital:

> When first you join the Army, on the Army you are keen.
> You polish up your buttons and you keep your rifle clean.
> You like your work and do your best to earn your daily bob,
> And you never think of looking for a
> > Nice Soft Job.
>
> But when you have ploughed a month or two through Belgium's miles of mud,
> With ammunition on your back it seems to cool your blood,
> And you start to think with longing of a
> > Nice Soft Job.
>
> Then if your star is lucky and you 'cop a souvenir'
> And get carted back to Blighty and the things that make life dear
> And plan ways of thanking for a
> > Nice Soft Job
>
> Oh it's great to be a service man, home and wounded from the Front,
> To know you've had a smack at it and faced the battle's brunt;
> To criticise the 'Bookies' who regard you as a Nob
> But best of all is to have a
> > Nice Soft Job.[21]

59   *A group of patients and nurses outside Tofts Hall.*

However, even in Norfolk, bombs were a risk. Edith Upcher recorded a discussion in her hospital in March 1916:

> In the event of Invasion that the Hospital men to be returned to Norwich (how?!) and that the detachment takes work at a dressing station 8 miles behind firing line. Nurses to volunteer for the work. In case of bombardment the Hospital might have to be used first as a dressing station (? If it was left standing!).

The hospital in Overstrand Hall was closed in October 1916 because of the danger of its being bombed.

Another upper-class family that fully embraced nursing work was the Amhersts. Lady Amherst and her daughters ran a hospital at Tofts Hall in Buckenham Tofts. This family, too, had suffered a personal tragedy: Lady Amherst's nephew, William, was killed at the Battle of the Aisne in 1914.

Letters of thanks to Lady Amherst and her daughters give a good impression of their work, and of some of their patients:

From Private H. Alcock, in Salonika with the Royal Fusiliers 27 June 1917 –

> Sorry I have not written to you before to thank you very much for the two parcels. I received them both quite safely. I ought to have written to you before to thank you for your kindness. It is extremely kind of you all but you must excuse my neglect,

60   *Wounded soldiers enjoy the Norfolk air.*

and the magazine I received safe. It is very good of the Parishioners to knit the mittens. I hope you are all well, the Ladyship and Ladies and also the staff of the Hall. I am well myself at present. It is very hot out here now, to hot to work in the day time…. I hope to live through it all and meet you all and tell you some of the tales of this country.

From Private J.H. Twigg, of the RAMC, in the NWH in Thorpe –

Yours to hand with many thanks. Thanks very much for tobacco. I have been in bed for a week my chest has been so painful and my cough does not seem to improve. Bogg told me about the Pictures thanks very much for sending mine home. Had another letter from Sister Joy she starts day duty on Friday. On Thursday next is the Sports Day. There was a concert in the Hall this afternoon but I did not go. I thought it would be to close. It would have been on the Recreation ground if weather

61 *Albert Eagle at the Pyramids.*

[words lost]. I hope we shall soon get a change, no chance of me getting any better while it lasts. On Thursday the Nurses play another match with Patients who have not played Cricket before, to wear skirts and sun hats. Bogg still going on alright. You would see the difference in him now.

From Private D. Bogg, Royal Fusiliers, also in the NWH –

Just a few lines hoping this will find you quite well, as this leaves me fairly. Oh this Place is a Prison to your lovely hospital. I was in agony last night, they took no notice of me. I have had nothing done for me since I have been here so I am getting out as soon as possible. No sugar in our drink. Now Dear Matron I must thank you very much for your kindness and looking after me as you have done.

(These two letters are not dated but a drawing by Twigg probably enclosed with the letter is dated 7 April 1916.)

From Private J. Armiger back on active service, 25 February 1917 –

I beg to thank you very much for your kindness in sending me the knitted woollen wrapper & cocoa & tea tablets which I received yesterday, they will come very useful. We have had some sharp frosts and cold weather, but it is now much milder, although we are at present getting very little sun. We have had a spell in the trenches and are having a short rest. We had our blankets & clothing

62   *Interior of Kirstead Hospital, 1915.*

disinfected today & have been & had a shower-bath so feel much fresher & clean & comfortable.

From Isaac Eagle, of the RAMC, Citadel Hospital, Cairo, 11 October 1915 –

I thank you all so very much for your kind and generous gifts I safely received the other day. I shall reserve them for the front, where I may soon find myself again. I may find myself on the way there any time now, one never knows when he may be called upon to leave, for the front. I am glad to say that I am feeling extremely fit and well. So far Egypt has not affected my health. I have done my best to observe all the rules of health as laid down by the authorities for our personal benefit. But unfortunately a good many have been laid low with that awful dysentery, caused sometimes by indulging in eating too much native fruit, and as you know well enough the natives are none too clean personally. I believe they have a dislike for soap. There is one good point in their religion which compels them to wash, otherwise I do not think they would wash at all.

From Mrs Emma Kirk in Scunthorpe, about her son –

Thank you very much for you writing to me & was pleased to hear from you. Yes I am glad to say I feel a little better but still I feel upset after the air raid that we had at Scunthorpe. I have never been the same since. I am glad to hear that my son is getting better again, but he is still without his voice. It seems a long time coming back to him. I know it is a long journey for him & very bad weather too, I know & he longs to see me & I should like to see him. Will you tell him to rest contented and not to worry over me … PS You see it is 12 months since I saw him.

63   *Outside Kirstead Hospital.*

In a later letter (both letters are undated), Mrs Kirk writes –

pleased to hear that my son is on the improve, as it has worried me to think that
he has suffered so much & not able to go & see him, you see it would be such an
expense to me. Still I am longing to see my son. I think if I could only see him I
should feel much better as I often sit down & have a good cry over him.

From Sapper Wilson of the Royal Engineers, written in Southampton 8 May 1916 –

i am so very sorry at not writing sooner i have had so many Friends to see that
the ten days Leaf i had from Tofts Hall has all most gone before i knew where i
was i received your twine all write and i am on the next Draft for Active Service i
shall arrive in France about Wednesday and i feel in the Pink i must thank you for
that i think i never felt better than i did under your Care what a Roaving
Commission i had at Buckenham Toffs Hall for inever seen any Finer Estate in
my Life i have seen the prettest Estates in Cheshire and Derbyshire but not one
to Beet that what grand water for the trout and that is what the Peasants like Best
i think if there is a nice swamp the Peasant clames it And it is the Finest Shooting
for the Wild Duck and Snipe and Good Sandy Ground for the Rabbits and for
the Covers there is fine woods and grand Timber i am sorry our Leaf was so
soon i will nit you those nets and Plenty others when i get settled over in France
you might tell me if the Ones you have are Big Enough i will send you my
French Adress as i Expect to go over any time Give my Best Respects to any or
the Nurses and Sisters if you should come across them i am sure they would
Laugh at the Funny Remarks i made and i hope you have kept my secret about
the Smokey Chimdney Don't Lite the Fire and then you are on the Safe Side if
Ever i have the chance to come over from France on Leaf i would not mind to

come and Have a Look at you but i shall have to Chance my Luck i was very Lucky Chap the Last time i hope my Little Friend is going on i mean the Boy Freeman he did Enjoy a walk with Wilson he told me i was the Best in the Lot i shant forget when i stole him that Hot Cross Bun and You Matron Found it when we was beiign Photografth So i must Close my Letter and Get Ready for another Rough job and they want the Men Like Wilson is Excuse me not writing Sooner But i will send you my Settled Adress in France.[22]

The names of the Norfolk Hospitals appear on a large banner that was presented to Norwich Cathedral by the Red Cross in 1919. Curiously, in 1959 the Cathedral authorities had it taken down, and they returned it to the Red Cross. However, in 1989 the Cathedral once again accepted the banner, where it provides an important counterpoint to the regimental banners also held there.[23]

Norfolk women worked at Hospitals elsewhere in Britain too: Henrica Bulwer, the wife of Edward Bulwer of Heydon Hall, was commandant of Freeford Hall Hospital in Staffordshire. Patients there included Belgian soldiers wounded in 1914, several of whom were later to return to the Belgian army.

During the war the Germans, of course, were making their own arrangements for their wounded. Beatrice Gurney was working with the Church Army in Namur, Belgium in 1919:

Miss Gregory and I came across some soldiers living on an old German hospital barge & they showed us all over it. It must have been a heaven for the patients, tho the German wooden beds were not so nice as our iron ones & of course it was not nearly as spick and span

"THE GODDESS (?)"

64   *The Goddess (?)*.

65   *The linen room, Freeford Hall hospital.*

as it would have been as a hospital, but the hugeness width and height of the place amazed one. I shd like to have seen it fitted up. They used to tow lots of them to Germany with a steam tug.[24]

Hospitals needed not just nurses but all sorts of ancillary staff, and women volunteers – some members of the VAD filled these posts. Ruth Hewetson, the brother of Philip Hewetson whose career is described in chapter seven, worked at Fargo Military Hospital on Salisbury Plain. Her letters home describe her life:

66 *At work in the kitchen, Freeford Hall hospital.*

Yesterday was certainly a different Sunday for me (so used to a different dress, a best hat, Church and S School & lots of hymns) – I was up by 6 cleaning my hut – and by 8 I was thoroughly grubby & glad of a whole breakfast. This was my 1st public meal & I won't deny I was rather terrified especially as sugar and marg were not doled out till Tues & I had to rely on other people (therefore I got more than I wld otherwise I suspect!).... Last night there was a farewell party to Asst Matron (who is going off to Salonika) & a lot of Med[ical] Off[icers] came in. Oh dear!!! I shan't get married <u>here.</u>

Added to this we have 200 German wounded – awful cases – <u>very</u> young – only captured on the 23rd, only allowed to be nursed by men, it seems very wrong to send here.

They say we're going to have 300 British Wounded sent here – I hope not, it is far too isolated for them – & the Hospital is already understaffed. There are crowds of Germans (the last lot very bad) I believe here now.

It is a nuisance that after all our care in choosing my work (rejection of WAAC [Women's Army Auxiliary Corps] etc) I shld have landed in something wh seems none too satisfactory – but still I suppose I shld meet w the same difficulty in any Body of Women nowadays.

Now about my change of work –

There are two alternatives:

1) <u>Kitchen</u> to work under Miss B (who is very fond of me – she told me so last night – & I of her), learn 'mass cooking (I call it) – (have the cleaning of one large range).

2) Be 3rd in <u>the Mess</u>. I prefer Mess work – <u>but</u> Miss Tottenham is going to be Head in Mess – she's already started planning all her alterations (awfully bad form as Miss Allsopp's nowhere near going yet) & I shall sure to be annoyed by her.

Tomorrow I start work in the Kitchen! ... I'm to be 3rd in there – so no ranges – a certain amount of cleaning, & cooking!

There is a very bad epidemic of dysentery in the Hospital – in fact all leave for the staff has just been stopped. Men are coming in fast (48 last night!) & there have been several deaths.

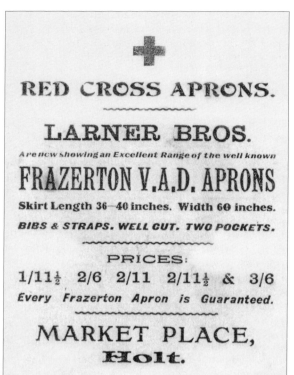

67   *Aprons for VADs.*

My new work is very nice – absolutely different, & honestly I don't consider anyone really works until they get in a Kitchen … I am entirely responsible for the boiler (in wh now milk is sterilised) must be lit & clean by 6.30 – & then kept up all day – then also I have charge of 2 larders & Sister's store room – passages betw these too – they get filthy w meat & fish & all food – those are regular undisturbed duties then I do anything to help in Kitchen (all vegs except potatoes) any fruit cutting – salad etc. Last Sunday we took 3½ hrs to cut beans for 116 staff for midday!! – today I did apples for puddings & then 4 (!) cucumbers for salads. If 'on' afternoon (2 a week I am alone) there's often porridge – all kettles for lots of teas – milk & water to sterilize & things to prepare for supper.

Ruth, like many women, found that her work in the war was making her much more of an independent person. Her life would never again be the same:

I do get teased here – you know – I'm very much treated as a 'baby' in many ways & yet I'm sure I'm much more capable etc than I used to be … I think I now have my full share of 'self confidence'. … You see for the last 7 months I've been living in an atmosphere where everyone is out to 'get on w it at all costs & never mind how' & it is so different from dumplings! It is difficult to explain in a letter but don't think I mean I never want to do my old works again it is not that a bit, it is just that I've seen how very different people can be from Salhouse. See?[25]

Influenza

The last year of the war, 1918, saw the outbreak of a virulent form of influenza, commonly known as Spanish flu as it was wrongly supposed to have originated in that country. The epidemic spread across the whole of the world, killing more people than had died in action in the war. It spread among the prisoners of war in Germany in July. Ralph Wilson wrote:

The camp was over-run with an epidemic of Spanish grippe – at a time when our vitality was almost at its lowest ebb. The additional misery it brought about I would like to forget, though it is difficult to obliterate from my mental picture of that dark past the sight of mere spectres of human beings, fellows with hollow cheeks, attenuated limbs, and frail bodies, with their skin dried like parchment for want of fat, lying or walking about in a condition that was ghastly and horrible. There were fortunately only a few deaths at this time, but it was an anxious period for every man who caught the disease – and nearly every man was affected. To have been half-starved was terrible enough, but to have to combat this epidemic in that condition was immeasurably more fearful.[26]

By August, Ruth Hewetson was experiencing the disease in Fargo Hospital on Salisbury Plain:

> Just at present we're fearfully busy because there's a <u>very</u> bad outbreak of flu on the Plain – it has been in London & is supposed to come fr Spain. The Hospital is crammed – 2 or 3 new wards opened & today men lying out on the grass waiting for beds! The Nursing Staff have been recalled from leave etc & now number over 100 w only 14 of us – so we <u>are</u> busy especially as the meals are all irregular w lots of ones & twos always coming in late etc. Some of the Staff have got it now – luckily it only lasts 3 or 4 days but is quite bad then I gather.
> The epidemic is raging <u>furiously</u> in the Hospital. Men in 20s & 30s from all over the Plain. 6 staff borrowed fr other hospitals. All working w'out time off & late on into the night – new wards opened. Said to be <u>very</u> bad – I don't know the cause.[27]

On 21 November 1918, Bill Carr wrote home from Eton College to his mother in Ditchingham, Norfolk:

> I am so very sorry that I have not written before this week, but I have been so very busy avoiding the flu and playing football etc. we have got the flu rather badly here, in one house they have got 28 cases, I do so hope I shall not get it.[28]

The disease was active in Norfolk too, including within the Military Hospitals. Eight soldiers died from influenza in the Town Close Red Cross Hospital in Norwich in November 1918: before this, only two soldiers had died in Norfolk's Red Cross Hospitals during the whole war. Dr Lawson McClintock, who ran the Red Cross Hospital at Loddon, died from influenza on the very last day of the war, 11 November 1918.[29]

Four

The Home Front:
War Comes to Norfolk

Invasion

The fear of invasion from Germany was a very real one in 1914, and Norfolk, only 80 miles across the North Sea from the enemy coast, was one of the most likely places for troops to land. The initial sense of panic is reflected in a letter to Laura Upcher at Sheringham Hall from a cousin in the Admiralty in November 1914: 'Dear Laura, I don't think the Germans will come but if they do it is nothing to make a fuss about. You must take it all in the day's work'.[1]

As with so many things in the First World War, plans for what to do in the event of an invasion were improvised at a local level. Yarmouth issued instructions to every household:

KEEP THIS IN A PROMINENT PLACE

Directions to the Public, in the event of Bombardment or Invasion

In case of BOMBARDMENT do NOT go into the STREET, but *keep*
In your cellar or *on the ground floor of your home.*
In case of a hostile landing and the necessity arising of leaving the town,
VEHICLES from *YARMOUTH* must travel by CAISTER ROAD.
FOOT PASSENGERS from Yarmouth must proceed past VAUXHALL
STATION on to the ACLE NEW ROAD.
Both Vehicles and Foot Passengers from **SOUTHTOWN**
AND GORLESTON must use the road to ST OLAVES via BRADWELL AND ASHBY.
It must be borne in mind that in case of any of the roads being required for the movement of Troops, civilians must be prepared to move off the roads temporarily into adjacent fields if necessary in order that they may not hinder the movement of the Troops.
Persons leaving the town should provide themselves with *food* and *warm clothing.*
If you wish for *advice* ask one of the SPECIAL CONSTABLES who will be on duty in case of danger, and be prepared to obey the directions given to you.
If any alarm comes during school hours, the *children attending the elementary schools* will be sent home at once.

DAVID McCOWAN,
Mayor.

TOWN HALL
GREAT YARMOUTH
6th February 1915.[2]

68   *Unexploded bomb that fell from a Zeppelin at Heacham in January 1915.*

At a district level, special constables were responsible for evacuation procedures:

POSSIBLE GERMAN LANDING
INSTRUCTIONS TO EMERGENCY SPECIAL CONSTABLES
For the parishes in the AYLSHAM Police District No 2

In the event of a landing, an instruction will be sent to the special constables by the police either to PREPARE or TO ACT at once.

TO PREPARE, will mean that special constables give notice to the inhabitants to make preparations in case they have to leave the district.

These preparations will consist in getting together horses, mules & donkeys, & any things they can move in their carts.

TO ACT at once, will mean that Special Constables are requested to inform the inhabitants who wish to leave that they are to get out of the district as quickly as possible with their horses and carts, that they are to destroy all petrol, spades, picks, saws and axes, that they are to render useless or destroy carts, blacksmiths' forges, and by removing some of the machinery to render corn mills & traction engines useless, but not to burn the mills. The Special Constables are to arrange to leave no horses, cattle or sheep, for the use of the enemy. The inhabitants must on no account travel to NORWICH & main roads should be avoided.

People are advised to make their way by bye-roads to the South-west where possible, but which route is to be taken must depend upon the direction of the enemy's advance, & the best advice will be given at the time.

Stock, STACKS, buildings & other property are only to be destroyed by order of the Military & receipt forms will be provided for use in case of the destruction of property by order of the Military authorities.

KEEP THIS IN A PROMINENT PLACE.

Directions to the Public in the event of Bombardment or Invasion.

In case of BOMBARDMENT do NOT go into the STREET, but **keep in your cellar or on the ground floor of your home.**

In case of a hostile landing and the necessity arising of leaving the town, VEHICLES from **YARMOUTH** must travel by CAISTER ROAD.

FOOT PASSENGERS from Yarmouth must proceed past VAUXHALL STATION on to the ACLE NEW ROAD.

Both Vehicles and Foot Passengers from **SOUTHTOWN AND GORLESTON** must use the road to ST. OLAVES via BRADWELL AND ASHBY.

It must be borne in mind that in case of any of the roads being required for the movement of Troops, civilians must be prepared to move off the roads temporarily into adjacent fields if necessary in order that they may not hinder the movement of the Troops.

Persons leaving the town should provide themselves with **food** and **warm clothing.**

If you wish for **advice** ask one of the SPECIAL CONSTABLES who will be on duty in case of danger, and be prepared to obey the directions given to you.

If any alarm comes during school hours, the **children attending the elementary schools** will be sent home at once.

                                        DAVID McCOWAN,
TOWN HALL,   *Mayor.*
    GREAT YARMOUTH.
    6th February, 1915.

69   *Bombardment or Invasion warning poster.*

All owners of stock are recommended to mark their stock with the letter 'B' to denote their district & also with their private mark, & to register the latter with the police to facilitate compensation claims.

Should orders be given to destroy cattle the Committee are advised the following method will probably be best: -

The cattle to be driven into boxes or small enclosures as close as they can be packed so that there is no room for any of them to move. The stock should then be shot behind or near the ear with an ordinary shot gun held at a short distance.

Special Constables are requested to inform the police of any excessive light in their neighbourhood.

The Special Constables are to make arrangements for & to see that the above instructions are carried out, & it will be well for them to instruct the inhabitants at once in what they may be called upon to do, & in the event of an enemy's landing, they should be the last persons to leave the district, after seeing that there [*sic*] duties have been carefully performed.

(Approved by the Chief Constable of Norfolk & by the Aylsham Emergency Committee No 2 District)

COUNTY OF NORFOLK

General Line of evacuation of the civil Population & transport & also, beyond 10 miles from the East Coast, of all Horned Stock, approved by General Sir Horace Smith-Dorrien, GCB, D.S.O., Commanding 1st Army Central Force, Cambridge.

No. 1 Acle.	To Norwich. No stock to be moved.
No. 2 Aylsham.	Towards Kings Lynn and Terrington.
No. 3 Dereham.	Swaffham and Downham Market.
No. 4 Docking.	To Kings Lynn and Terrington.
No. 5 Downham.	To March.
No. 6 Harling.	To Thetford & Newmarket.
No. 7 Holt.	To Rudham, Hillington, Kings Lynn and Terrington.
No. 8 Loddon.	North of Loddon, Brooke to Norwich. South of that line to New Buckenham Harling Thetford.
No. 9 N Walsham.	To Norwich.
No. 10 Norwich.	East of Norwich to Norwich. Rest to Hingham & Watton.
No. 11 Pulham.	To Harling, Thetford & Newmarket.
No. 12 Swaffam.[*sic*]	To Downham Market & March.

No. 13 Terrington.	If necessary, to Wisbech or Spalding way.
No. 14 Walsingham.	To Kings Lynn and Terringyon [sic].
No. 15 Wymondham.	To Hingham, Watton, Mundford & Littleford [sic].
No. 16 Norwich.	To remain. But those removing to go via Hingham, Watton & Mundford.
No.17 Yarmouth.	If the landing is in Norfolk to go via Suffolk. If the landing is in Suffolk, to [go] via Acle to Norwich.
No. 18 Kings Lynn.	Through Terrington to Wisbech or Spalding way.[3]

Detailed procedures in case of invasion were arranged at a village level. In Lyng, for example, a Parish Emergency Committee was formed. The first meeting was on 12 February 1915, and they then met every fortnight. On 10 March 'the special constables handed their lists of families, stock, & impliments [sic], as far as they could obtain the same. The various families to be removed in each wagon & the drivers' lists were drawn up.' On 15 April, these lists were agreed and it was decided to prepare cards to give to the families concerned.

No meetings are recorded for the next three years. However, the German successes in France in 1918 revived invasion fears and the Committee met again on 26 April 1918. On 17 May they drew up new lists. The men to dig defensive trenches was revised and now consisted of: Walter Curson (in charge), J. Bunnett, D. Welton, Ed Cranmer Goddard, Tom Skipper, G. Allison, Parker, J. Blythe and Skipper Beales.

Wagon owners			Drivers
Mr Cobon	2		Speakman & Emerson
Mr Nicholson	2		Browns
Mr Wm Dann	2	2	Browns
Mr H R English	1		Parden & Thompson
Mr H English	1		E Frost
Misses English	1		Turtle
Mr Comer	2		Melton
			Patrick & Reeves

The Special Constables present undertook the following duties:

Mr Walter Curson	In charge of Trenchdiggers
Messrs Greaves & Pye	Charge of stock & horses
Mr Buck	Food
Mr Nicholson	Destruction of wheels etc
Mr R Melton	In charge of the wagons & to act as Headman of the Convoy
Mr Allen	Loading of wagons

However the next meeting, on 28 May, was to be the last. As the German advances in France came to a halt, it became clear that there was no longer any danger of invasion.[4]

There were rumours of invasion in Sheringham in February 1916. Edith Upcher recorded in her diary for 24 February:

Good deal of agitation about. Many soldiers on Links and round Hospital. Found out from outpatient that a landing was expected. All the soldiers had been out all night & not come in for morning rations … We took this quite calmly, but found

70 *Defending the country: a First World War pillbox beside the Acle Straight. Very few defensive sites from this war still survive.*

that the inmates were dreadfully unnerved and expecting bombardment, invasion, and all the horrors of war at any minute … Le Gros came with wide open eyes to announce that Germans <u>had</u> landed at Weybourne! 'How many?' 'Ah, that's the worst of it no one knows & they are in khaki & it will be a very difficult thing to find them among the other soldiers.' 'But it's quite impossible.' 'No not at all, & they are so clever.' The rumours were soon found to be false and the excitement died down.[5]

Fear of invasion led to the construction of defences in the county. Lines of trenches were dug, and heavy guns placed to defend the beaches. Pillboxes were built so that men could fire at the invading troops from defended positions. Some still survive, including the six-sided pillboxes on either side of the Acle Straight outside Yarmouth, and several round ones along the river Ant. These are some of the very few physical reminders of the invasion scare of 1914-1918 still to be found in Norfolk.

Other defences were more temporary, such as the deliberate flooding of the marshes at Salthouse. The only reminder of this today is in the churchyard: the grave of Walter Potton. He was a private in the 7th Essex Regiment who died when his bicycle wheel caught in the planks of the raised walkway put over Beach Road because of the flooding. He came off the walkway and was drowned.[6]

The coast in wartime was very different from its peacetime appearance. William Harbet visited Great Yarmouth in April 1918. He noted in his diary:

I saw the masts of several ships sunk in the Roads and all the beach is barb wire entanglements to stop the Germans if they land.[7]

Air Raids

The First World War was the first war in which citizens in their own homes, many miles away from the battle zone, faced the risk of sudden death. About 2,500 people in Britain were killed as a result of bombardment from the air or the sea. These figures now seem small because we naturally compare them with what was to happen in the Second World War. At the time it was a completely new experience – and one that created a strange and terrifying uncertainty, sometimes leading to outright panic. The parts of Britain closest to Germany were obviously the most vulnerable – Kent, London and East Anglia. Norfolk suffered several times during the war, as did Suffolk – raids on Bury St Edmunds are described in my book *A History of Bury St Edmunds* (Phillimore 2002).

The first air raids on Britain took place at Dover and Kent on 24 and 25 December 1914: there were no casualties. The first casualties were on the night of 19/20 January 1915 during airship raids on Norfolk. The raid was carried out by two airships (a third had to turn back because of engine failure). The Norfolk ports were targeted. Seven bombs were dropped on Yarmouth, killing two and injuring three. Eight bombs were dropped on Lynn killing two and injuring thirteen. The raid was described in detail in the local press, and the inquests on the four victims were also fully reported.

The victims at Lynn were a 14-year-old boy, Percy Goate, killed as he was sleeping, and Alice Gazeley a 26-year-old widow. She had just finished having supper with a neighbour in Bentinck Street and was buried by falling rubble as she returned to her house. Alice's husband had recently been killed in France. The Lynn Inquest report openly refers to a Zeppelin raid.

The Yarmouth victims were Samuel Smith, 53, a shoemaker, of St Peter's Plain, and Martha Taylor, 72, who lived with her sister in the nearby Drake's Buildings. The Coroner said that both were killed by the same bomb falling on St Peter's Plain. Other bombs were thrown from the same aircraft, exploding near the Fish Wharf, in Crown Square and in Norfolk Street. Most witnesses at the Inquest said that the bombs were from an airship. However, one police witness, Charles Brown, was sure it was an aeroplane, showing that even the most apparently reliable eyewitness cannot automatically be believed.[8]

In a letter to the *EDP* published on 23 January, Mary Telford of Horsey School House wrote that she saw the Zeppelin over Horsey at about 8.15 pm on 19 January:

> The searchlights were very powerful and gave a weird appearance to the sky. It was, to me, a black leaden mass, which was all I could see of the object. It seemed to waver over the village as if uncertain of its route, and was flying very low. Its noise was terrific.

Detailed reports survive among the Yarmouth borough records, assessing the damage caused by the air raid:

Damage by German Air Raid, January 19th 1915

Estimated cost of damage

Race Course	£75
Fish Wharf Refreshment Rooms	£125
Fish Wharf Stores	£75
Fish Wharf Coffee Tavern	£20
13 St Peters Road	£20

	£	s.	d.
Total damage to Corporation Property	315	0	0
Fish Wharf belongong to Port & Haven Commissioners	550	0	0
Broken glass and woodwork Southtown Rd and Ferry Hill	40	0	0
Damage Pestells property	400	0	0
Do. St Peters Villa	180	0	0
Do. St Peters Parsonage	18	0	0
Do. St Peters Church	120	0	0
Do. 3 & 4 Lancaster Rd	110	0	0
Do. Corner house, Drakes Buildings	140	0	0
Do. Fishing premises ditto	40	0	0
Do. Glass and sashes ditto	12	0	0
Do. ditto King Street	30	0	0
Do. ditto Dene Side	10	0	0
Do. Cycle shop, St Peters Road	28	0	0
Do. Mr de Caux's house	10	0	0
Do. Royal Standard and other property, St Peters Road	40	0	0
Do. St Peters Plain, South end	8	0	0
Do. Water Works Coys premises	25	0	0
Do. 14, 15 & 16 St Peters Road	25	0	0
Do. Lancaster Rd, South side	30	0	0
Do. ditto North side	40	0	0
Do. ditto East of Nelson Road	45	0	0
Do. ditto Backs of houses	25	0	0
Do. York Road ditto	25	0	0
Do. York Road	42	0	0
Do. Drill Hall	15	0	0
Do. Cycle shop next Drill Hall	12	0	0
Reported damage to boat in harbour	130	0	0
Contingencies	35	0	0
	2500	0	0

J W Cockrill, Borough Surveyor & Architect 25 January 1915.

The house at St Peter's Plain in which Samuel Smith died now carries a plaque recording the fact that it was the first house in Britain to have been damaged in an air raid. An inventory made at the time lists the damage, and incidentally shows how few possessions a lower-middle-class household in the early 20th century owned:

John Beazor, Licensed Valuer, February 1st 1915: Valuation of damaged furniture for Mr W Scott at 18 St Peter's Plain, Great Yarmouth, caused by bomb raid, Tuesday January 19th 1915.

	£	s.
Sideboard, badly damaged and glass broken	1	10
2 mahogany chests of drawers damaged		10
Hair covered couch damaged by water		15
16 prints and photographs, all glass broken,		
some of the prints with holes in	1	10
2 Toilet sets broken		10
Sundry ornaments broken		15
Treadle sewing machine	1	5
Corner whatnot		8
Mangle damaged		10
Small mahogany stand table and dressing glass		15
9 chairs damaged by water	1	10
Large dressing glass		15
3 mattresses badly damaged	1	5
Pair of curtains, clock, brass lamp,		
green dessert service		15
Carpets 30/- 2 Rugs 12/-	2	2
Stair carpet 15/- Linoleum 15/-	1	10
Hood of pram		7
Lady's coat, badly damaged	1	0
3 beds spoilt by water	1	5
	18	17[9]

An airship raid on the North Norfolk coast in 1916 inspired Edith Upcher to start keeping a war diary:

Perhaps the Zeppelin raid makes a good landmark – or war mark – at which to begin. Jany 31 1916: Feeling weary, tumbled on to my bed after late lunch on return from Hospital, and slept like a log. Woke up, room rather unusually dark. Elizabeth came in. 'Is it time yet, time to get up?' 'Tea time and an hour after, and didn't you hear that horrid thing go over?' There being only one 'horrid thing that goes over' I got out of bed dressed and went to Drawing room for cold tea. Father, mother, Lily quite 'normal conditions' I could see having heard nothing. The servants had heard the Zeppelin and also seen it going quite low over the wood near the house.

I made no remark but in an hour's time heard a suspicious purring of engines, tho not like the threshing machine noises of late 1915. Lil, father and I exchanged glances. The noise became more distant, seemed following the coast for a bit, then – crash, bang, shake, a loud explosion, every door and window in the house struggling to break free, another and another – then louder. Mother thought first of a Naval Engagement but we told her it was Zeppelins and at first thought of our guns firing at it. Barford soon came along, we knew that bombs were being hurled from the sky somewhere in Holt direction. A lull in the banging then Harman's quiet voice at the door asking 'what about the jewelry'. Very thoughtful but what a comparative value jewelry seemed to have when one felt what are the bombs doing and whose turn next.[10]

The bombs dropped by this Zeppelin fell around Bayfield Lodge, most falling in fields where they made '8 large holes in which 22 men could stand'. Defences against this new threat appear to have been distinctly amateurish. Edith was told that the guns on the cliff and at Bodham had failed to go off 'so they had to have a man from London who knew more about guns than what these soldiers do'. An anti-aircraft party was said to have panicked and fled to Holt, leaving their searchlight turned on Holt Lodge!

A schoolboy writing home to his parents in Ipswich gave his account of the raid:

> We were just going out of the last lesson at 6 o'clock and were going out to tea, when we heard a buzzing and —— told us that a Zeppelin had been sighted at ——— at 4 pm in broad daylight, but they had done no damage. We came out of tea at 6.30 and we went out to see what was happening. We heard the Zeppelin plainly, and suddenly a bomb burst about two miles away; then eleven more all in succession, so quickly that it seemed like one bright flash. Then we saw some more flashes, and we counted twenty-four. We went off to see the damage next day and lots of boys found pieces of bomb. One house had all the windows broken and half the slates off. The only casualties were three sheep, one heron, thirty sparrows and a pig.[11]

Other places suffered from air-raid damage, including East Dereham where five people died in a Zeppelin raid on 8 September 1915. Ernest Tovell, a child at the time, later recalled:

> as a boy seeing the damage I had to have a look round. First I had to pass the bomb hole in outside the Guildhall Entrance gates, it knock down the wall & made holes in other buildings. It also took some stones & cement work off the Bell Tower, next bomb was outside Hammerton's shop it took the front out & done a lot of damage. Allso Mr Cave's next door was also damaged. There was a fire in the warehouse of Bradley's, Iron mongers. There were three people killed in that raid. One was a soldier, I see his uniform jacket & cap hanging on the railings which ran from the Market Place to Quebec Street.[12]

A grave at the Rosary Cemetery in Norwich records a tragic coincidence. Private George Garrod was killed by enemy aircraft while at Felixstowe in July 1917. A quarter of a century later, his widow Lily was to be killed in the Baedeker raids on Norwich in April 1942: they are buried in the same grave.

Bombardment

Towns on the East Coast of England, including Norfolk, also had to face bombardment by German warships. As early as 3 November 1914 a force of German ships bombarded Yarmouth and Gorleston. On 25 April 1916 a naval attack on Yarmouth and Lowestoft killed four and wounded nineteen. The bombardment was described in the local press:

> Firing began at a quarter past four, when it was broad daylight, but daring inhabitants who ran to the sea front could only see the flashes emitted at each discharge of the guns, no enemy ships being visible to the naked eye. Every house in the town seemed to be shaken, and the inhabitants had an anxious ordeal. Some people dressed and set out for the country with the object of putting distance between themselves and the shrieking shells; others left their houses for the marshes, and no one was able to sleep through the terrible clamour made by

the constant report of big guns. The firing subsided at a few minutes after five, whereupon nearly all the population turned out to see what damage had been done. This proved to be remarkably small for the vigour and extent of the cannonade. A block of fishing premises was set on fire and partially destroyed, the roof of some other premises close by was struck and collapsed, letting part of a stock of barrels roll out onto the road, but for the rest the actual damage was small in comparison to the number of shells fired. Windows were blown out and brickwork damaged here and there, but there was no outstanding ruin wrought anywhere. There were some large shell holes in gardens, but not a single person was reported to have been hurt, and the town had a marvellous escape. Some portions of shell were picked up in the neighbouring villages of Bradwell and Corton, some large pieces weighing as much as 40 pounds. Children found it a profitable occupation to search for shell fragments which were sold to souvenir hunters who gave anything from 1 shilling to 10 shillings for a piece according to its size.[13]

Will Copeman was at Caister-on-Sea at the time, and he wrote an excited letter to his brother Tom in Norwich:

I expect you know that we had plenty of excitement about here early this morning. About midnight we were awakened by bombs dropping 'tidy' near. The whole place shook, & soon we heard the engines of a Zepp as she passed overhead.

After this we all got two or three hours sleep, & then about 4 am a terrific cannonade began & we were all soon awake. My little cottage & the shed were shaking like anything. I soon dressed & got my bike out & started of for the beach to try to find out what it was all about. By the time I got near the railway station I met a lot of people running away from the sea shouting out that the shells were falling just out to sea.

I did not get much further, for just then there was a report louder than any I had heard at present & a cloud of black smoke rose from the direction of the Manor House Hotel. It was the first shell that burst at Caister. I thought it was getting a bit too thick, & so started off home, the guns still firing as hard as ever, & the crowd of refugees going west still increasing.

As soon as I got home, the rest started dressing, with the idea of clearing out. A few minutes later, the cottage was shaken by an explosion which nearly knocked me over & sent poor old Mike banging against the wall. At the same time mould & stuff rattled against the window & a dense cloud of black smoke rose from some back gardens just opposite. A shell had burst within a hundred yards of our cottage. Grannie, Aunt D, Uncle Gilbert, Charles & Tip were soon up to ours & went on ahead. We soon followed & by this time, east Caister was practically evacuated.

When we reached the top of the hill, we saw over the sea what we at first took to be a number of enemy aeroplanes, but what we soon saw were puffs of smoke caused by shells bursting round one of our aeroplanes. The firing continued gradually getting more distant, till at about 6 am we began to move east again. Yarmouth was entirely hidden by a huge cloud of smoke, & we heard reports from one frightened refugee from that town, that hundreds of shells had dropped and done a tremendous lot of damage.

We found a crowd round the garden opposite ours where the shell had made a hole about 10 ft deep by 15 or 20 ft across. It is thought by the large cylindrical shaped pieces of this shell that were picked up that this must have been a 15 incher.[14]

71 *Scouts' bicycle patrol.*

There was another naval attack on Yarmouth on 14 January 1918: six people were killed and another six wounded. Nation-wide, a total of 157 people died in England as a result of naval bombardment during the war.

In the days before radar, the only way to have advance warning of bombing raids, whether by enemy ships or from the air, was physically to keep watch. The church towers along the Norfolk coast were ideal for this, and the best watchers were boy scouts. Their printed diaries included images of allied and enemy aircraft for identification purposes. Access to the coast was banned to ordinary people, but the scouts were given special permission to go there: 'Scoutmaster Bellerby Lowerison is engaged in Coast Watching service under the Admiralty, which necessitates his visiting the beach at Heacham and elsewhere at all times of the day or night.' [signed] Basil Hall, Commander, Competent Naval Authority. The local authorities responded with an appreciative nod to Lowerison's local knowledge:

> Sir, The Commanding Officer thanks you for your letter of the 5th inst. We have arranged with 2nd Lieutenant Pearce at Brancaster that a Pass should be sent you for Patrolling the beach in the neighbourhood of Heacham and should be glad if you will co-operate with our men on duty there.
>
> In case of a German raid we should be glad if you will co-operate with our men in the capacity of Guide, in view of your knowledge of the local country. Will you please arrange this with Sergeant Boddy the NCO in charge of our men c/o Mrs Thompson, Westgate, Hunstanton?
>
> The Commanding Officer much appreciates your offer to help with regard to the Minature [*sic*] Rifle Shooting practice which will be permitted to our men at Hunstanton and (if arrangements can be made with 2nd Lieutenant Pearce) for the men at Brancaster as well.
>
> Kindly answer the following questions
> 1. Have you a Motor Cycle or push cycle?
> 2. What rifle have you got?
> 3. What will the cost be for firing on the range?
> [signed] R W Spielman, Lieutenant, for OC 3rd Provisional Cyclist Company, Wells, Norfolk, 8-5-16.[15]

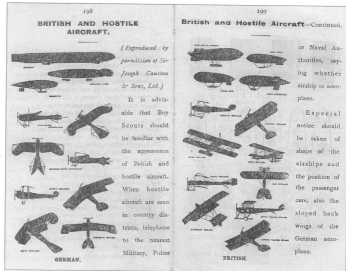

72 *British and hostile aircraft, from a Boy Scouts' diary.*

One of the boy scouts, William Glew, kept a diary of his watching work at Morston and Blakeney in 1918. Typical entries read:

14 March: 6-8 Watch – saw 3 Hospital Ships

3 April: 6-8 Watch. Saw airship. Went for row. Saw monitor. Signalling with OP soldiers.

17 May: Camp Orderly. Saw flying boat, 2 monitors & obs balloon. Cooked outside.[16]

Lights

An obvious defence against night attack from the air was to put out the lights. Again, this was regulated at a local level, with some areas being very slow to introduce blackout orders. Norwich and Norfolk, however, were quick to introduce lighting regulations after the airship raids of January 1915.

> LIGHTING ORDER FOR THE CITY OF NORWICH (22 January 1915)
>
> It is ordered
>
> (a) That all outside lights, other than those maintained by the Corporation and Railway Companies, shall forthwith be kept extinguished.
> (b) That all the lights inside any building whatsoever, excepting churches, shall be extinguished are [*recte* and] covered by blinds or are constructed of such material as will effectually prevent light diffusing through them.
> (c) That in the case of factories with glass roofs, care must be taken to screen all lamps, whether gas, electric or oil, in such a way that the light shall not appear through the roof.

20,000 copies of this order were distributed in the city. A total of 4,042 people in Norwich were summoned for breaking lighting orders during the war – they were normally fined ten shillings or so for the offence.

ORDER AS TO LIGHTS IN THE COUNTY OF NORFOLK (25 January 1915)

1. The public lighting shall be reduced to the minimum consistent with safety. All powerful lamps shall be extinguished, lowered or obscured; and lamps shall be shaded so as to cut off the light from the direction of the sky.
2. All sky signs, illuminated fascias, illuminated lettering, and powerful, external lights used for outside advertising, pr for the illumination of shop fronts or other establishments or premises, shall be kept extinguished.
3. The intensity of the inside lighting of shop fronts shall be reduced from 6 pm so that no bright light is shed outside.
4. All public and private lighting visible from the direction of the sea shall be kept extinguished or effectively obscured from one hour after sunset each night.
5. Upon being informed by the Senior Police Officer that there is danger of an attack from the sea or by hostile aircraft, all lights shall be immediately extinguished, and electric light and gas companies shall take such steps as will ensure this being rapidly done.
6. In all places where the lighting of the streets has been reduced the use of powerful lights on motor or other vehicles is prohibited

The rules involved inconvenience, of course. On 3 October 1915 Canon Aitken preached at St Paul's in Great Yarmouth: 'The church was carefully darkened … unfortunately to make assurance doubly sure they turned out all lights but two during the sermon and I had to preach pretty well in the dark'. In 1916 he was at his home in The Close in Norwich when he heard airships overhead, on their way to the Midlands where 54 people were to die from their bombs – 'places will have to follow the example of Norwich and go in for darkness … It is clearly evident that the Hun will stick at no act of down-right murder or pitiless destruction'.[17]

Submarines and Mines

Civilians have always been at risk in wartime, but usually only those who are unfortunate to be living close to the battle zone. In the First World War this zone was enormously expanded for the first time, as the two sides tried to starve each other into defeat. The British were first in the field, declaring the whole of the North Sea a military zone. This meant that merchant ships for Germany, Holland and the Baltic had to go through the narrow Straits of Dover, where it was easy for the British to stop and search the vessels, and confiscate any contraband cargo. One response by the Germans was to build enormous submarines that could carry cargo from the United States to Germany. The first of these was the *Deutschland*, launched in 1916. After the war it was shown to the public in Yarmouth, where it caused a sensation.

The Germans also responded by declaring the seas all around Britain a war zone: their submarines sank all the shipping they could in this area. This reached its controversial climax on 7 May 1915 when the passenger ship, the *Lusitania*, was sunk by a single torpedo off southern Ireland: over 1,200 of the 2,000 people on board died, including 128 American passengers.

The disaster had Norfolk connections, naturally stressed by the local press. One Norfolk resident among the passengers was Miss Constance Barber who lived with her aunt at Green Hills in New Costessey. She had been travelling in Canada and the United States for two years. Her plan was to come home on the *Tuscania*, but she made a last minute switch to the *Lusitania* so that she could have a few extra days in America. She was drowned. Other Norfolk connections among the passengers included Thomas Bloomfield, a New York solicitor and brother of the Yarmouth boat owner, James Bloomfield, and John Thurston, the son of John Thurston of Forncett St Peter. Also on board was Mrs Finch of Lynn, Massachusetts, who was travelling to England to see her father Walter Howard of the *Britannia Tavern* in Botolph Street, Norwich. None of these people survived the disaster.

One Norfolk man did survive, and his experiences were published in the *Eastern Daily Press* on 14 May 1915. He was Thomas Pitcher of Yarmouth. The family had moved to Yarmouth fairly recently and Thomas' father, Charles, was serving on the Cross Sands lightship. Thomas had been doing casual work in America for two years and, deciding it was time to come back to England, he signed on as a working passenger on the *Lusitania*. He was working in the carpenters' shop when the torpedo struck: 'the lights went out, things toppled off the shelves, and there was a rush to the boat deck, but he saw nothing of a submarine or any torpedoes. This was the only explosion he heard. The boat he described as already listing to starboard.'

Pitcher helped to launch the last lifeboat and was trying to release a collapsible boat when he found that the water was lapping at his feet. He found a lifebuoy and 'leapt into the sea and struck out as well as he could to get clear of the sinking steamer. The funnel only missed striking him by a couple of yards, and when the great hull was immersed he was drawn down by the vortex. He was only under for half a minute when a rush of air and steam sent him to the surface again, desperately gripping his lifebuoy. The scene was terrible with drowning folks, and it was only then he really heard the first cries of distress and the screams of the perishing people.' He was helped on to an upturned boat, then on to the collapsible he had been trying to release earlier, and was finally rescued by a trawler, which took him into Queenstown.

Curiously, the name Pitcher does not appear on the passenger or crew lists of the *Lusitania*. Possibly the man was spinning a yarn, but it is more likely that the lists are not totally accurate for crewmen – or perhaps, for some reason, Pitcher had given a false name when he signed onto the ship.

The sinking of the *Lusitania* created a scandal because there were American passengers on board, but it was only one of many such tragedies, some of which caught up innocent Norfolk people. A memorial in the Rosary Cemetery in Norwich commemorates Isabella Bilby who died when the liner *SS Persia* was torpedoed in the Mediterranean on 30 December 1915. Three hundred people died in this disaster: the U-boat had given no warning.

The submarine and the mine were also terrifying new hazards for those people who made their living from the sea. There were large numbers of fishermen and merchant seamen operating from Norfolk coastal towns, and many lives were lost. The first fishing trawler to be sunk off the Norfolk coast was the *Copious*, which struck a mine on 3 November 1914: nine members of the crew were killed. Nine more people were killed when the Yarmouth steam drifter *Seymolicus* was blown up by a mine on 18 November.

In June 1916, the Corton lightship was struck by a mine and blown up: five of the seven crew members were killed. The two survivors were George Jackman of Yarmouth and Alfred Morris of Gorleston. One of them described the event:

[The Master] looked over the bows when he said 'Here's a mine'. It exploded in a
moment, and the forepart of the ship was blown to atoms. I felt the glass from
the lantern on the mast come showering down all over me like rain.

He found himself in the water. When he looked back 'the lightship went to pieces
like a box of matches and there was no piece bigger than a chest of drawers'. The
two survivors were picked up by a patrol boat within ten minutes.[18]

The North Sea was a battlefield with innocent lives at stake. The advantage was
with the German submarines. On 11 August 1915 no fewer than seven fishing boats
were captured by them about 20 miles off the coast north-east of Cromer. In each
case the crew were forced to abandon their ship, which was then blown up. Submarines
sank three Yarmouth fishing boats, the *Petunia, Good Design* and *Renown*, in July 1916.
The British responded with patrol boats like the one which rescued the Corton
lightship survivors. They had some successes. On 29 July 1917 the Lowestoft-based
torpedo boat *Halcyon* sank the German submarine *UB 27* over Smith's Knoll off
Winterton. The *Halcyon* caught the submarine on the surface: she rammed her and
then dropped depth charges. All hands on the submarine were lost.[19]

One Yarmouth fishing boat, with a crew of nine, had the misfortune to be at sea
on the day of the bombardment of the town at Easter 1916. They saw the German
battleships in the distance, then a torpedo boat came up to them and ordered them
off their ship. The fishermen were not prepared for an emergency like this. They
launched the ship's boat, but it at once filled with water. They then tried to launch
their raft, but it capsized and floated upside down in the water. The Germans forced
the crew onto the raft but did not destroy their ship: presumably any noise would
have drawn attention to the presence of the battleships. After drifting in the water
for a long time, the crew managed to get back to their ship and three of them were
able to climb back on board. The other six died from drowning or exposure, one as
he was actually being hauled back on board.[20]

Mines could cause problems to civilians on land too. On 11 March 1916 one
washed up at Sheringham. Edith Upcher recorded the incident:

At 5 past 8 a resounding bang and windows rattled furiously. Of course no one's
suggestions were the right ones. A floating mine had come ashore. It was seen for
2 hours but no steps were taken to prevent disaster … The inevitable had
happened and the mine had burst. The spot it chose was the town drain pipe …
the inhabitants being told of its nearness to the beach, and the likelihood of its
bursting, assembled to look at it, and were allowed to do so unmolested. The
desire for breakfast at the magic hour of 8 am proved stronger even than curiosity
and 8.05 saw everyone seated around their breakfast tables, safely housed when
the worst came … Windows broken wholesale, 3 at the Hospital, any amount
down Cliff Road … Beach stones and bits of mine and drain thrown great
distances … The excitement was to find bits of mine as it was said in the event
of it being an English mine the Government would have to pay damages.[21]

Five

The Home Front:
Living and Working

On the Farm

The policy adopted by both sides of trying to starve out their enemy meant that it was vital for the country to produce as much food as possible at home. Norfolk, as a predominantly rural county, had a key role to play in this. Within a week of the outbreak of war, the shortage of farm workers was being noted:

> Owing to the recent mobilisation, the countryside is being almost denuded of its rural workmen. The effect of this on the harvest is already felt. In many districts operation[s] are in progress, and with a scarcity of men great difficulties are confronting the farmers. In some cases half the labourers on a single farm have left to join their regiments.[1]

With the introduction of conscription in 1916, it was clear that the shortage of male farm workers would build into a crisis. The solution was obvious: to use women. The leader of the farm workers' union in Norfolk, George Edwards, made a dramatic appeal to them:

> To my fellow working women of Norfolk, the wives, mothers and sisters of our brave boys who are now so gallantly fighting for their country in France, Belgium and other parts of the world, I feel constrained to make an appeal to you in the hour of our national danger to seriously consider the gravity of the situation and what it would mean to this country (especially the working classes) should Germany and her confederates win this war. Everything that is dear in our English life will be destroyed; all our hopes for improvements in our national life will be blighted; the working classes will be thrown back into far worse conditions than they were one hundred years ago; all our liberties so hardly won for us by our forefathers will be lost.
>
> THE SACREDNESS OF DOMESTIC LIFE IN DANGER
> I ask you to consider for one moment what has taken place in Belgium and France. Towns and villages, the homes of the poor, have been robbed and destroyed by fire and sword. Old men and women have been murdered in cold blood, women and children outraged and killed, mothers separated from their children and wives from their husbands, not knowing whether they are dead or alive. What these people have suffered is a small thing in comparison to what would happen to us should our enemies reach these shores, and they will unless we are able to defeat and destroy the cruel and barbarous military power of Germany. Do you wish your daughters outraged, your children slaughtered? Would

you like to see our old veterans of industry murdered, our homes burnt, villages and towns made desolate? No, I know you would not. No women are more devoted to their home and loving to their children than the women of Norfolk. The danger, however, is very great, and it can only be prevented by everyone doing all that lies in their power to help the nation in its hour of distress. It is for the protection of our hearths and homes that we are engaged in this terrible war. Hence the great call on the manhood of this country. And now the time has come when the women of the nation have to be appealed to and I am making a particular appeal to you, the women of my own county, to come forward and help in the present crisis.

THE CALL TO YOU
In making this appeal to you I am asking you to do what I hoped you would never have been asked to do again, and what I am thankful to say the improved conditions of labour have made unnecessary. But the crisis is so great, and the danger of losing all that is sacred and good in our national life is so pronounced, that I venture to make this appeal to you to offer your services in cultivating the land in order that as much food can be produced at home as possible.

HOW YOU CAN HELP
There will be a great deal of work to be done in the spring, such as hoeing, weeding, getting the land fit for the turnip crop, and many light jobs which hitherto have been done by men. You can also render good help during the harvest. You can also do good service on farms where cows are kept, in milking and other light work in connection with dairy business.

A FAIR WAGE WILL BE GUARANTEED
The service you are asked to render will be paid for at a fair and living wage. You have your own representatives of labour on the various committees that will have to deal with these matters and your interests will be well looked after.

THE FIRST ESSENTIAL IN LIFE
One of the first essential things in life is food, and unless this can be provided then a great disaster is staring us in the face. In order that this may be avoided the land must be cultivated, the crops must be put in, and the corn harvested when ripe. But this cannot be done without labour.

A SHORTAGE OF LABOUR
There will no doubt be a great shortage of labour in the near future. If only half of those are called up who have enlisted under Lord Derby's scheme, many of the villages will be denuded of labour. This is a most serious problem for unless some means can be found to replace the labour that will be taken from the land, it cannot be cultivated. It will mean a great reduction in our food supplies and will bring starvation to the poorest of the poor.

THE NATION WANTS YOUR HELP
England stands today at the crisis of her help, and she depends very largely on the womanhood of the country to help her in her hour of need, and she appeals to you at this critical moment to come forward. Yes the blood of your sons, husbands and brothers who have given their lives for the protection of your womanhood and the upholding of human freedom cry out to you to render all

73 *'Lily' in the uniform of a postwoman, February 1917. She sent this photograph to her boyfriend who was serving with the Norfolk Regiment in Mesopotamia.*

74 *Ethel Barnes, Farm Worker, February 1917.*

the help you can. Will you allow the voice of the dead to be raised in vain? No, I am sure you will not. I know you honour and love too much those who have given their lives and shed their blood in such a righteous cause not to take your part in this great conflict and I appeal to you in the name of God, who made you free, and in the interest of your children, to respond to the call that is made upon you, and in doing so you will not only help the farmer, but you will be doing something to help your country to crush and lay low the greatest foe of humanity the world has ever known.[2]

The phrase 'God who made you free' has a special resonance in Norfolk, as Edwards was undoubtedly aware. It was the rallying cry of Robert Kett, the Norfolk rebel of 350 years earlier. Edwards' appeal was heard throughout the county: 50,000 copies of it were distributed to Norfolk schools.

75   *Landworkers at Swannington.*

The appeal was successful: the female land worker was to become a familiar figure on Norfolk farms. An undated Roll of Women Workers in Brampton contains nine names, including three with the surname Watts. The women were aged between 19 and 50, and they expressed their willingness to work between four and six days a week. Seven women wanted to do farm work, and one to do vegetable and fruit gardening – the ninth hoped to find work in her current occupation as a grocer's assistant. Some of them had had a little experience at farm-related work, having weeded for farmers or done fruit picking, but at least one admitted to having no experience at all.[3]

A pioneer in this field was Gilbert Overman, who had taken on women farm workers to replace men on his farms in Weasenham as early as the autumn of 1915:

76   *Work on the farm at Sporle 1.*

What they have done has been an immense surprise to some of Mr Overman's friends, many of whom, after being consistently sceptical are at last showing signs of conversion by plying him with all sorts of curious enquiries. 'You'll never get 'em to do muck spreedin' said some. Anyhow, they spread two thousand loads of muck between harvest and Easter and no one could wish it better done. Besides they did twenty acres of turnips and carted them and most of the mangels as well.[4]

Sir Ailwyn and Lady Fellowes of Honingham Hall were the main organisers. In July 1917 they reported that over 5,000 women were registered as land workers in the county, and that probably there were many more who were not registered. 'Under the national Service scheme, centres for training girls for work on the land had been opened as follows: Mr W. Case, Gateley – accommodation for 12 girls; Mr G. Overman, Weasenham – 4 girls; Mr W.R. Harvey, Illington – 6 girls; Miss Godfrey, New Buckenham – 1 girl; Mrs Oswald Ames and Mrs Betts, Thornham

77   *Work on the farm at Sporle 2.*

– 2 girls each. These girls were trained for four weeks, after which situations were found for them for various works on the land. Should no situation be available they remained in the hostels until places where open. They were provided with an outfit, and their railway fares were also paid. Though it did include breeches, she (Lady Fellowes) thought there was nothing in the outfit to which the most particular person could take exception. It was a very pretty costume. Besides the training centres, they also had a bursar scheme working.

Sir Ailwyn commented,

A few months ago a certain amount of prejudice existed amongst the farmers of Norfolk, as it did amongst farmers in other parts of the country, to the employment of women labour. He was glad to find that prejudice was gradually disappearing from our midst ... There was some feeling that women could only work on the land during the summer months. He desired to contradict that statement in the strongest possible manner. A farmer living in the Fakenham district had employed women year in and year out. During the winter months they were engaged in feeding his stock, in milking his cows, and in doing half a hundred other things which the farmer wanted done during that time of year. To his mind it was not at all derogatory to a woman to ask her to work in winter months to help to promote the food supply of the country'.[5]

Three months later the War Agricultural Committee was told:

Excellent reports have been received from farmers employing Volunteers of which the following are unsolicited testimonials 'I have great pleasure in saying that Volunteer —— who came here 3 weeks ago as a woman Milker has proved to be a most excellent hand at the work. I have not had my Cow House kept so clean before, she is also very good at feeding young calves and most willing and obliging. I have raised her pay to 25/- per week as I consider she is worth it'. 'Just a few lines to express my sincere appreciation of the work done on my Farm by members of the Women's Land Army. The Volunteers you have sent me have given every satisfaction, and although I have asked them to do all manner of jobs, from spreading manure to driving cattle, I have never heard a grumble or a complaint, but have always found them very willing. My weeding was all done by the Volunteers, and also most of the root hoeing. They also did most of the

Every woman who helps in agriculture
during the war is as truly serving her
country as the man who is fighting in
the trenches or on the sea.

Walter Runciman
President of the Board of Trade.

Selborne
President of the Board of Agriculture.

78   *Farm Work Certificate.*

loading during Haysel and Harvest, and since then have spread manure, cleaned out and whitewashed cattle boxes, carted roots, and in fact done anything that was wanted. Two girls drove a lot of cattle 17 miles and arrived at their destination with both themselves and their cattle fit and fresh.

More controversy has taken place on the subject of Uniform for Village Workers and there is a strong feeling prevalent that all legitimate land workers should be supplied with this, irrespective of wages.

It is estimated that the average wage of the Volunteers of the Women's Land Army is £1 per week. The unanimous opinion of the Executive Committee decided against any attempt to raise the wage of the Land Army at the present juncture

Returns were handed in for 5553 Women working on the land, and some hundreds more are known to be at work on the land.

Another source of labour was that of soldiers who were not fit enough to be at the front. A circular letter from the Norfolk War Agricultural Committee on the use of soldiers on farms in October 1917 said: 'a number of soldiers will shortly be available at this centre who have some experience of horses but none of ploughing. We are anxious to have these men taught and they are wishful to learn … The farmer will have nothing to pay for a man whilst being taught, and when the weather prevents ploughing he can have free services of the man for ordinary work along with his other men or, preferably, to help the horseman. When any ploughing is going on however, [he works] with a competent ploughman, getting properly taught. When his fortnight's training is completed, the farmer will forward a short statement of his progress and if he is fit to be sent out as a ploughman'.[6]

However these soldier workers were not always much use. In January there were complaints by Norfolk farmers, Mr Keith and Mr Thistleton Smith. The latter said that 'he could not cultivate 2,500 acres because of the inferior character of the drafts he had been receiving. It was most disheartening to have men who had never seen a farm, and also to get a second time men he had returned because of their utter uselessness'.[7]

By the summer of 1918 men were still needed for the front, but the importance of getting in the harvest first was understood by the military authorities. In August 1918 'the Secretary [of the War Agricultural Committee] reported a report by the National Service Department to fix a date for the end of harvest, as he had

79 *'The Lady Carter'.*

instructions to call up certain men after harvest. Resolved to reply that September 15th was the appropriate date. The Secretary also reported that the National Service department had instructions to call up for grading all men born in or since the year 1888 but that men should not be called up for this purpose without the consent of the Executive Committee. Resolved that the committee do not consent to any such men being called up during harvest'.[8]

Work

In all situations in life there are winners as well as losers. Many Norfolk firms were able to benefit from the war by supplying items needed in the new situation. Caley's chocolate factory in Norwich was just one example – 'Norwich-made chocolate bars were popular with British troops during the first world war. Thousands of bars of Caley's famous marching Chocolate were sent to the front, starting their journey in the firm's own solid tyred vans'. Chamberlin's of Norwich, clothing makers, found that their oilskin waterproofs were much in demand – the War Office and the Admiralty requisitioned their entire stock. They also made clothing for munitions workers,

IT ISN'T A CASE OF

IF the Cap

Fits

IT

DOES

FIT

New Blue Grey
for R.A.F.
Now Ready

GK
-18

H. RUMSEY WELLS

4 SAINT ANDREW'S STREET, NORWICH

80 *If The Cap Fits ….*

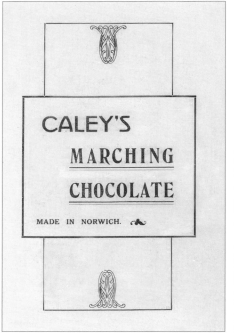

81 *'Caley's Marching Chocolate'.*   **82** *Munitions girls at Laurence and Scott, 1917.*

and later 'demob suits' for soldiers returning to civilian life. The grocers' firm of Copeman supplied rations for the War Office; at one time they were running canteens and supplying rations for 30,000 troops stationed in Norfolk before going to the front.[9]

Norwich's boot and shoe industry also prospered during the war. Howlett and White supplied 453,000 pairs of boots and shoes for the British Army, 32,000 pairs of boots for Allied Armies, and 21,000 pairs of British Aviation Boots.

The making of weapons and armaments was a key element of life in the war. The shortage of shells for the heavy guns on the Western Front became a national scandal. In February 1915 employers and trade unions came to an agreement that women and boys could work with machinery normally operated by adult men. In March the unions gave up the right to strike. In the summer the Government set up the Ministry of Munitions, creating new factories and encouraging standardisation in the private ones. Women made up 60 per cent of the workers in the metal trades – by 1918 the figure was 90 per cent, including 70 per cent of the people engaged in the manufacture and filling of ammunition. However this only happened while the men were away at the front: within one year of the Armistice three quarters of a million women had been dismissed.[10]

Great Britain was divided into 42 Boards to direct the making of munitions. East Anglia came third in the 'League Table' of these Boards in terms of munitions produced. This may seem surprising, but in fact the many firms producing agricultural machinery and related products were easily converted to war purposes. East Anglia

produced the cheapest munitions of all, no doubt
a reflection of the traditionally low wages paid in
the area. Eight Norfolk firms made munitions,
including Laurence Scott of Norwich who made
shells for giant 60-pounder guns, Burrell's of
Thetford who made shrapnel, and Norwich
Components Ltd, who made fuses – including the
new 106 percussion fuse which was a key factor in
improving dramatically the gunners' ability to cut
the enemy's barbed wire. The firm made more than
two million fuses. A report of February 1918 said
that there were 7,650 munitions workers in
Norwich alone.[11]

Munitions work could be as dangerous as
serving at the front. The *Norwich Mercury* carried a
sensational story in January 1917:

83 *'Our Girls in Wartime', drawn by a patient
at Sheringham Hospital.*

A few minutes before 7 pm on Friday a
disastrous explosion, the cause of which is
apparently not discernible, occurred at a
munitions factory in the East End of
London. Severe damage resulted, and when
the death roll and the number of injured are
finally known, it is probable that the human
toll will reach 500. The force of the explosion may be judged from the fact that
the concussion was felt and the glare of the subsequent blaze was seen in many
parts, even so far distant as Norfolk and Lincolnshire … a most searching enquiry
is to be made, and Dr Addison assures munition workers that there is no cause
for alarm.[12]

This is a remarkably frank account of a disaster in a munitions factory, doing
everything but actually name it (it was, in fact, the Brunner, Mond and Co factory in
Silvertown). It contradicts the claim in several books that explosions in munitions
factories were never reported in the press. As so often, it is much better to use
original archive material of the kind that forms the basis of the present book rather
than rely on secondary sources.[13]

There was no such disaster in Norfolk, but the Norwich Components factory did
burn down on 9 September 1917 after an electrical fault:

A few minutes before midnight on Sunday the fire hooter at the works of
Norwich Components Ltd, near Foundry Bridge, brayed forth, and ten minutes
later the compact but commodious building of five stories was a blazing cauldron,
with huge tongues of flame leaping skywards, and lighting up the city as though it
was daylight. A fuse in the second floor is supposed to have started the fire, and
the rest was only a matter of seconds, for the contents of the works were such
that it required little to set the seal to a big blaze. At the time the machinery was
in full swing with several hundred employees engaged, including a night shift of
150 young women … It was a fitting setting to the darkness of the night, and the
curve of Prince of Wales Road and further afield the spire of the Cathedral were
thrown up in relief as in a gold and silver setting.[14]

84   *The Working Woman: Ministry of Munitions publicity photograph.*

Although munitions were not actually mentioned, any reader noting that the factory was working at full stretch at midnight would have drawn their own conclusion. The force of the fire threatened nearby houses too, which had to be evacuated as a notice in the next day's *Eastern Daily Press* implies: 'The women living in Foundry Bridge Yard wish to thank Mr and Mrs Silkwood of the *Railway House*, Foundry Bridge, for the great kindness shown to them during the great fire; also for refreshments given to the women and children'.

The importance of munitions work is implied in the speed with which the firm re-established itself. Within three months they were up and running once more, this time using the city's skating rink as their factory.

There are no mentions of any casualties in the report. Obviously this could be because none were reported for propaganda reasons. However, I have checked the Norwich Inquest papers for the period and there were certainly no deaths in the incident. One Norfolk man who *was* killed in munitions work was William Ward, born at Thurlton in 1879. He died in an explosion at a munitions factory in Nottingham.

Some Norfolk firms were slower to adapt to wartime conditions. Lane writes of Burrell's of Thetford: 'There is no evidence that the Directors, like many of their contemporaries, made any serious attempt to secure work to aid the war effort. It was not until twelve months later in 1915 that the Government stepped in, compelling the company to undertake the manufacture of munitions'.[15]

The importance of the work of women in munitions factories to the war

85   *A Short 183 seaplane at Mudros in the Mediterranean.*

effort was summed up by a statement in Parliament by the Minister of Munitions, E.S. Montagu: 'Our armies have been saved and victory assured by the women in munition factories.'[16] One of the other main contributions to the military effort in Norfolk was the building of aeroplanes. Boulton and Paul made them from 1915, firstly at Rose Lane and then at Riverside: their airfield was on Mousehold Heath. They made 550 FE 2Bs, 1,550 Sopwith Camels and 430 Snipes during the war: by the end the firm was turning out 45 aeroplanes a week.

Mann Egerton of Norwich also made aeroplanes, including Short bombers and seaplanes. They had an enormous hangar on the Cromer Road: this was not pulled down until 1984. Aeroplanes were also made in King's Lynn, by Savage's, more famous for making traction engines and roundabouts. The firm had closed down in 1910 but had been revived by, among others, the chief electrical engineer for Lynn, John Pilling. Pilling went to France and met the legendary aviator Louis Bleriot: he secured manufacturing rights for the Voisin Type LA biplane. Eighty acres of land near the factory were purchased for use as an airfield.

Boulton and Paul also built huts, hangars etc for airfields, hospitals, army camps and prisoner of war camps. They supplied many miles of barbed wire. The Norfolk Ironworks (Barnards) supplied over 7,000 miles of wire netting to the War Office and the Admiralty. Although the wire was mainly used in defending the trenches against enemy attack, the netting had another important use: in the deserts of the Middle East the wire was laid on the sand to make a track for marching upon. Crane's of Dereham made 27,000 gun wheels during the war, including all the wheels for the guns made by the Vickers armaments firm.

Men who worked in their home country rather than fight in the trenches were always liable to be publicly humiliated. Clayton wrote of the Norfolk Post Office engineering staff: 'By 1915 the remaining external staff had to wear armbands to show that they were on work of national importance, for any able-bodied man walking the streets of Norwich was generally regarded as a fugitive from the armed forces and was abused and insulted as such.'[17]

Tommy 'Well an' what d'yer think yer doin'?'

Conductress with sarcasm 'Aw can't yer see I'm on me 'oneymoon.'

86   *The Conductress.*

Norfolk's brewing industry suffered from the restrictions imposed on beer drinking in the war. The duty on beer was raised in 1914 from 7s. 9d. to 23 shillings; by 1920 it was 100 shillings. The price of raw materials – malt, sugar and hops – also rose massively due to supply shortages: the local industry, like the national one, responded by making them go further, that is, by making weaker beer! In addition, afternoon closing of public houses was introduced and 'treating' (buying a drink for another person) was forbidden. These measures had a drastic effect on the industry: for example, Steward and Patteson of Norwich produced 67,000 barrels in the year ending November 1918, about half of what they had produced in the year before the war began.[18]

Wages rose rapidly during the war, but prices were rising too. There was some industrial unrest. In October 1916 there was a strike by 3,000 juvenile factory workers in Norwich: they claimed that they were entitled to a war bonus. The spark was lit when clothing factory workers were deducted five weeks' unemployment insurance contribution: this was to bring clothing workers in line with the provisions of the Insurance Act. Five hundred female workers at Harmer's factory in St Andrew's downed tools and marched to the Market Place to protest. The employers said: 'the view of the firm is that no case for a war bonus has ever been made out, as the girls earn considerably higher wages than in pre-war days, and they have been well treated in various ways, notably by the payment of an average week's wages to every employee when the factory was closed down for a week in August'. However, another 500 girls in Chamberlain's clothing factory in Botolph Street also went on strike and joined the Harmer's strikers in the Market Place.

The trouble spread to boys working in shoe factories on the following day: boys from local shoe firms, some 400 in all, joined in. Men in the factories were asked to undertake the boys' work, but they refused and the factories ground to a halt on Wednesday. After a bout of window smashing and mud throwing, the boys soon returned to work. They claimed that the average wage for 14 to 18 year olds was only 16 to 18 shillings a week. However G.E. White of Howlett and White said that they were earning as much as 25 shillings a week at the ages of 17 and 18: 'many of them are earning a good deal more than is good for them. They pay little of the money into the home, and in many cases nothing at all. Wanting time to spend their earnings, they take occasional days and weeks off. The more they have the more they want. Lately they have been suffering from a war-bonus fever. The fathers are away, and domestic discipline has broken down. The truth of the matter appears to be that in the present demand for labour we have had to employ a great many boys of a different type than has hitherto been customary in the boot and shoe trade and that the better class boys are subject to the intimidation of the poorer element'.

The boys, however, claimed that by the time they were entitled to their war-bonus they would have been called up into the army! Whether it was the force of this argument, or the shortage of labour, is not clear but the youngsters, both girls and boys, won their case, and were given a war-bonus, graduated according to their age.[19]

There were, of course, many accidents on farms and factories, some of which were fatal. These people can be regarded as war victims, just as much as the soldiers who were killed in action. However, it must be remembered that safety regulations in the working environment were incredibly primitive by the standards of a century later. Deaths at work were very common, among men and women, before, during and after the war.

We can take just one example of such an industrial accident as typical. In Great Yarmouth, Milly Barber of Row 123 was killed in September 1916 when she fell into a vat of boiling dye at Grout's factory in the town. The coroner said that it was all the more sad because she was taking over a man's job. Milly was just 20 years old: she had been due to be married the following week. Her name does not appear on any war memorial.[20]

Douglas Haig, the Army Commander, recognised the importance of the workers on the home front. He wrote a public letter to Henry Tillett in December 1916: 'You can tell Labour at home that the best of all Christmas presents they can give to their comrades in the field is the assurance that so far as in them lies nothing during the coming year shall hinder the regular, constant and increasing output of munitions and material. The workers have done splendidly in the past: we look for ever greater efforts in the future. If the men and women workers at home and the troops in the trenches pull together, the triumph of our cause is certain.'[21]

Food

The problem of how to feed the people of Britain was a very real one. Farm production went down, partly because the men were away at the war, but mainly because horses and donkeys were commandeered by the Army. Even more important was the loss of imported food – German U-boats tried to starve Britain and almost succeeded. (Of course, the Allies were trying to starve Germany too.)

The authorities did not ration food until 1918. For the first three years of the war they tried price control, fixing the maximum prices of key foodstuffs to prevent profiteering. These maximum prices were altered each week. In August 1914 these were

Granulated Sugar	3¾ d per pound
Lump Sugar	4¼ d per pound
Butter (imported)	1s 6d per pound
Cheese (colonial)	9½ d per pound
Margarine	8d per pound
Bacon, by the side	
Colonial or Continental	1s 2d per pound
British	1s 3d per pound.[22]

ECONOMISE IN GAS.

87   *'Economise in Gas'.*

In spite of these measures, there was a crisis of confidence. The *Eastern Daily Press* reported:

THE PRICE OF PROVISIONS PURCHASERS IN A PANIC

In a course of a look round the provision shops of Norwich yesterday it appeared evident that the public are taking the present crisis with too much precipitation. Orders were being given with reckless prodigality. The assumption appears to be that within a week or two we may expect to see a bivouac of foreign jabbering troops at the corners of our sweet suburban roads and that therefore it may be desirable to have a good supply of eatables up the chimney, under the bed and down the cellars. Said a certain merchant to our enquirer 'I have just had in my shop a lady from quite a small household buying two sides of bacon. Mere recklessness! Before she has eaten a quarter of it the remainder will be unconsumable'.[23]

As the German blockade began to bite, some food items were in short supply. It was the poor who suffered first. In December 1916 there was a heated argument amongst the Wayland Guardians of the Poor as to whether the inmates of the Workhouse should continue to receive butter, or whether it should be replaced with a cheaper substitute in the form of margarine.. It became a battle between two clergymen on the Board. The Rev. Thorns was in favour of margarine, arguing that £70 or £80 a year would be saved. However, the Rev. Kent was against 'forcing on the old people in the infirmary, who were under their care, what they had never eaten before'. The master of the Workhouse asked if the rule would apply to the staff as well – he pointed out that they had already made sacrifices, giving up eggs, bacon and sugar. By the casting vote of the Chairman it was decided that both staff and inmates would have margarine.[24]

Nine months later, the Aylsham Guardians had the same debate. It was said that butter was currently costing 2s. 4d. to 2s. 8d. a pound, whereas margarine was only 11d. a pound. Several of the Guardians said they themselves were now using margarine, and Mrs Buxton said that almost every other Workhouse now used it. Mr Herbert Cook pointed out that 'thousands of soldiers were having margarine, and he did not think that any hardship would be imposed upon the inmates of the house'. However, several of the Guardians were opposed to the change, including Mr

Eglington, who said that margarine was only a substitute and substitutes were dearer in the long run: anyway 'no-one knew what the margarine was made of'. The proposal to change to margarine was defeated by 12 votes to ten.

The inmates in Great Snoring Workhouse were already receiving margarine instead of butter: in the same month the Medical Officer recommended that the children there should have butter instead 'as he considered it better for the growing child'. The Guardians agreed and the change was made.[25]

By January 1918 there was a meat shortage in Norwich. The *Eastern Daily Press* told the story:

LOCAL MEAT SUPPLY
HOW A SHORTAGE IS BEING MET
ENSURING THE SUNDAY JOINT

Housewives in Norwich have been experiencing an anxious time this week in getting butchers' meat. Monday is generally an 'off' day, but supplies have been so greatly curtailed that on Tuesday and Wednesday many of the shops had to be closed. Our representative, doing a tour of inspection yesterday, observed that most of the shops were closed, notices in the windows stating 'Sold Out', 'Open Thursday' or 'Closed Until Friday'. The last mentioned announcement was posted at the central meat shop of the Norwich Co-operative Society.

'For the first time we today had a queue', said Mr W.J. Algar of St Stephen's. It was about noon when our representative visited his shop. All the meat had been sold and the establishment was about to be closed. Mr Algar explained that he and other butchers endeavoured to keep open for a part of the time every day, but in other cases, owing to failing supplies, this was not possible. In order to facilitate matters, it was explained that stewing beef was cut up beforehand into half pounds and roasting beef into quantities of two pounds. 'When our regular customers who have placed their orders with us the day before have been supplied' said Mr Algar, 'we serve the public generally.' Some purchasers of his surplus meat came from as far away as London.[26]

Behind the self-sacrifice and community spirit shown by most people in the war, there was a darker side. A combination of detailed regulations and real shortages offered opportunities for crime. Where there were fixed maximum prices, there was

NOTICE

To the Members of the Congregation.

An appeal in the Nation's hour of need. — Eat less Bread. —

THE sinking of foodships by German Submarines and the partial failure of the World's wheat crop have brought about a scarcity of wheat and flour which makes it imperative that every household should at once reduce its consumption of **BREAD**.

The Food Controller asks that the weekly consumption of Bread throughout the Country should be reduced to an average of 4 lbs. per head.

In order to get down to this average everyone must eat less bread than before, and must reduce his or her consumption by at least one lb. per week. Every possible step must be taken to AVOID WASTE.

COMPULSORY RATIONING will be costly, difficult and extremely irksome Let us all try our utmost to avoid it by **VOLUNTARY RATIONING.**

Will you start Rationing in your Home at Once?

This announcement is posted at the request of the National War Savings Committee, Salisbury Square, London, E.C.

88   *'Eat Less Bread'.*

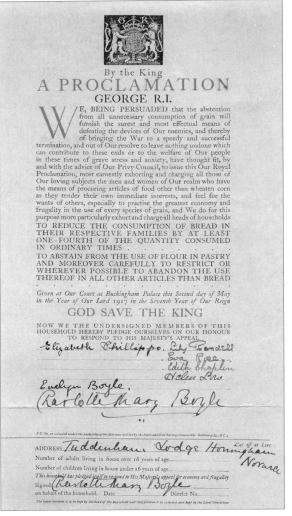

89 *Pledge to Eat Less Bread.*

always the chance of making a quick buck. In September 1917 Walter Calvert of Outwell was charged with selling 15 tons of seed potatoes and almost 10 tons of 'ware' potatoes to London dealers at £2 or £3 a ton above the fixed prices, making himself an illegal profit of over £108. His defence council pleaded for leniency: he said that Calvert had never been to school, had started working at the age of seven, and was ignorant of what the maximum prices were. He had seven children, the eldest of whom was serving in France. Calvert was fined £140.[27]

It may have been genuine hunger, or perhaps just boyish high spirits, that led two Holt boys into trouble in December 1917. Macdonald Weston and Henry Howard were summoned for stealing two parcels of food intended for soldiers at the front. The parcels had been packed by Jane Youngman, wife of a miller at Weybourne, for her son who was serving in the Egyptian Expeditionary Force. Her daughter, Myrtle, handed the parcels in at Weybourne post office. Later Myrtle found a chocolate box from one of the parcels by the side of the Holt Road: it was empty. The two boys, both aged 13, had the job of carting sacks of post from Weybourne to Holt. On being arrested they confessed to opening up several parcels and eating chocolate, apples and cake.

The Court was shocked: 'the Chairman of the Board very much regretted to see two young lads pleading guilty to what he regarded as a most atrocious offence, viz stealing parcels containing articles and food which were being sent to our soldiers who are fighting for us abroad, robbing them of what they had been hoping to receive from their friends this Christmastide … Indeed he could hardly conceive that boys who had been educated in a good school like the accused should have done such a thing.' The boys were sentenced to a punishment characteristic of the early 20th century, six strokes of the birch. Weston's father said that his son suffered from asthma and he was not sure he was strong enough to take his punishment: the court ruled that a doctor should be present to decide about the boy's fitness.[28]

As it was difficult to obtain food from overseas, it was vital to make full use of home-grown produce. Newspapers constantly offered housewives advice on how to

make best use of the food they had. 'Juliet' had a regular
column in the *Norwich Mercury*:

TEA TABLE TALK FOR LADIES

Life is not very easy for any just now: for some it is
terribly hard. Even on those who are supposed to be
comfortably placed, and to have few big difficulties to
tackle, petty worries are often showered – worries
which take all the edge off life and obscure what is
good and satisfactory. It is the peculiarity of the crowd
of small worries that it can obliterate the sunshine –
cut off a much greater stretch of it than its own bulk
would appear to make comfortable.'[29]

The higher the
price per pound
the less the cost
per cup

CEYLINDO TEA

International Stores

THE BIGGEST GROCERS IN THE WORLD
TEA · COFFEE · GROCERIES · PROVISIONS

90   *The rising price of tea.*

Recipes appeared in the column on a regular basis. Those
in October 1917 included:

Here is a delicious mixture to spread on toast, as a change from bacon for
breakfast. Peel a sufficiency of tomatoes by first dropping them into boiling water.
Chop them with some onion. Melt a little butter into a frying pan and fry them
for five minutes. Add seasoning and a slightly beaten egg. Stir over the fire until
the mixture is thick, then spread on toast. Serve very hot. In this way one egg will
serve two or three people.

A cheap and savoury roll can be made without meat if you proceed as
follows. Take a cupful of lentils, a turnip, 2 cupfuls of breadcrumbs, ½ a cupful
of grated cheese, and salt and pepper to taste. Soak the lentils over night, then
cook in very little water till soft. Boil the turnip and mash it. Mix all together and
form into a stiff roll. Place in a tin with a little dripping and bake for half an
hour, basting frequently. Arrange fried tomatoes round, and serve with mashed
potatoes.

Other local newspapers were not short of advice either:

STOCK YOUR LARDER FROM YOUR GARDEN! WAR-TIME PICKLES
AND PRESERVES TO CARRY YOU THROUGH THE WINTER

'Look ahead!' That should really be the housewife's motto in these days of war
economy, and those blessed with even a small patch of garden should try to
imitate the canny squirrel, and from its produce lay in a store of fruit and
vegetables for the winter months, or for times of scarcity and very high prices.
On account of the sugar shortage it may not be possible to make jam, but fruit
and vegetables can be preserved 1) by bottling 2) by drying. We shall tell you how
to do it every week in this column. Cut the Notes out of this paper and paste
them in a book ready for use as the various vegetables etc are fit to be treated.[30]

The Royal Horticultural Society issued advice too, such as this:

PRESERVING BLACKBERRIES
WITHOUT SUGAR

Fill the bottles as full as possible, place in a steamer until the fruit looks cooked –
or place bottles in a saucepan with hay in the bottom (to prevent breakage) in *cold*
water and boil for five minutes; take out one bottle at a time, fill up with boiling
water and cover with bladders (or screw-on tops). Bullock bladders, obtainable

91   *Ploughing up the woodyard at Carrow for food production.*

from a butcher, should be used, and should be washed and soaked in warm water to soften them before use. They should be tied on with string and cut into pieces of such size as will leave a fair sized piece below the string after tying.[31]

Clearly it was essential to make use of as much land as possible for food production. In January 1917, a plan to plough up parts of Cromer and Mundesley golf courses was hotly debated by the War Agricultural Committee. In the end it was decided that although it would indeed be possible to use the land to grow oats 'the gain to the country was not equal to the loss to the district'. A month later, nine acres of Eaton Park in Norwich were divided into allotments and let out to 60 people.[32]

Each local WAC [War Agricultural Committee] tried to make sure that land was properly exploited. A good example is a draft letter from Mr Bird, a committee clerk, dated 20 March 1918:

Dear Sir

Food Production

I am instructed by the local WAC to inform you that your land Garden and Greenhouses must be fully used for the production of food forthwith.

   Kindly inform that this will be done. If you are unable for any reason to do this yourself or to arrange for it being done and can suggest any way in which the Committee might be able to assist you, please let me know. Please let me know and tell me the name and address of your landlord.[33]

A voluntary rationing scheme was introduced in February 1917, under the guidance of Lord Devonport. Many people now argue that the war economy actually resulted

92 *National Ration Book.*

93 *Purchaser's Shopping Card.*

in a more healthy diet, especially with the limitations on the consumption of sugar products. This seems to have been recognised at the time by some people. When a mother was before the Norwich bench charged with failing to send her daughter to school, she said that the child was ill, suffering from bilious attacks. The magistrate replied 'she will not get bilious attacks if you stick to the Devonport rations'.[34]

The first case in Norwich to be brought under the food orders of Lord Devonport was in May 1917. Bessie Lines of Catton Grove Road, Norwich, was charged with feeding bread to her bulldogs. She said that she bought bread that had been nibbled by mice to give them. Her baker confirmed that he supplied Bessie both with normal bread and with bread damaged by rats and mice. 'He would not consider the bread produced fit for human food. Rats and mice carried infectious disease.' However, she was convicted, and fined £2 with a guinea costs.[35]

Voluntary rationing proved inadequate. It was followed by rationing of meat and fats in London and the Home Counties in February 1918. This was extended nation-wide in April. The *Eastern Daily Press* announced:

Meat rationing will come into force over the whole country on Sunday. Supplementary rations for those engaged in bodily work will begin on 14 April; supplementary ration of five ounces of bacon or equivalent will be available for boys between 13 and 17 years old.[36]

The people of Britain now faced something completely new to them, the ration book:

MINISTRY OF FOOD
NATIONAL RATION BOOK (B)
INSTRUCTIONS *[Read carefully]*

1. The person named as the holder of this Ration Book on the Reference Leaf (page 6) (Green) must sign his name in the space provided on that leaf, and must copy in the space provided for it on the Reference Leaf the Serial Number appearing at the head of this cover.
2. The Book must be registered at once for the purchase of **Sugar, Fats (i.e. Butter, Margarine and Lard), Butcher's Meat and Bacon.** To register for Sugar the holder must sign his name and enter his address and date of signing on the Sugar Counterfoil (Yellow), and take the book to the sugar retailer. The retailer will enter *his* name and address in the proper space (numbered 1) on the inside of the cover and on the back of the counterfoil, and will detach and keep the counterfoil. Registration for other foods will be effected in the same way, by use of the counterfoils for Fats (Blue), Butcher's Meat (Red), and Bacon (Red).
3. Persons living in hotels, boarding houses, hostels, schools and similar establishments should not register their Ration Books until they leave the establishment.
4. The Ration Book may be used only by or on behalf of the holder, to buy rationed food for him or members of the same household or guests sharing common meals. It may not be used to obtain rationed food for others.
5. The Ration Book may only be used while the holder is living in Great Britain, is not drawing Government rations, and is not in an institution (hospital, asylum, workhouse etc). If he dies or joins the forces, or enters an institution, the book must be given up to the proper authority, that is to say, the Registrar of Deaths, the naval, military or air force authority, or the head of the institution, as the case may be. If the holder is leaving Great Britain for a period exceeding four weeks the book must be given up to the Aliens' Officer on embarkation. During a shorter absence from this country the book may be retained, but must be produced to the Aliens' Officer for inspection on embarkation; it must not be used during absence, and all the coupons for the period must be detached and destroyed. Any book not given up to the proper authority in any of the above cases must be returned at once to the nearest Food Office.
6. Any leaf with its coupons can, if desired, be detached as a whole, by cutting along the line **x x**, and can be deposited with the retailer with whom the book is registered for the food in question, provided the holder first writes his name and address and the serial number of the book on the leaf to the left of the coupons, and that the retailer enters the words 'Leaf deposited' and the number of the leaf, below his name and address in his space on the inside of the cover. The leaf and coupons so detached cannot then be used for purchases at any other shop, or to obtain a meat meal.
7. **Coupons can only be used for purchases if the book is presented as a whole or if the leaf is deposited in the way described in the last paragraph. Coupons already detached are invalid and cannot be used for purchases.**
8. The leaves, spaces and counterfoils marked 'spare' are for use if other foods are rationed.

9. **It is a summary offence punishable by fine up to £100 or six months' imprisonment, or both,** for any person –

(a) to apply for or hold more than one ration book;

(b) to retain a ration book which ought to be given up;

(c) to use a ration book for purchases when it may not be used;

(d) to use the ration book of another person, except for or on behalf of that person, or to lend or give his own ration book to any other person;

(e) to purchase more than the proper ration in respect of any coupon or space;

(f) to use coupons for purchases without the leaf to which they belong, or in the wrong periods;

(g) to deface a ration book or without authority alter any entry made thereon; or otherwise to contravene any of these instructions or any of the provisions of the Rationing Order, 1918, under which this book is issued.

Alongside the ration book came the shopping card:

MINISTRY OF FOOD
RATIONING ORDER, 1918
PURCHASER'S SHOPPING CARD
MEAT

The card is valid only with the Butcher who issued it, and whose name appears below. If you change your Butcher, a new card will be issued by the new Butcher.

A BUTCHERS'S NAME AND ADDRESS
Your Butcher must stamp his name and address below before issue, otherwise the card will not be valid.

Norwich Co-operative Society St Stephen's

A PURCHASER'S NAME AND ADDRESS

Mrs Flood, 25 Geoffrey Road, Lakenham.

THIS CARD IS VALID ONLY WITH THE BUTCHER WITH WHOM THE RATION CARDS OF MEMBERS OF THE HOUSEHOLD HAVE BEEN DULY REGISTERED.

INSTRUCTIONS

1. This card is issued by the butcher on the authority of the Ministry of Food, so that he can check how he distributes the butcher's meat supplied to him for his registered customers.

2. Any household registering five persons or less with a butcher will receive from him one card. It the number is more than five, but not more than ten, two cards will be issued, and so on. The spaces not required must be cancelled by the butcher before he issues the card.

3. YOU MUST PRODUCE THIS CARD ON THE OCCASION OF EACH PURCHASE, AND SEE THAT YOUR BUTCHER MARKS OR CANCELS THE APPROPRIATE SPACE OR SPACES.

4. THIS CARD IS VALID ONLY WITH THE BUTCHER WHO HAS ENTERED HIS NAME ON IT. The name and address of the butcher must be entered at A by the butcher before issue, and may also be entered at C.

5. The butcher will enter on this card at D the number of persons to whose ration of meat it applies, and the total value of their weekly rations of meat.
6. Enter your name and address on the front of the card at B.
7. This card by itself is no authority to obtain meat, and your butcher may, therefore, before serving you require the production of the Ration Cards (N. 86) of the persons included on this card.
8. If any person stated on this card as registered with your butcher is temporarily away from home, and therefore takes his Ration Card with him, meat may not be obtained for him on this card. If any such person is away from the household for four weeks or more, you must tell your butcher who will amend this card accordingly.
9. The butcher may be informed at any time by the Food Office that a member or members of the household formerly registered with him, has ceased to be so registered. In such case the butcher may require surrender of this card, with a view to its re-issue as amended, or to the issue of a new card.

PENALTY FOR MISUSE – £100 fine or 6 months' imprisonment, or both.[37]

The system was quite complicated. Each ration card had four meat coupons. Three would be used on the meat ration which was fixed (at first for London and the Home Counties only) at 1s. 3d. worth of meat weekly per head. The fourth coupon could be used for an issue of other meat (bacon, ham, poultry, game, rabbit, prepared meats) to correspond to five ounces of uncooked butchers' meat. Child's coupons entitled the child to half the adult amount of meat.[38]

Meat rationing could cause serious hardship. When William Harbet stayed with a friend in Yarmouth in the spring of 1918 he recorded:

We have a rabbit for dinner Nelly gave 5/- for it and had to beg for that. She has a little bit of salt pork 2/- lb and a small piece of beef about 2lb 4/6d. That's all she can get for the week for 3 of us they wont let her have more. It is now Sunday and I have not had any meat since Thursday dinner when I left camp.[39]

Some people thought that rationing would lead to riots or even revolution. In February 1918, Ralph Mottram wrote:

Mr Hotson Palmer caught me up as I came back from Chapel this morning & said 'Well Mr Mottram – which is coming first – peace or revolution?' Sometimes I think it is a toss up which it is to be – I can't think of anything more likely to bring about the last than the severe (& necessary) rationing now going on & yet I cant bear to think so meanly of our people as that they cant endure a few months of being hungry most of the time – I mean the general public – not the soldiers who ought to have all that they need, seeing it is they who are actually doing the job, whether at home or abroad.[40]

The concerns of Norfolk people can be seen in the 'Letters to the Editor' section of the local press. On a typical day in February 1918 there were five letters:

1. Cannot something be done to limit current consumption. In one house five stones of flour is used weekly by seven people, including three children. In another, a month's supply has been accumulated by using less than the

ration of three pounds a head. In time this accumulation would be penalised as 'hoarding'. While the consumer of three times his share goes unpunished. There is something wrong here. [signed] FAIR PLAY.

2. Could not something be done to prevent the waste of light in Norwich shops. The public are constantly being urged to economise in the matter of lighting, yet in a shop in London street on Saturday last there were some thirty lights inside and twelve outside lights burning at 2 pm. [signed] AC

3. Ethel Reeve complained that pet dogs and racehorses were consuming food that could be used to help small poultry farmers – 'English people have given their husbands and sons to their country; and shall it be said the women will give up their men kind but cannot part with their dogs.'

4. H. Goude had advice for people growing their own food; he recommended the Dutch brown haricot bean for its cropping powers over any other haricot bean.

5. ECONOMIST returned to the canine theme: 'What about the absolutely useless dogs that exist in every small parish … Ought not a drastic order be given that those dogs shall at once be destroyed? Last week I saw a woman feeding her dog with chocolates. Poor children cannot afford such luxuries.'[41]

Sparrows also caused concern. The Norwich Food Production League claimed that house sparrows consumed 185,000 acres of cereals each year. However 'Hedge Scholar' looked more deeply into the matter: he pointed out that 'all grain-eating birds feed their young on insects', so that if all the sparrows were to be killed then the crops would instead be destroyed by a plague of insects. Such ecological debates were vitally important in a national context when the survival of the country depended on the quantity of food it could produce for its human inhabitants. They set the scene for similar debates, in a global context, a century later.[42]

Housing and Health

One effect of the war was to draw attention to the poor health and housing conditions of many of the working classes. This was first demonstrated when it was found that many of the men who volunteered, or were called up, were simply not healthy enough to join the Army. The men of Eastern England were rather less healthy than the national average:

Health Category	Eastern England	National Average
1	31.8%	36.0%
2	25.1%	22.5%
3	31.3%	31.3%
4	11.8%	10.3%[43]

These judgements were not made after a thorough medical, but simply based on measuring the height, chest size and weight of each man at the time he enlisted, or was called up. Grade 1 men were 'fit', grade 2 men were fit enough to walk six miles with ease, grade 3 men were unsuitable for combat, and grade 4 men were 'utterly unfit'.

The health of children was a matter of special concern in the war years. In 1915 Fred Henderson commented on the annual report of the City of Norwich Medical Officer: 'He could not let the report pass without calling public attention, very urgently and very emphatically, to the continued very high proportion of children in their schools who were insufficiently nourished and improperly clad. It did seem to him that when a public body was faced with the fact that children in elementary schools were nearly one in four returned as under-nourished, and between one in six or seven were insufficiently clothed, that the public should be asked to pay attention to that fact. In these times when we had come to see that the physical condition of the manhood of the country was not just a matter of private interest to the parents of the children; we had come to see that the physical condition of the children and our men was, in the last resort, our greatest national asset. What an enormous proportion of men who had offered their service to the country had been rejected on the ground of physical unfitness.'

J.T. Hotblack, another committee member, disagreed with Henderson, blaming the children's poor health on 'Citizen' life, by which he meant living in the city rather than the countryside: 'this has as much to do with it as malnutrition. As to that, as I walk about the streets, every day I see bread and bread and butter thrown away by schoolchildren.'[44]

The report of the School Medical Officer for the year 1916 blamed the parents. It said hat 4,591 schoolchildren had been inspected in the year and 548 (about 12 per cent) needed medical treatment. 'We experience great trouble with some of the parents owing to differing professional opinions as to the urgency, or even desirability, of operations for, say adenoids and enlarged tonsils etc, and yet more from ignorant prejudice. The bugbear of the administrative SMO's life is the commonly ignorant, but sometimes, I fear wilfully obstructive attitude assumed by a number of the parents.'[45]

The most famous children in Norfolk in the war years were those attending the Burston Strike School. Tom Higdon and his wife Annie had become teachers at Burston in 1911. They had previously taught at Wood Dalling where they outraged the authorities by encouraging farm labourers to join the Union, and also to get themselves elected to the parish council. They repeated the process at Burston, making enemies of the rector, Charles Eland, and some of the farmers. Higdon expressed his empathy with the poor in a long poem, *The Labourer*:

> With tattered shoes the children trudge to school
> Along the lane's wet slush and muddy pool,
> Prey to diseases springing from their chills
> And to the more preventable of ills
> All for the labourers' lack of means to buy
> Clothing to keep his children warm and dry!

In April 1914 the Higdons were dismissed on a series of trumped-up charges. However, they had the support of most of the children in the school, and of their parents. The children went on strike, refusing to attend the official school. Instead they continued to be taught by the Higdons, at first on the village green and later above a carpenter's shop. Despite the distractions of war, their cause was supported by many working men including trades unions, especially the Agricultural Labourers and the Railwaymen. Money was raised to buy a site by the green and a new school – the Burston Strike School – was built. It opened with a grand flourish in May 1917: the ceremony was attended by notables such as George Lansbury and Sylvia

THE STRIKE SCHOOL   — AND —   ITS MASTER (MR. T. G. HIGDON).
Will never be forgotten so long as Burston people live.

94   *Burston Strike School and its Master Tom Higdon.*

Pankhurst. The school continued to teach practical socialism throughout the war, and almost into the next one. It closed when Tom Higdon died in 1939. The building can still be seen today. The strike split the village into two factions, especially after the rector, Charles Eland, evicted strike supporters, including Harry Garnham, from land owned by the church.

Several men of Burston naturally joined the Army when war broke out. These included Eland's son, Arthur; George Durbidge (although he was 46 years old), with his son George; and Herbert Garnham, whose memorial was to cause controversy, as described in chapter nine. George Durbidge senior wrote to Tom Higdon from Malta in 1916:

I thank you very much for the nice letter that you sent me and I am Pleased to hear that you and Mrs H are in the Pink. Well Tom as I will still call you I was very pleased to hear such good news about the doings at the old strike school. I feel quite proud of you all. You deserve a medal as large as a plate but I know your old heart is in the right Place and to stick to the one thing that you have Battled for the last two years. that is justice which is a thing we seldom get. But at the same time unity is strength and strength means victory for the Burston Allies. Dear Tom I am very proud of our good and brave companions that have taken such interest in our fight for freedom from the vile and unjust persons that are surrounding us. It seems quite to me that A dark Cloud is hanging over their heads which no doubt they are expecting a severe storm from … . I am also very

Pleased to hear that the site is purchased for the school and the noble sum that is raised for that purpose it will be a bone for them to pick for years to come no dought [*sic*] they thought that they were playing their cards quite alright. But they were not aware of your holding a trump card in your hand.[46]

There were no benefit payments as such in 1914-1918. Soldiers' wives and their children needed to live: they were given a *separation allowance*.

Wife	12s 6d
Wife and one child	17s 6d
Wife and two children	21s
Wife and three children	23s
Wife and four children	25s

These allowances were considered to be generous: 'recruiters should find considerable assistance in their work from the new conditions, and especially the improved position given to dependants of those who enlist, while there is no doubt the country will gladly bear the added financial burden.'[47]

Along with the money came supervision, which caused much resentment. Local newspapers contain a large number of cases where women, whose husbands are at the front, are accused of gross neglect of their children. These prosecutions were usually instigated by inspectors from the National Society for the Prevention of Cruelty to Children, and often make comments on the separation allowance. A typical case is that of Gertrude Brewster of Suton, wife of an army reservist, who was summoned for neglecting her six children, aged between three and 10 years old. She was prosecuted by George Bainbridge on behalf of the NSPCC. Gertrude's husband, George Brewster, had worked in a stone pit, earning 16 shillings a week. Now that he was on active service Gertrude received 26 shillings a week separation allowance.

> The possession of so much money led to her degradation to a large extent. She had been drinking a great deal too much, and had given way to immoral habits, and neglected her home.
>
> The children had been left alone in the house for hours together, and there were instances in which they had been left from 10 o'clock in the morning to 2 o'clock the following day with no-one to look after them. On several occasions there was no food nor fire in the house. It seemed to him that there had been a great outcry against police supervision of soldiers' wives at home, yet this was an instance in which supervision might have done a great deal of good. The children were fairly well-clad and well nourished, but they, together with the house, were in a most filthy state. There were only two beds and the woman and two children slept in one, and the other four children in the other. A doctor was called in and he said that 'the two beds were dirty … the condition of the mattress and bedding on which the defendant slept was filthy. The other bed was also sodden and in a most indescribable state'.

Gertrude was sentenced to four months in prison with hard labour. The children had already been taken to the local Workhouse: the court ordered that they should stay there until their father returned from the war.[48]

Violet Nichols was another woman accused of spending her separation allowance on drink. She was 27 and lived at Leighton's Row, Trafalgar Street, Norwich. She was summoned for neglecting her children Grace Watling (9), Gladys Nichols (6) and Katherine Nichols (21 months). Mr Reeve, for the NSPCC said that the defendant's husband had joined up in the previous August. Violet received a separation allowance of 23 shillings a week. An NSPCC inspector had visited the house three times and found the children dirty and verminous. He called in a doctor who found that Grace was:

> pale, thin and anaemic looking. Her head was verminous and full of nits. She was suffering from advanced scabies, and had also large boils upon her back, the clothes were dirty, the stockings and boots were in holes and unfit to be worn, the child's body was filthy and covered in verminous bites.

Gladys and Katherine were not in quite such a poor state, but both also had verminous bites. The doctor continued: 'the bedroom was in a disgusting state. There were two bedsteads. One with nothing on it, and the other with one mattress and two feather beds in a terribly filthy condition. The whole place was unfit for human habitation.' The doctor sent the children to Norwich Workhouse infirmary.

Mr Reeve said that it might be asked why a woman could not keep three children decently on 23 shillings a week: 'The answer was that she spent her money in drink … Instead of looking after her children she also had soldiers and other men come to her house at all hours of the night'. Violet stated that, in fact, her money had recently been reduced to 19s. 6d. a week. When asked why, she said 'Because my husband has not allowed me out of his money'. Reeve retorted, 'Perhaps he had an idea what you were doing'. Violet was sent to prison for three months with hard labour. The children were ordered to be kept in the Workhouse for 12 months.[49]

Some families were actually worse off with the separation allowance than they had been before. Emma Bedwell of Queen's Place, Southtown, was charged with neglecting her seven children. Her husband, George, was in France with the Royal Engineers. He had been a bricklayer earning £2 a week. Now Emma received 31 shillings a week, out of which she had to pay rent of five shillings a week. In this case the court was sympathetic: they postponed any punishment to see if the condition of Emma's children improved.[50]

In many of these cases there were hints and allegations of immoral behaviour, and dark tales of association with soldiers and sailors. The separation allowance could actually be stopped if immoral behaviour was suspected. Lily Clapham, married woman of Cooper's Yard, Barn Road, Norwich, had had her allowance stopped in 1916, in consequence of her [unspecified] conduct. In January 1918 she was summoned for neglecting her child, Maud Patteson, aged six. Lily had married six years earlier and her husband had joined up in August 1914. Maud was illegitimate.

Dr Henry Watson said that he visited the house in Dial Yard, Oak Street, where Lily and Maud were living:

> the child was sufficiently clothed but the underclothing was dirty and the skin suffered in consequence. The head was also dirty. The child was poorly nourished, but not badly nourished. The atmosphere of the house was horrible. Apparently only one bedroom was in use and this was in a dirty condition. In his opinion the child was suffering as a result as the condition of the house and through want of attention.

Lily's landlady said that the child always appeared weak, and that she had twice seen the mother drunk in the year that she had been her tenant. Another witness said that Maud was often left alone on Saturday afternoons and evenings: however, after an intervention by Lily, she admitted that she had never said that the child went without her meals.

Detective Sergeant Goldsmith said that he had known Lily for three years. He had visited the house three times in one day. On the first occasion Lily was out and Maud was playing with other children in the yard. The third time that he called, Lily was in: 'with her in the house was another woman, a sailor and a soldier'. An NSPCC inspector had visited the house and it was he who had decided to prosecute Lily.

The court was not unsympathetic to Lily's difficulties: 'The Chairman said the Bench was sorry to hear of the life the defendant had been living. It must more or less have had a bad affect on the child'. They in effect put Lily on probation, saying that if in five weeks 'she showed an improvement and a willingness to do her best for her child, she would probably hear nothing more of the case'.[51]

Malicious rumours of scurrilous behaviour could put enormous pressure on these women and their children, which occasionally was too much to bear. Edith Hunt of Great Yarmouth was living on the separation allowance: her husband, Edward, was serving in Salonika. In June 1917 she killed her son with a mallet and then stabbed herself, dying before a surgeon could arrive. She left a letter to her parents, beginning, 'I am writing to let you know how horrified I am to learn what people are saying about me, but as God is my judge there is no truth in it. If I had been guilty of wrong-doing I would own it, and not die with a lie on my lips.' The previous night Edith had told a friend that she would feel better when the war was over and her husband was back. Edith's own mother had climbed through the window of the house at Say's Corner at 6.30 in the morning to find the boy dead and Edith dying; Edith said to her: 'honour is better than life. I have done no wrong'.[52]

Poverty could occasionally lead to deliberate abuse of the system. In 1915 Florence Chaplin was accused of falsely obtaining money from the Local War Relief Fund. Her husband had enlisted in the Royal Field Artillery on 14 December 1914, and she was given credits worth 15 shillings a week. However, when the husband was discharged on the grounds of ill health on 1 January, Florence did not tell anyone and continued to receive the credits. Florence admitted her guilt: she said that she needed the money to buy her children boots and clothes. The magistrates considered sending her to prison, but instead fined her £1 and ordered her to repay the money in instalments.[53]

As several of these cases demonstrate, many houses in which the poorer people lived, in both town and country, were in a very poor state. No one was prepared to spend money on housing improvements during the war, so they inevitably deteriorated further. The village of Burston provides a good example. At a Parish Meeting in 1914, a Mr Sutton moved a resolution:

> That this parish meeting supports the Parish Council's endeavours to obtain better and more adequate housing accommodation in Burston and confirms the urgent necessity which exists for such provision being made. Mr Higdon, the schoolmaster, remarked that there were many cases where better accommodation

was required in Burston and the matter constituted a great trial and trouble. Some of the conditions under which people had to live were deplorable, but they had no choice in the matter. Mr Johnson asked why the Inspectors were not made to do their duty. Mr Sandy replied that owners were not treated alike. He was made to do what was directed, but the 'big men' were not compelled to carry out the work detailed in the notices served upon them. He instanced a case where during the rainfall of the previous evening the water ran down the walls of a cottage, also of buildings which were ordered to be thatched where the work was only partially carried out and he added that some of the cottages were not fit to keep a monkey in. (Laughter and applause.)[54]

These conditions could have tragic results. Three children of James and Christina Blyth of Loddon died within a week of each other in May 1915: they were aged between four years and just four months. It is thought that they caught typhoid from their drinking water, which came from the village pump.[55]

The Liberal politician Arthur Samuel, writing to Fred Henderson, linked the war directly to the housing situation: 'I am at work here, unpaid of course, in the purchase of weapons and explosives … if we had our equipment ordered <u>before</u> the war the Difference … would have paid for enough new cottages to have solved the whole housing of the poor problem.' George Roberts' election manifesto in 1918 offered a solution:

> The question of Housing, both urban and rural, urgent before the War, is intensified owing to the fact that the exigencies of War have arrested building operations. It shall be my endeavour to expedite the erection of well-planned, roomy and sanitary houses in adequate State-aid so that they may be let at reasonable rentals.[56]

A local child in whom Norwich took a special pride was one of the city's winners of the Victoria Cross, Harry Daniels. This was because he had been brought up at Norwich Boys' Home. (His cousin, Robert Snelling, who was in the Home at the same time, won the Distinguished Conduct Medal for bravery at Festubert in December 1914.)

On 15 March 1915 Daniels was at Neuve Chapelle, serving with 2nd Battalion the Rifle Brigade (the Prince Consort's Own). The company commander ordered Daniels to make up a party to destroy the German barbed wire ahead of them. Daniel just turned to his friend Tom Noble and said 'Come on Tom, get some nippers'. The two men jumped from their trench and began to cut the wire. Both were hit by gunfire. Noble died and Daniels was in No Man's Land for four hours before he managed to crawl back to his trench. Both men were awarded the Victoria Cross.

Daniels spent several weeks in hospital. Eventually he came back to his home town of Norwich, which he had not visited for 11 years. He was greeted as a local hero, and many functions were held in his honour. On the last day of his visit, the sheriff presented him with a 'purse' containing £20. Cheering crowds lined the streets as he went to the station to catch a train back to London and from there to rejoin his battalion.

A few orphans may have had a good war: unfortunately the war created many more orphans. The Sheringham branch of the National Children's Home opened in June 1916. An appeal for funds in the *Norfolk Chronicle* on 13 July 1917 read:

PEOPLE OF NORFOLK! Do you know that in your midst at beautiful Sheringham is a branch of the National Children's Home entirely reserved for THE SONS OF OUR GALLANT FIGHTING MEN with upwards of thirty boys – many of them fatherless – already in residence? Standing on Hook's Hill the House is described as a 'Children's Paradise'. It commands a fine view of the sea, to defend whose freedom their gallant father's [*sic*] died. May we claim your kind interest in this House? Its little inmates are your guests: will you help to make them happy? Visitors are welcome. Gifts (of money or of clothing) may be left with the Sister in Charge or sent direct to the Principal, Rev. W. Hodson Smith.

The victims of war were growing in number. By 1917 the Ministry of Pensions had responsibility for over 670,000 disabled men, widowed women and orphaned children. The Minister of Pensions explained the position in the House of Commons:

NEW PENSIONS SCHEME EXPLAINED

MEN BROKEN IN THE WAR

CLAIMS OF WIDOWS AND ORPHANS

In the House of Commons yesterday, on a Supplementary Vote for the Ministry of Pensions, Mr George Barnes, gave an interesting account of the work and scope of the new Government Department.

Mr Barnes said the care and welfare of disabled men was, perhaps, the most thankless part of the work of the Pensions ministry. He paid tributes to the work in this direction done by Sir Arthur Pearson at St Dunstan's. Out of 600 blinded men 200 had already passed the hospital and 300 were still there. The Star and Garter Hospital at Richmond had 600 paralysed men. Already 6000 limbless men had passed through the hostel at Roehampton. Of these 1216 had been trained to new occupations, and about 2000 had been found other positions in the trades to which they belonged, and the remainder had been sent to the care of various centres. He had considerably modified his views as to the length of time men should be kept in military hospitals. He believed that some men had been kept in hospital so long that their recovery had been absolutely delayed. He was not sure that some had been not kept so long that recovery had been prevented.

Barnes said that the Ministry had charge of the following: Disabled men 140,275; children of disabled men 157,544; widows 62,796; children of widows 128,294; dependants of deceased men 29,832; total on the books 518,741. Besides these, there were 125,000 widows who had not reached the pension stage; 65,000 men in hospitals; and 65,000 men medically unfit.

These figures brought the total number of men, women and children up to 673,741.

He announced a new pension rate for a disabled man, ranging from a minimum of 27s 6d a week up to 75 shillings a week, depending on previous earnings. Allowances for children of disabled men were also increased, so that a man with four children would receive 15 shillings instead of 10 shillings.[57]

Fund Raising

The Great War was funded to an extraordinary extent by voluntary contributions. Even schoolchildren took a keen part in this. After the war, Norwich Municipal Girls Secondary School summed up its achievement in this field:

95   *'Remember Our Women'.*

Our War Work
Being the Head Girl's Report for the period of the War, 1914-19.
The object of this Report is to preserve a Record covering the entire period of
the war.

FIRST	£	s.	d.
Belgian Girl Hospitality Fund	70	15	1
Form Money Boxes Fund	111	11	3
Entertainment Fund and Sales	181	15	4
Miscellaneous Activities	38	2	5
Contributions to Hospital Garments' Material	34	16	9
Total	437	0	9

The money has been devoted to the following Relief Funds: Lord Mayor's
National Relief, Princess Mary's Sailors' and Soldiers' Christmas, Blue Cross,
Belgian Relief, Poland and Galicia, Servian, Red Cross, Star and Garter Building,
Camps Library, Edith Cavell Memorial, EDP Plum pudding, King George's for
Sailors, Daily Telegraph Naval, Halifax Disaster, St Dunstan's Hospital for Blinded
Soldiers and Sailors, To equip a Hut for Sailors from torpedoed merchant vessels,
Christmas gifts for wounded in Norfolk and Norwich Hospital, Lakenham
Hospital; Norwich Hospital Charities, Jenny Lind Infirmary, Norfolk Regiments'
Prisoners of war in Germany, League of Mercy, Voluntary War Work Association,
Castle Street Hospital Supply Depot, Toys for Jenny Lind Xmas Tree.

96   *Carrow girls making sandbags.*

SECOND
Form Miscellaneous Activities have been: Egg collection (1,023), magazines for
wounded, sandbags, two prisoners of war in Germany adopted, meat coupons
checked for the Local Food Control Committee.

THIRD
Needlework Guild. – Between 3,000 and 4,000 garments, sewn and knitted, have
been made, and distributed as below: The Lady Mayoress' Needlework Guild,
Wounded at Norfolk and Norwich Hospital, Jenny Lind Infirmary, Servians, Lady
Leicester for the 1st Norfolks, Cambridge Needlework Guild, The Grand Duke
Michael for the Sailors, Voluntary War Work Association.

FOURTH
The School has been responsible for the Swab Department at the Castle Street
Hospital Supply Depot, working there on Saturday afternoons from November
1915 to December 1918.

FIFTH
War Savings Association – Grand Total £2,693 13 0

The duration of the Association has been exactly three years. In the early part of
the present School year, the armistice was arranged, and soon afterwards the
pressure of work which all had experienced during the war began to decrease and

the available labour began to be directed into its normal channels. In response to the changed conditions, the committee felt that the time had come for the 'winding-up' of the Association. Consequently, all members have completed their certificates, or withdrawn the balances due to them. The need for thrift both from the national and individual point of view is still acute, and it is sincerely hoped that all will continue to save as much as possible and to invest their money in War Savings Certificates through the Post Office.[58]

Many people in Norfolk are familiar with the Shell Museum at Glandford, but few are aware that it began in the First World War as a way of raising funds. The *Eastern Daily Press* noted:

A very enterprising step has been taken in North Norfolk, with a view to the perpetual aid of the Norfolk and Norwich Hospital. A gentleman living thereabouts who has for forty years made a hobby of collecting shells, has built and equipped, within the precincts of Glandford-cum-Bayfield church, a museum, in which his treasures will be displayed.[59]

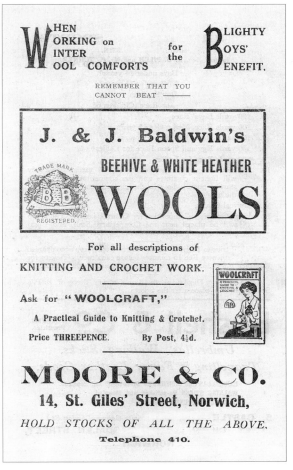

97   *Baldwin's Wools advertisement.*

Norfolk led the way in fund raising through Farmers' Red Cross sales. One held at Fakenham in January 1916 raised £4,050, a record for England. This was beaten when a sale at Lynn in February 1916 raised £4,711, and even this record was broken in Norwich in April when £6,326 was raised.

One good way of raising money was by means of a 'Tank Week': a tank was on display and formed the centre of fund-raising activities. On 1 April 1918 it was reported:

The tank arrived in Norwich yesterday. Brought down by rail from London, it was soon pieced together, and between three and four in the afternoon it ambled out of Thorpe station and made its way to the quarters it is to occupy until the end of the present week. This was a cumbrous and leisurely proceeding, for its utmost rapidity seems to be about a mile an hour. An enormous crowd of the usual Sunday afternoon character watched it with curiosity and delight.

The tank went along Prince of Wales Road, London Street and into the Market Place, finishing up in front of the Guildhall. A musical celebration followed, with contributions from Marcelle Molray, a Belgian soprano who was herself a refugee from Antwerp, and a tenor named William Forster. The Tank was moved to a place in front of the Shire Hall for a few hours during the week so that the county rather than the city could join in. The object, of course, was to raise money for the war effort and the great question was whether the sum of £1 million would be raised during the week. It was a close run thing but it was done and Norwich became the 33rd city where tank week had raised this magical sum. The actual sum raised for War Bonds was £1,057,382. In the previous month Yarmouth had held its own War Bonds Week: £217,000 was raised.[60]

Tank Week in Norwich coincided with the German attacks in the spring of 1918. These led to increased appeals for aid. A typical appeal was that of the Belgravia War Hospital:

> The monthly record of the Belgravia War Hospital Supply Depot: if ever there was a time when the splendid work of the BELGRAVIA War Hospital supply Depot should be loyally supported, it is the present, when the country is passing through the darkest hour of its history. Never has it paid such a toll in flesh and blood and suffering.
>
> Convoy after convoy of wounded is pouring in from France. The need for plain dressings alone has multiplied, heaven knows how many-fold, during the last terrible six weeks, both here and across the channel. Not only has the demand increased but vast supplies on which the army counted for the immediate relief of our wounded have fallen into the hands of the enemy. Ambulances, field dressing stations, casualty clearing stations, full of healing appliances have had to be abandoned, surgeons and staff accounting themselves fortunate if they could get away their wounded before the advancing flood overtook them. In many case, alas! they did not succeed, and doctors and men are enduring the unspeakable horrors of german activity. Unfortunately, for all the yearning in our hearts, we can do little to help them. But the many, many thousands who have been brought back into safety from the fields of blood are claiming and must receive the nation's zealous care.
>
> Every conceivable article that a wounded man may want for the alleviation of his sufferings is urgently needed.

Women responded at a local level. Between January and the end of March 1918 the ladies of Syderstone, to take just one example, had made:

Dressings	990
Triangular bandages	55
Slipper soles	61
Mittens	11 pair
Socks	35 pair
Mine sweepers gloves	6 pair
Mufflers	13
Cap	1
	1172 articles

In April and May, about twenty women were attending meetings in the village and making over 200 dressings a week, together with a small number of other articles.[61]

Six

I Spy Strangers

Refugees

Britain was a much less cosmopolitan society in 1914 than it was to become later in the 20th century. However, there were plenty of 'foreigners' living in the country, including Norfolk, who were treated with suspicion and sometimes downright hostility during the Great War, whether they originated from enemy, neutral or even friendly countries.

One of the main public reasons for the war was to fight in defence of 'gallant little Belgium'. As the Germans conquered almost all of their country, thousands of Belgians fled, and some wound up in Norfolk. The first refugees arrived in the county at the beginning of September 1914. The *Eastern Daily Press* carried the story:

> BELGIAN REFUGEES ARRIVE AT NORWICH
> PARTY OF TWELVE HOUSED IN THE COUNTRY
>
> Yesterday afternoon twelve distressed Belgian refugees arrived in Norwich. The first-comers were a family of the name of Biddeloo who alighted from the 1.30 train from Liverpool Street, due at Thorpe at 4.30. Mr and Mrs Geoffrey Birkbeck were on the platform to meet them. Monsieur Biddeloo, who is a working tailor by trade, was accompanied by Madame and their little girl, all of them wearing a button hole or a rosette of the Belgian colours, and looking a little strange and anxious in their new surroundings. They had been living in Brussels, whence they had fled in a state of much loss and distress almost at the moment of the German occupation … Mr and Mrs Birkbeck took them to the Thorpe refreshment room, and subsequently drove them to Stoke Holy Cross, where they will be housed at all events for the present with Mrs Birkbeck's head gardener.
>
> The remaining nine of the party consigned to Norwich arrived at Thorpe by the train due at 3.37 pm. They consisted of a family named De Jongh, husband, wife and three children; and a family named Raymackers, husband, wife and two children. These persons come from the environs of Antwerp, which city they appear to have left just before the arrival of German troops before the city.[1]

Mrs Birkbeck was president of the Norwich branch of the Women's Catholic League, working under the War Refuge Committee. The De Jonghs and the Raymackers were placed by the Birkbecks in a vacant farmhouse they owned in Poringland. An auction for the Belgian Relief fund held at Norwich on 14 January 1915 raised £396 14s.

On 15 October 1914, 1,350 Belgian refugees were landed at Lowestoft in fishing boats. An eye-witness wrote:

98   *Trawlers from Ostend carrying refugees.*

Look! There are women amongst the number … Now I understand. She is from Ostend with Belgian refugees on board. Yes I see them plainly – truly a pathetic sight … A friend has just called with the information that several boats with refugees have reached the harbour during the day. The quays and jetties are lined with townsfolk who give the refugees a most tender and sympathetic welcome. Better still, food, shelter and warm clothing are being provided.[2]

All foreigners in Britain needed to register with the authorities, including the Belgian refugees. One of them, Frans van Wanroy, wrote to the *Eastern Daily Press* after a mix-up with his registration: 'all civilian citizens of Norwich are very patient towards myself and other unfortunate Belgian refugees'.[3]

The most well-known of these Belgian refugees to stay in East Anglia is a fictional one: Agatha Christie's detective Hercule Poirot. He and six other refugees were housed in the Essex village of Styles by the kindness of the local lady of the manor. One reminder of the Belgian refugees' brief presence in Norfolk is in the church at Sidestrand. The memorial to Sir Samuel Hoare, who died in 1915, takes the form of a *rood*, a crucified Jesus, with St John and the Virgin Mary. It was designed by a celebrated Belgian carver, who was himself a wartime refugee.

Aliens

Under the Aliens Registration Act passed in August 1914, Germans had to register with the authorities by 17 August and Austrians by 24 August. The fear, of course, was that these foreigners would be 'the enemy within', acting as spies or saboteurs. Group Captain Lancelot Tomkinson remembered spy panic in Yarmouth at the beginning of the war. He was duty officer at the Coast Defence Station on the very day that war broke out. Flashing lights were reported from a seafront hotel. He gathered up some men and wanted them to go quietly and secretly to the hotel:

But, true to their traditions, the Royal Marines had to march ... In file, boots ringing on the pavement at regulation pace, we marched, with the result that as the rumour had got around, we soon attracted a following of children and our arrival at the hotel was greeted by subdued cheers from a sizeable crowd which by now had collected to see 'the fun'. It turned out that a small boy, on holiday with his family, had been playing with a torch he had just been given for his birthday. The boy, his mother and sister burst into tears when confronted by the marines, but his grandfather remained calm – 'putting one hand on my shoulder and shaking me vigorously by the other he said in solemn tones, 'Allow me to congratulate you, sir. The British navy – always on watch'.[4]

99 *Arthur Fosser, a Belgian refugee who was at Freeford Hospital. By the time this photograph was sent to Mrs Bulwer, Fosser was back with the Belgian army.*

Attitudes to aliens at the beginning of the war were summed up in a local newspaper report in early August. Four young German prisoners were brought to Norwich Market Place under armed guard: 'there were various rumours, the chief of which was that they had been tapping telegraph wires. From all accounts the men were German reservists who had been engaged as waiters'. The four were made to sit around a market stall and a local hairdresser was fetched and their hair cut. They were then marched to the railway station 'followed by a booing crowd' and taken to London.[5]

There was a special unease about aliens in Norfolk because of its proximity to the North Sea. In November 1914 the Chief Constable of the county had a letter published in the local press, intended to calm the situation. He said that there had been about 176 known Germans and Austrians in Norfolk before the war, but that now there were only 32:

Germans: 4 males, 17 females

Austrians: 1 male, 10 females

Of this number one male German is a pauper in a workhouse, a very old man, while the other three German males have been found to be perfectly harmless after thorough investigation.

The Austrian male has been vouched for by the members of the club at Hunstanton of which he is steward, and his case has been fully investigated.

The female aliens have all been under full reviewing. About half the number consists of English women married to Germans, and inmates of Convents. The others are governesses and domestics vouched for by responsible persons.

The case of one German, John Lichtens, was specifically raised: he ran a lodging house in Sheringham. As he was of an age to serve in the German Army, many Norfolk people were saying that he should be interned. However, the Chief Constable said that he was unfit for military service and so could not be interned. In any case he was now earning a living: if he was interned he would become a burden on the state.[6]

Austrians and Germans were subject to persecution – even those who joined the British army! The *Eastern Daily Press* carried this story in January 1915:

ALIEN IN THE RANKS
GERMAN CHARGED AT NORTH WALSHAM

Otto Fredericks appeared before the North Walsham magistrates wearing an ASC uniform. He was charged with as an alien failing to notify his change of address last November; travelling more than five miles from his registered place of residence without a permit; entering a prohibited area, to wit the county of Norfolk, without a permit; and using an assumed name at the start of the war.

It emerged that Fredericks was born in Konigsberg in Prussia in 1890. He had been in England since was two years old. He was now married with a child and lived in Peckham. He had grown up in England and had forgotten his German origins; when the war broke out 'it was impressed upon him that he was a German and he did not like it'. He had joined the Army Service Corps because all his pals did, and no one had asked him if he was an alien: however he did adopt his wife's maiden name of Bennett when he enlisted. 'When the spy scare came about he thought about giving himself up, but he liked the work very much, and all were very fine fellows with him, and he had not the courage to surrender himself.'

The magistrates were not sympathetic. They took the view that it was 'a most serious case' and sentenced Fredericks to three months' imprisonment with hard labour.[7]

'Aliens' included not just citizens from enemy countries, who might be spies and saboteurs but citizens of neutral countries were also subject to restrictions in their movements. In January 1918, John Carlsson of 6, Garden Place, Thetford, came before the local magistrates charged with failing to register himself. He was a painter by trade and of Swedish nationality, having been born in Malmo in 1880, and had served in the Swedish army. He had registered on 8 January, claiming that he had only arrived in the district at the end of December. Eventually he admitted that he had been in Thetford for a rather longer time: his employer, Albert Goodlin said that he had been employing Carlsson for the last 2½ years, and found him totally reliable. Carlsson claimed that he did not know that he was living in a restricted area. He was fined £2. Carlsson's landlady was charged with failing to keep a register: she said that she only had two lodgers and did not know that she was supposed to keep a register of any aliens: in any case she had had no idea of Carlsson's nationality. She was fined five shillings.[8]

Even citizens of countries on the same side in the war as Britain could be the subject of harsh treatment. In September 1917 Gargis Barzdatis, 47, a Russian Pole, was charged at Lynn Police Court with failing to register under the Aliens Registration Order. Chief Constable Hunt stated that from information received he had visited the shop of Mr Love, tailor, Norfolk Street, and there saw the defendant. In response to questions he stated that he had come from Norwich, and that he had been in the town for three weeks. He said that he left his identity document at 158 St George's Street, Norwich. He had filled up a registration card at his lodgings in Lynn, but admitted that he had not notified the police in either Norwich or Lynn of his change of address. Hunt said that he had now received the documents from Norwich and from this it appeared that Barzdatis had served in the Russian Army and had lived in Norwich since 1902. He was fined £1 and sent back to Norwich. But bureaucracy had not yet done with him: he was arrested next day and charged with not informing the Norwich police of his movements. Barzdatis pointed out that he had just been fined for this in Lynn! The Chief Constable said that under these circumstances he would not press the case, but the Norwich Bench still imposed a further fine, albeit of only 2s. 6d.![9]

There was spontaneous anti-German rioting in several towns in Britain after the sinking of the *Lusitania*. Philip Hewetson, in Felixstowe waiting to embark for France, wrote home on 16 May [1915]: 'I had another run into Ipswich yesterday. We went to the Hippodrome and when we came out there was a huge crowd in the main Street engaged in breaking the windows of a German butcher's shop.' *The Eastern Daily Press* reported that the shop was in Carr Street and belonged to a Mr Scheuermann.

On 18 May two Lynn fishermen, Charles Hornigold and James Ward, appeared before the local magistrates charged with breaking the windows of the photographic shop of Leopold Vilenkin of 60, High Street. Vilenkin was not a German at all: in fact he was a Russian and had served in the Russian army. He had lived in England for the last ten years.

The defending counsel said there was no disputing the facts: the windows had indeed been smashed. 'The cause might be attributed to the feeling which existed against alien enemies throughout the country. The same feeling existed in King's Lynn. Evidently the accused acted under a misapprehension.' Hornigold had three sons fighting for his country, one wounded at Mons, one in the 1st Norfolks, one in Kitchener's Army.

The Chairman said that the men 'had evidently allowed their feelings to break over their better judgement. To break windows as they had done was a criminal matter. Probably they thought Vilenkin was a German or Austrian. All knew that the feeling in the country was screwed up to the highest point it could be for the murders committed by their enemies upon land and sea.' The men were discharged provided they paid 25 shillings for the damages, which they had already agreed to do.[10]

People of foreign origin were subject to all sorts of more subtle persecution. Abraham Feldhun had been convicted in London of an unspecified crime: he was sent to Wormwood Scrubs prison. 'Signs of mental trouble becoming apparent', he was removed on a judicial order to the Home of Detention at Kenninghall. 'Here the mental trouble increased and the man was removed … to the County Asylum.' Norfolk County Council claimed that the London County Council should be paying for his maintenance. They argued that 'it would be monstrously unfair in cases like this one if the authorities in large towns and cities could remove such individuals as Feldhun at their will to these Houses of Detention, which are almost always situate in rural districts, and when the cases needed removal to an asylum, that the local or county authority for the area in which the House of Detention was situate, should be liable for the maintenance of them.' The magistrates adjourned the case for a week, when the County Council accepted that we would have to pay for Feldhun's maintenance in the asylum. It is doubtful whether the matter would have caused much debate if the man had not been an alien – Feldhun was a Jew from Warsaw.[11]

In the same way, although many hundreds of people in Norwich were fined for breaking the lighting regulations, one man's treatment seems especially harsh. Luigi Tonrascelli, alias Luis Thomas, a confectioner of 195 Sprowston Road, Norwich, was summoned for an offence under the Lighting Order. William Brewster said he saw a green flash from Thomas' premises, followed by a light one which showed on the gable of an adjoining house. Alfred Palmer, a tram conductor, said he saw three flashes, all white. He knocked at the door and challenged Thomas who replied, 'I only struck a match to see the way to feed my pony. Can I go in the dark at twelve o'clock in the night?'

Elizabeth Warminger claimed to have seen a red light at 10.45 pm and what appeared to be a blue light at 11.30. In court, Thomas behaved with the volatility of a son of Italy. Saying that all he had done was to strike a match, he suited the action to the word, drawing a box of matches from his pocket and striking one. Thomas was fined £1 with 7s. 6d. costs. At the same court 12 other people were charged with breaches of the Lighting Order: they were fined ten shillings each. It is interesting, too, that it was not the police who were the witnesses against Thomas, but his own neighbours who 'shopped' him, no doubt suspecting that he was a spy signalling to enemy aircraft.

Those aliens who were from enemy countries and of military age were interned in camps, of which the largest was on the Isle of Man. In April 1918 it was reported to the Agricultural War Committee that an alien camp was being established at King's Lynn: the Committee resolved to ask the Board if their labour would be available for farm work.

Prisoners of War

In March 1916, Mr F. Clifford Turner wrote to a local newspaper suggesting the use of German prisoners as labour:

> If a soldier could be sent to guard, say to every six prisoners, probably provision could be made for his accommodation with the prisoners, with strict orders to enforce obedience or shoot. It seems that it would be necessary to send men who have some little idea of agriculture or turning their hands to anything, and that it would be best to pay them something (say about one shilling a day) and the remainder of what the farmer paid to go for board and lodging.'

The paper picked up on the idea – 'English prisoners of war in Germany are being used in that way to assist German production; on the face of it there is every reason why the prisoners we hold should be set to work in the same way here. There is an urgent need for increasing our production of food in this country; and with the

100 *German prisoners in Norwich Market Place in August 1914.*

101   *Prisoners of war at work in Norfolk.*

departure of so many agricultural labourers for war services, it is important that means
should be devised for utilising the energies of the large numbers of prisoners of war
in this direction. Our army is suffering by reason of the loss of the services of the
great number of men who have to be retained for work on the land; and the reports
of the proceedings of the Tribunals in the rural districts emphasises the needs for
adopting whatever means may be effective in releasing more of them for the military
service in which they are so urgently needed'. The newspaper saw that a major problem
was finding guards for the prisoners, and suggested that the scheme should be organised
by the War Agricultural Committees rather than by individual farmers.

Mr Turner's inventiveness was not yet exhausted. Another letter by him was
published on 9 March. He wrote:

> I know it is a most difficult question to see that these same Germans are well
> guarded … Since writing my Saturday's letter I hear that many disabled soldiers
> are being drafted in our neighbourhood. These men, although quite unable to do
> heavy work or even continue their drilling, would in necessity be able to guard
> prisoners and see that they did their duty to the farmer, and by making use of
> these wounded men we might increase the proportion of English to German a
> good deal, and these same guards would be able to do a little work on their own
> account to pass their time, but they must be armed … With the disastrous Fen
> flood now taking place, it seems that a good number might be usefully employed
> in that neighbourhood preparing and strengthening the banks.[12]

The responsibility for placing prisoners on farms fell on the Agricultural War Committees. They met in January 1917 and decided that accommodation might be provided for prisoners at Shrub Hill Farm, Feltwell for Southery drainage work; at Costessey Hall, Hellesdon Mills, Gayton Workhouse, Lakenham Mills, Rockland, Kenninghalll and Swaffham Workhouses and Geldeston Mills for drainage work on the Wensum and Waveney, and at Buxton Mills or Lammas Hall at Oxnead Mill, at E.T. Learner's barn at Burgh, Colonel Kerrison's Racquet Court at Burgh Hall, G. Durrell's Farmhouse at Aylsham, G. Dunham's Farmhouse at Ingworth, Blickling Mill, and at G Hawkins' farm barn at Itteringham for drainage work on the Bure. It was later resolved that their rate of pay for piecework should be the same as that paid to Norfolk labourers. The Board decided the rate should be five pence per hour for 'efficient agricultural labourers' and four pence per hour for unskilled labour, with piecework 'at ordinary rates'.

In February Colonel Dawson reported that he had been to Kenninghall Workhouse where there was accommodation for 410 people, and Manor House, Stratton St Mary, where there was accommodation for 110. There were prisoners at Narborough by June – a letter from the Commandant of the Camp said that 80 prisoners could be sent out daily but no transport was available.[13]

Norfolk farmers wanted to use the prisoners on drainage work. The Norfolk War Agricultural Committee said that drainage work along the river Yare was needed. The Chairman said labour could be provided by German prisoners. William Carr stressed the need for immediate action 'because German labour would not be available in the winter, as the men would have to be accommodated in tents'. Three weeks later, the Depwade War Agricultural Sub Committee received a letter from the County Committee. It said that 150 German prisoners would probably reach the district about the first of August, and asked if they could arrange for any suitable work for them within a distance of three or four miles, as it was important that every use should be made of such labour. The Secretary was instructed to inform the County Committee that the German prisoners would be much better employed in clearing out the Waveney.[14]

It was decided that the prisoners should work the hours customary in a particular district, and in gangs of five. Food would be provided by the military authorities. The men were not always welcome. When the question of prisoners of war was raised at the Erpingham War Agricultural Committee, Mr Collison said that they could be used to improve the condition of the waterways. Mr Owles responded that this was more wanted in other parts of the county, and the Chairman agreed that 'in all probability there would be little demand for it in this district'.[15]

There were prisoners at Kenninghall by early August. It was suggested that handbills be distributed advertising that the prisoners were available, and on 14 September it was decided to put an advertisement in the *Eastern Daily Press*. On the same day, a letter was read to the Committee from a Mr Giles about the prisoners working on drainage of the Waveney. He said that they were working satisfactorily and did not require much supervision. It was resolved to ask for a further 40 prisoners for this work. However on 13 October it was reported that these prisoners had been forbidden to smoke while at work, and that they had been warned that unless their work was more satisfactory their rate of pay would be reduced. By this time there were also prisoners at Shouldham Hall.

There were several other camps for prisoners in Norfolk – in 1918 there were 42 prisoners staying at Houghton Hall stables. However, a proposal to house prisoners at Marlingford Hall stables was turned down by the Quartering Committee 'owing to the bad drainage and insufficient water supply'. At the same time, the Board were told that the Military authorities would not allow the use of prisoners in migratory gangs: they could supply soldiers instead. They offered up to 1,000 men 'below category A' who would be released on agricultural furlough for harvest work.

In September 1918 the Executive Committee received a letter from the Mitford and Launditch Committee saying that 'they were of the opinion that it is impossible for Prisoners to do satisfactory work on the present rations'. The War Office must have agreed as later in the same month they issued instructions for the midday ration to be increased. The Kenninghall prisoners were working on the 1918 harvest in 62 working parties – Captain Byng was given authority to hire a car so that he could go round them all. The prisoners were still there in December, when they were used in an experiment in the reclamation of sandy soil.

Inevitably, some of the German prisoners of war died during their exile in Norfolk. Otto Kohnert died on 9 January 1918, and Ludwig Wingert six days later, both at Kenninghall. They were buried in Kenninghall churchyard, and the vicar was paid five shillings a year by the then Imperial War Graves Commission to maintain the graves. They remained there until January 1963 when the German authorities decided to centralise the graves of their war dead: the bodies of the two men were exhumed and taken to the German War Cemetery at Cannock Chase in Staffordshire.[16]

Seven

Four Case Studies

The war had a dramatic effect on the life choices of many Norfolk people. In this chapter, four particular examples are examined: the Abigail family which produced several brave soldiers, and also the only man in the Norfolk Regiment to be shot for desertion; Philip Hewetson, whose letters home convey a brilliant – and cheerful – impression of life on the Western Front, but whose war was to end in imprisonment and death; George Roberts, MP for Norwich, whose uncompromising support of the war drove him away from his comrades in the Labour Party; and Edith Cavell, Swardeston-born nurse, who was to die before a German firing squad for her wartime activities.

The varied responses to the experience of war can be seen in the fate of the members of the **Abigail family** who served in the front line. Consider these two commemorations, taken from the web site of the Commonwealth War Graves Commission:

IN MEMORY OF
PRIVATE JOHN HENRY ABIGAIL

9694, 8TH BN., NORFOLK REGIMENT
WHO DIED AGE 20
ON WEDNESDAY 12 SEPTEMBER 1917.
PRIVATE ABIGAIL, SON OF JOHN JAMES AND SUSANNAH MARIA
ABIGAIL, OF 17, DISTILLERY YARD, OAK ST., NORWICH.

REMBERED WITH HONOUR
ESQUELBECQ COMMUNAL CEMETERY.

IN MEMORY OF
PRIVATE FREDERICK ALBERT ABIGAIL

15029, 8TH BN., NORFOLK REGIMENT
WHO DIED AGE 20
ON SATURDAY 1 JULY 1916.
PRIVATE ABIGAIL, SON OF ROBERT AND ELIZABETH ABIGAIL, OF
53, MUNDESLEY RD., NORTH WALSHAM, NORFOLK.

REMBERED WITH HONOUR
THIEPVAL MEMORIAL

The two memorials sound – deliberately – much the same but they conceal a great contrast in the fate of the two men. Frederick was one of almost 20,000 men killed

102 *Britannia Barracks, Norwich. The army career of thousands of Norfolk men began here.*

in action 'going over the top' at the Somme on 1 July 1916. John was shot by a British firing squad for desertion during the Battle of Ypres in 1917. He was one of about 340 men in the British army to suffer this fate in the war, and the only one from the Norfolk Regiment.

Abigail is a relatively uncommon surname: there are 64 Abigails in Norfolk in the 1901 census, and almost all are living in, or have originated from, the North Walsham/Bacton part of north-east Norfolk. Here we look at two sets of Abigail brothers, one from Norwich and the other from North Walsham.

John Henry Abigail was born in Thorpe Hamlet in 1897. He was the son of John Abigail, a carter for Norwich Corporation, and his wife Susannah. The father was part of the north-east Norfolk Abigail family: he had been born in Bacton. John was their third child: his brother William was born in 1894, and his sister Elizabeth in the following year. She was baptised at St Matthew's church in Thorpe Hamlet on 13 November 1895. The family lived at Gypson's Yard, off what is now St Leonard's Road.

William was keen to be a soldier: he had become a Territorial in 1911, when he was sixteen. He was a smallish lad; his papers give his height as 5 feet 4 inches. However his vision is described as 'normal' and his physical development as 'very good'. He was then working as a labourer for a Mr Edwards, who also lived in Gypson's Yard.

Another branch of the Abigail family lived at 53, Mundesley Road, North Walsham. Robert Abigail was a bricklayer, born in the town: his wife Elizabeth came from nearby Ashmanhaugh. Three of their sons were involved in the war.

The eldest brother, Walter, joined up first: he went into the Royal Field Artillery and served in France from 30 May 1915 until 11 October 1916, when he was wounded in the left wrist and buttock by a shell. He returned to the front on 16 May 1917. In

September, however, he was again sick: he was reported to be suffering from *shell shock*. This term was first used in 1915. It was applied to soldiers who suffered a nervous breakdown while at the front. The name stems from the belief that the physical force of shell explosions was the cause. However, it soon became clear that it was psychological – men who had not actually been under shell fire could equally well be the victims of shell shock. Walter's case was less serious than many others. He was able to return to the Front within a few months. In January 1918 he was wounded once more, suffering an injury to his left foot. This was to be the end of the war for

103   *'Shellshock', drawn by a patient at Sheringham Hospital.*

Walter Abigail: he left France on 31 January and did not return.

Two younger brothers followed Walter into the Army. Frederick, aged five at the time of the 1901 census, joined up at North Walsham in September 1915. His elder brother Robert was a married man and living in Warwickshire: he also joined up in North Walsham in September 1915, but he did not go into the Norfolk Regiment.

Frederick and John Abigail both served in the 8th battalion of the Norfolk Regiment. The battalion took part in the Battle of the Somme on 1 July 1916. The day is vividly described in the Regimental diary, now at the National Archives. The battalion was to attack German trenches north of Carnoy and south-west of Montaubon. The battalion diary gives the timetable for the early morning:

> 5.30am. Teas served out
> 7.20 am. Artillery commenced intense bombardment, enemy retaliated
> 7.27 am. A mine and two Russian saps were exploded. At the exact same time the first wave of C and D companies climbed over the top and laid out in the open about 30 yards in front – they were not fired on.
> 7.30 am. The assault began, with the remainder of the two assault companies moving forward in four successive waves. Within 10 minutes they had reached the German lines at Mine Trench and Mine Support. The artillery had done its job: the German barbed wire had been 'completely destroyed' and those Germans in the trench still alive were 'thoroughly cowed' and surrendered. At 8 am Bund Support was reached.

So far, so good for the men of the 8th Norfolks. However, during the next step forward, the two companies came under heavy machine gun fire from Breslau Support and Back Trench. Many officers were killed and the other ranks were reduced to 90 or 100 men in each company. The left leading company reached Pommiers Trench about 10.30 am. The right company was held up by machine gun fire, but eventually reached the trench too. At 3 pm both companies advanced towards Montaubon Alley, their final target of the day. They again came under machine gun fire and were held up until a bombing party gained entry to the trench. The Alley line was taken at

104   *Ypres – the Menin Road.*

5.45 pm. The day was over but the cost was great: three officers and 102 men had been killed. Frederick Abigail was among them. His body was never recovered: his name appears on the great monument to the missing at Thiepval. He was 20 years old.

For John Abigail, the horrors of the first day of the Somme were too much to bear. He deserted in the aftermath of the battle. He was caught and sentenced to 10 years' penal servitude, which was later suspended.

The 8th Norfolks were once again selected to 'go over the top' in the British attack at the third Battle of Ypres on 31 July 1917. For John Abigail this was the last straw. When his company was gathered together ready to advance to the front, Abigail was missing. He was found three days later, well behind the lines and without his rifle. A Court-Martial was inevitable: it met on 22 August 1917. The President was Lt Col Hill, DSO, of the 8th Suffolk Regiment. The other members were Capt. Richardson, MC, of the 6th Royal Berkshire Regiment, and 2Lt Whiting of the 10th Essex Regiment.

On 24 August Abigail was formally charged: 'When on active service deserting His Majesty's Services in that he in the Field on the 30th July 1917, absented himself from his Battalion after having been warned for the trenches, and remained absent until apprehended without arms or equipment by the Military Police on a tour behind the lines at about 4.30 pm on 2nd August 1917'. The Court Martial papers, held at

105 *Ypres – a camouflaged tank at 'Clapham Junction'.*

the Public Record Office in Kew, record the details in staccato fashion: each of the four witnesses gave a very short statement, and Abigail's response was the same each time: silence.

FIRST WITNESS: No. 20962 Cp W. Ellwood, 8th Norfolk Regiment
Between 3 and 4 pm on July 30 Sergeant Barnes, my platoon sergeant, warned the platoon to be ready to move to the trenches in fighting order, all packs to be handed to the QM [Quarter Master} stores by 6 pm. About 8 pm I noticed Abigail had not handed in his pack and searched the camp but could not find him. Witness did not see him again until he came back under arrest.

Accused declined to cross-examine the witness.

[Ellwood himself was to be killed in action on 21 March 1918: his body was never found. His name is recorded on the Arras Memorial.]

SECOND WITNESS: No. 30306 Pte H. Livings
Barnes gave the warning about 3.45. Abigail was only two yards from Barnes. Abigail was absent when we handed in our packs and still absent when the platoon moved off.

Accused declined to cross-examine the witness.

THIRD WITNESS: No. 22854 Pte C.E. Broughton
Barnes gave warning about 3.30. He also ordered us to collect wood for making breakfasts with the next morning after zero. I myself left for the camp before the platoon marched off to the forward area.

Accused declined to cross-examine the witness.

FOURTH WITNESS: No. 2875 Cp H.N. Stallworthy MMP
On Aug 2 about 4.30 I was on duty near Staple. I met the accused walking along the road. I stopped him and asked him if he was on duty. He replied 'No, I am looking for my battalion, they were billeted near here and I have been out for a walk for two hours and when I came back they were gone'. He was unable to give me any further accounts as to the whereabouts of his battalion. I conveyed him to HQ 2nd Army where he was detained. He was without any equipment whatsoever.

Accused declined to cross-examine the witness.

The prosecution case was closed. Abigail made no attempt to justify his action: he declined to make any statement or call any witnesses.

His past record in the army was then considered. It was not a good one: he had had four earlier brushes with authority. We have seen that he had deserted once already in the previous summer. While at Felixstowe in the winter of 1916-17, he had offended three times. On 19 December 1916 he was found to be absent from parade at 9 am. He remained absent until apprehended by the civil police at Norwich at 4 pm on 27 December. He was sentenced to 168 hours' detention and to forfeit nine days' pay. No doubt he was homesick: after all this was Christmas and he was only nineteen. Still at Felixstowe, on 15 January 1917, Abigail was charged with having a dirty rifle on parade at 9 am. He was sentenced to five days' CB [Confined to Barracks]. As soon as he had served this punishment he ran away once more: on 22 January 1917 he was again absent from parade at 9 am. This time he remained absent until he surrendered himself at Britannia Barracks Norwich at 9.40 pm on 27 January. His sentence was 14 days' field punishment and the loss of six days' pay.

Inevitably, Abigail was found guilty of desertion. Sentence of death was passed upon him. On 9 September it was confirmed by Douglas Haig. Abigail was shot at dawn on 12 September by men from his own battalion: his body was buried in Esquelbecq communal cemetery. Like Frederick, he was 20 years old when he died.

The 8th Battalion was in the Rubrouck area until 23 September. On that day they marched to Esquelbecq, arriving at 1.45 pm and were there until 6 pm when they entrained en route for Poperinghe from where they marched to Road Camp. It is unlikely that any of them took the opportunity to visit Abigail's grave.

The church in Thorpe Hamlet where Abigail's sister was baptised is now used for offices. However, a new St Matthew's church has been built, only a few yards from where Abigail was born. The war memorial has been moved to a place of honour in front of the church, and has been lovingly maintained. Abigail's name does not appear on the memorial. Nor does his name appear in the original Norwich Roll of Honour. However his name *has* recently been added to the 'electronic' version of the Roll in the Castle Museum.[1]

Philip Hewetson was the son of William Hewetson, the rector of Wroxham with Salhouse. He joined the Loyal North Lancashire Regiment on the outbreak of war in 1914. He wrote a series of letters home to his family, which give a very clear picture of life at the front. He was later captured and the family papers give a picture of the distress this caused which must have been a common experience among Norfolk families. Very few collections of papers have survived that give so much detail.

The letters quoted here fall into two groups. The first group was written by Philip to his father or his sister, describing how he joined up, and what life was like in the trenches on the Western Front. The second group was written by other people to Philip's father, and describe in graphic detail his tragic fate.

106   'Philip' Hewetson.

Joining up

H S and I were going up to town as I had said to finish off our kit but thought we might just drop in at the LRB [London Rifle Brigade] Headquarters to see that everything was alright as we had been told. Comber & Carter both advised us to do so so we did. We arrived Liv St 12.40 and to 130 Bunhill Row EC by curious small and dirtyish streets. We went in and a sergeant directed us to a room upstairs where he said we should find the Colonel. We found him & 3 other officers surrounded by paperwork etc. I said that we had come just to see that everything was alright, and when they had asked our names they just looked blank. They eventually found a paper with the names of about 8 recommended subalterns, H S among them. They <u>said</u> they knew nothing about me and had got neither of our papers … They showed us the list and said that was all the subalterns they would want, they were sorry as they supposed we wanted to keep together, still they were full so 'Good morning' and – we went! We went back to Liv St and ate a dejected lunch. [Philip went back to Cambridge and saw Comber who was 'very annoyed' but who had friends in high places: he recommended Philip as subaltern to a colonel who was trying to find subalterns for 'a general, newly appointed over one of these new armies …] This means if all goes well a Commission in the New Army. Of course it means I shan't get to the front so quickly as if I were in Terriers, but I shall be in the Regular Army, and I suppose one simply cannot choose. It's a pity Hugo & I are to be separated and instead of going through together we had to say 'goodbye on Liv St station yesterday. He'll go fighting before I do now after all.

Life on the Western Front

PM 9 July 1915. Last night those horrible Germans thought fit to shell this place. And between 12 & 3.45 they sent from 50-100 (!!!) into it! I slept soundly at first until at 3.15 I was awoken by a huge sort of whistling swi…sh coming straight at me in a crescendo followed immediately by a <u>huge</u> report & bang then falling masonry!! You may think you can imagine my feelings but you can't. I lay in bed & didn't know what do to; as a matter of fact this one fell about 100 yds away in a house. You hear them coming with a huge whistle & don't know where they're going till they burst. Nobody pretends not to be frightened inside!! Very much so you feel powerless! Then followed a dreadful 10 minutes (for me at any rate as it was my baptism of fire). What it will be like to be bombarded by 100s of shells I <u>don't</u> know.

20 June 1915. Well in case we were being relieved for a long rest I determined to get into the firing line before we left. So I walked up there with the Major. As the crow flies it was only about 300 yards from our trenches, but going along all the zig zag communication trenches you walk quite a mile. You never go straight for more than 5 to 6 yards. They are as I said from 6-8 ft deep about 2 feet wide never more & like this & so on ad infinitum! Where we got to the Germans were 70 yards away. In this part of the line we are about 500 yards further <u>West</u> than we were in December, so if people in England think a rush is possible, well tell them that the opposing forces have sat opposite each other in this sector in exactly the same places since January in parts only <u>20 yards</u> from each other. Nothing but High Explosive will turn either out.

11 July. When you dig at night it's very interesting, lots of our guns are just behind us and keep going off with huge reports, first you see the flash, then you hear the huge cracking report of the gun, and this is the most interesting if it's a dark night & you are quick at looking up you can see the white hot shells as they pass over your head! You then hear them whistling away in the distance, then next you see their flash as they burst and some seconds after you hear the explosion. It all requires practice of course, and I'm not by any means an adept at it yet, but you get to be able to tell the burst of the shell from the report of the gun, whether when shells pass over head to some far target, they are your own going or theirs arriving; whether when you hear a German shell coming towards you it is going to pitch short, whether it is aimed at you or whether it is going to pass harmlessly over your head and hit some poor village behind. To be able to do this naturally saves a tremendous amount of unnecessary speculation & ducking behind cover. It's very fascinating in the trenches, you hear these big 'coalboxes' etc come whistling at you, you wonder when its coming, however some of the men know at once it will pass over, & the Tommies take no notice of them though they may be pitching 30-100 yards away only. A big shell always gives you plenty of time to flop down or dive into a handy dug out as you hear them coming 2 or 3 secs before they burst. That's why shrapnel is so deadly, it gives you no warning, you just hear swish bang, swish bang as they burst.

23 July 1915. I am enclosing some pcs of the village about ½ hours from here where we go & dig. There is not one house standing. There was some of the fiercest fighting of the war there last October when the French drove out the Germans by street fighting which lasted 5 weeks. It is a town of the dead, not a living civilian anywhere, just as if there had been a colossal earthquake. Houses with no roofs & no walls – everything overgrown. Rusty twisted unrecognisable pieces of furniture, wagons, farm machines etc. Telegraph poles broken in half with twisted wires all round them.

We have got our mess in a little cottage owned by an old couple of 85 & 83 respectively. Dear old people who have just settled down here as a last home bought out of their savings. It was I hear very pathetic to see them yesterday, when the place was being very heavily shelled for a short time, sitting together down in their cellar.

[One shell] unfortunately hit the barn in wh half my platoon were, it killed one & wounded 4. Another shell killed my servant. I am so sorry about it, such a nice young chap who left Felixstowe with me 7 weeks ago yesterday. I have written to their people & sent back a few little belongings such as letters found in their pockets. We buried one in the little Churchyard here. My servant died on the way to hospital.

31 July. During that time there was a terrific thunderstorm & torrents of rain for about ½ an hour. When I woke up about 5.15, the trenches were once more liquid mud & water, & all the wood for fires wet through, everything was <u>sopping</u> wet. However we slopped about as we did in the other trenches. The servants got us some tea somehow by 5.45. When the trenches are like that they are dreadfully uncomfortable & you are caked in mud very soon, or rather everything you touch is muddy.

1 Aug. You ask about washing – well the usual procedure is to have your bath <u>in</u> your basin or rather near the basin. You manage to wash all over but that's the only receptacle for water you have. You really get quite adept at that sort of thing. A 'toilet' in the trenches is really quite a work of art too!

9 Aug. The Germans opposite us were very lively at night & used to keep up a continuous pot-shooting at our trenches. During the day they were quieter. On Saturday night I was very pleased to find no shooting going on as I had to go with a small party of men to cut the grass in front of our barbed wire. However when we'd been there about ½ hour they seemed to suspect they were there. They sent up several flares in our direction & had some pot shots wh all went overhead. When they do this you just lie flat as a pancake face downwards on the ground & you can't be seen. You work on hands & knees. However a bit later they seemed to make up their minds we really were out & the shooting became more 'personal'. So as it was not worth losing a man for the sake of some grass I brought my party in all safe & sound.

19 Aug. The Germans are afraid to shell us too much as the lines are so close that a bad shot might quite easily hit their own front line, however we got some shells at us. Our gunners are apparently surer of their skill for they shell the German front line & sometimes it seems as if our shells are going to hit us from behind. What both sides trouble each other most with are trench mortars. The best of these is that you can see them coming – looking like a black oblong sausage about 2 feet long & 5 or 6 inches in diameter … It is most exciting dodging them when you see them coming.

21 Aug. I am caked in mud; it has rained & thundered most of the 48 hours we have been in so far, though today has been better. Again it's a case of us washing or shaving. The trenches are in a worse condition than they were those horrible 5 days before. This time however I'm rejoicing in the possession of my gum boots. They are solidly encased in mud. So are my knees & a few inches above them, solid caked mud. Hands, tunic, hat, mackintosh all mud.

Capture and Death

In June 1918, Hewetson's parents learned that their son was missing. His fate only became clear to them gradually in a series of letters they received over the next few months.

Letter from Central Prisoners of War Committee: Re Captain R.J.P Hewetson. 'In reply to your letter dated June 19th we beg to inform you that we have this Officer's name on our records as missing on 27th May and have wired to Copenhagen to ensure his name being placed on every searching list of the neutral Red Cross.' The family waited anxiously for news. On 19 August G.E. Grove wrote to Mr Hewetson that he had met Captain Padwick, who was transport to the 9th: 'he saw your son with his platoon in the line on the left of the battn – they were apparently behind a hedge – a short time after he heard that the Bosch had worked round behind the hedge and cut off your son and his platoon, so it looks as though it was almost certain that he is a prisoner'.

Constance Colt-Williams from Paris 14 October 1918:

I have only just got back from Germany where I have been a prisoner for 4½ months & am writing immediately to give you what news I can of your son Captain Hewetson, who was brought to our ambulance as a prisoner seriously wounded in the leg – we had to amputate immediately & he was doing very well, then we were all sent to another ambulance about 3 weeks afterwards & had to leave all our wounded in charge of the German doctors, & fortunately English orderlies. About 3 weeks after that I saw one of the orderlies, who told me that your son had never done so well after the English surgeons & I – who was the only English nurse there – had left – & forgive me for having to tell you such painful news – but he [*sic*] appears that he died of septic pneumonia about the end of June or beginning of July – the orderly told me that the German doctors did everything possible for him but he had had gas-gangrene & it was evidently too much for him – He is buried at Beaurieux, where he died … It may comfort you to know that he was operated on by an English surgeon – Major Handfield-Jones, who was taken at Beaurieux the same day as I was & with whom I worked for 6 weeks. He was therefore in our care for 3 weeks but it appears that he lost all heart after we left … As far as I could see, the Germans treat the enemy wounded like their own, every man who died was buried by the chaplain (German) just as if they had died in our lines & crosses were put over all their graves – they were perfectly in their conduct to us – there were only 3 nurses, 2 French girls & myself we never had any bother or insult – they certainly respect the Red Cross if nothing else.

The Hewetsons wrote to Miss Colt-Williams for contact details of people who had been with their son in the hospital and received replies from several of them over the next few months.

Sergeant G. Temple described Philip's moment of capture:

At 2.30 pm we started off going in the direction of Glennes but we had only been going about 20 minutes when the Germans came over the Ridge, the Capt gave the order at once to extend and get into position behind what cover we could find. Things got very hot for a time and then I began to look round and see how we were situated and found things very bad.

During all the time of the fight which lasted an hour and I may add the hottest hour I ever had in my 4 years service the Capt was stood up giving orders and encouragement to the men, he was absolutely fearless though he was staring Death in the face, he had a Rifle and Bullets which he used with great effect.

Things could not go on like there [*sic*] were we were losing men very fast and our ammunition was about done so the Capt gave the order to retire back to a

Road where we had a better chance and he stood there till every man had got to this place all the time the Germans were closing on us.

About 10 minutes afterwards things got terribly mixed so I went to find the Capt who was about 100 yds on my right and one of the men told me the Capt had got wounded in the leg but was still carrying on. It was while I was on my way that I met Mr Sinclair who was in a very bad state and just as I got near him I got hit myself and put out of action altogether.

I crawled away to see the Capt and found him lying with a Bullet in his leg which was giving him great Pain, I am telling you the truth as you want me to although it is hard when I think of that Brave and gallant Gentleman lying helpless but still wearing the old cheery smile which made him so well loved by all who knew him. It was about 3.30 when I reached the Capt and he said to me, 'Well dear lad do you suffer much cheer up and trust to God he will bring you safe through it all although it is hard to be taken Prisoner after the way the Men have fought.'

The Germans then came up and called on us to surrender which we had to do having no option, the[y] went to the Capt and searched him taking a lot of things away from him, what they were I could not see but I know they were papers of some sort then a German Officer kicked him and called him a Swine and I had a hard job to restrain him from picking up his Revolver and firing at the German which would have cost him his life there and then.

The German Red-Cross man came up to dress our wounds and though the Capt was very badly wounded he would not let them dress him first but made them attend to me and some more of the Boys who were laying there wounded.

The Capt laid there from about 3.30 pm on the 27th till about 9 pm same day when he began to be delirious so the Germans ordered some of our Men who were not wounded to carry him to Glennes and I was left by myself until next morning when I crawled away and landed in Glennes to the same farmshed where your Son was laying.

He seemed a bit better then and kept on cheering the Men who were getting downhearted.

The afternoon of the 28th your Son was taken in a Motor Car from Glennes to Beaurieux and I walked down there with the help of L/Cpl Neale.

G. Waton wrote on 7 February 1919: 'he was delirious for fully fourteen days before he died, with just short intervals before he died, the German doctor, who to give him due credit did all he could, told me that there was no hope for him. We could do nothing. After doing all we could, I could only sit and watch your son pass away. He gradually sank and finally died about 6 pm on July 3. Two days later we attended his funeral. The full burial service was read by a German priest. Personally I don't think anyone can say your son died of starvation. The food was good enough and sufficient to keep him alive … Truly I think that had he lived till he left our hospital he would have died later owing to the food he would have received then, as the food where we were, although not to be compared with the food in an English hospital, was better by far than the food given to prisoners at other camps and in Germany'.

Hewetson's family were worried about their son's diet in prison, unsurprisingly in view of the conditions for prisoners of war in Germany discussed in chapter one. A letter from W.J. Wheeler reassured them:

… as for the food I will try to explain as much as I can. About eight in the morning we gave him some coffee and some thin bread and butter and jam, and

107   *George Roberts campaigns in the country …*

at eleven he had some soup and then dinner at twelve. His dinner consisted of meat and vegetables & sometimes soup, made from barley. About four he had some tea and some small biscuits with jam, & of course if he needed a drink at any time we managed to get him one of some sort and a German doctor who could speak a little English brought him a small bottle of champagne once or twice. At this time your son was as cheerful as he could be, and as far as I can remember not once during his illness did he have to be fed. Unfortunately the English doctors were sent away to another hospital & from that time he seemed to sink & become depressed & just after he contracted dysentery which did a lot to pull down & to weaken him & I am sorry to say he never seemed to pull round after. We used to carry out both your son & Mr Sinclair out into the sunshine as often as possible & put them into a cool place under the trees … Your son seemed to become rather melancholy & to be very quite [*sic*] as if he did a great deal of thinking & he seemed to gradually get worse until pneumonia set in & he became delirious and he never recovered.[2]

Philip died on 3 July 1918: he was 24 years old. His body, with that of 15 other prisoners of war who had died in captivity, was moved from Beaurieux after the war and re-interred at Vendresse British Cemetery.

George Roberts was born in Chedgrave in 1869. He was a printer by trade. He was a member of the Independent Labour Party and became one of their first Members of Parliament when he won a seat at Norwich in the 1906 general election. He was still MP when war broke out eight years later. As we have seen, the party opposed the war, but Roberts was strongly in favour. This led to estrangement from

108   *... and in Norwich.*

his former colleagues and closer ties with the Liberal governing party. Indeed he was one of the few Labour MPs to take office when Asquith formed an all-party coalition in 1915. He rose even higher when Lloyd George took over from Asquith. Roberts became Minister of Labour and joined the Cabinet in 1917.

As a working-class leader in support of the war, Roberts was very important to the government, and they made much use of him. He was on the Committee appointed to inspect the camps where aliens were being interned:

11 March 1915: I am directed by my colleagues of the Internment Committee to draw your attention to the following matters:

During a visit made to the *Laxonia*, moored off Southend, complaints were prevalent respecting the quality and cooking of the meat rations. Investigation seemed to show reason therefore. We understand both the catering and cooking on this ship is contracted by the Cunard Co. Where supplies are directly secured and the cooking is undertaken by men selected from among the prisoners, conditions are much more satisfactory. As, for instance, on the *Royal Edward* and the *Quennia*.

We respectfully suggest too that greater variety might be introduced into the meat allowance, provided that the regulation cost is not exceeded. Beef seems to be almost exclusively used in some cases. If mutton, etc, could be substituted occasionally consistent with the reservation as to cost, we believe a dietary improvement would have been effected.

Though the use of ships of [*sic*] internment purposes is not a question directly concerning our enquiry, nevertheless we have thought you would like our opinion thereon. We think that while one, or perhaps two, might be retained for the accommodation of the better type of prisoner, and those who it is desirable to keep in especially safe custody, it would be better to transfer prisoners from the others to land encampments.

Adverting to the *Saxonia*. On this ship are several cases of venereal disease. The prisoners so affected are kept apart from the others. However, we believe the only effective method of dealing with such is to segregate all in some central hospital.

On behalf of the Committee,

Yours sincerely

Geo H. Roberts

The Committee also looked at prisoner of war camps. They produced a report on Donnington Hall, which was being used as a prison for German officers. Several newspapers had alleged that the officers held there were being treated with undue leniency. Roberts concluded: 'the exaggerated statements in the papers as to luxuries being supplied with a prodigal hand by the Government have no foundation in fact … But all the same I have seen less attractive places provided for our own wounded'.

Roberts was also used by the government to visit France and meet with labour leaders. His articles on France in War Time were published in the *Typographical Circular* between September and December 1915:

Owing to my association with a House of Commons Committee that visits the several concentration camps in this country I was much interested to learn how the French treated captured German soldiers. I found at one place two hundred captured Germans engaged on some works being constructed for the city of Lyons. These men were paid from 2d to 4d per day according to their skill. In this country interned prisoners have not been put to work. Difficulties of guarding, beside the danger of competing with organised labour, have rendered it impracticable. But they appear to have overcome these difficulties in France; at least, they object to keeping prisoners in idleness, and, as far as one could gather, the prisoners themselves preferred to do some work.

Sept 1915 – British gunnery is universally acknowledged to be most efficient, and it is lamentable that guns, as in this battery, cannot be more fully utilised. 'Why not?' will be asked, 'Lack of shells' is the answer. In this region it was known that the Germans were strengthening their trenches and fortifying every available eminence. With an adequacy of shells our gunners could check this. As it is, they stand by helplessly for the greater part of the time, knowing that the order to advance will demand a sacrifice of life and an expenditure of munitions which could have been avoided but for the present deficiency in shells.

The train drew in and, like children on holiday-making, these simple great-hearted fellows [artillerymen on their way to the front] clambered aboard. For hours I read and listened to their singing and shouting. At last they detrained. I got out, too; saw them form up and march out into the night. Inky darkness and a torrential rain made them look like a phantom army. Back in the compartment I occupied alone, I pondered the scene; visualised those lads in deadly combat, and wondered how many were destined to be maimed and killed, and whether many or few would return safely to England and home. Some jaundiced critics aver I have become a jingo. But I hate war more intensely than ever, yet say with my soldier friends – there is now no other way. Could these purblind creatures but understand, they would know their paltering makes for greater death and disaster.

Above flew a British biplane. Enemy anti-aircraft guns were firing at it. A shell exploded a little short of it. With consummate skill the bird-like machine was made to soar higher and higher till beyond the deadly range.

A walk through the town revealed the fact that neither church nor cottage had been spared – everywhere was ruin and desolation. All civilians had been evacuated, and the place was occupied exclusively by British and French soldiers. They hailed us with laughter and cheers. But a little distant, shells were bursting. Whether or not these men were victims seemed a matter of mere chance. Considerable risk attended us. However, given immunity for an hour or two, we should pass out of the danger zone. But these men must remain. Only the sight of a Red Cross van speeding stricken heroes to a hospital served to remind that 'In the midst of Life we are in Death'.

In the course of my speech I told of the 979 controlled establishments employing over 1,000,000 workpeople, 600,000 of whom are women, and of the 20 national shell factories at work, and the 18 more in the process of construction. How that we started a new programme of heavy guns and consequent heavy shells. For the manufacture of the latter 11 national projectile factories had been erected, these factories being under the direct control of the Ministry of Munitions.

109 *The Image of War: George Roberts and Arthur Henderson, leaders of pro-war Labour.*

Roberts aroused controversy as the letters to him preserved at the Norfolk Record Office reveal:

J.G. Chapman, of Norwich High School for Boys to Roberts, 17 Dec 1916:

> I am writing to offer you my heartiest congratulations on taking office in the New Ministry, composed mostly of men of action, grit & determination like yourself … The citizens, among whom it is my lot to mingle, have nothing but praise & satisfaction at the manly, patriotic & statesmanlike manner in which you have acted all through the period of this horrible war. You have won the goodwill & respect of most, if not all, of the thinking & honourable men of our ancient city.

Timothy J. Wood to Roberts, 6 May 1918:

> I have often heard you lately say when defending the action which has separated you politically from some of us 'You hope we do not hate you'. No, that would

only be the negation of all the principles we hold dear, & I take this opportunity of saying that however much we may differ I have nothing but Christian love & the highest regard for you.

E.B. Reeve to Roberts, 6 June 1917:

I don't often take people to law, but should rather like to see your starchy cuffs & collar in the defendant's box, with that immaculate umbrella hanging over your arm by its well fitting crook … You are having a good time just now George, but the workers here are DAMNING you to H..L and will have your measure presently.

James Holmes, Organising Secretary of the National Union of Railwaymen to Roberts 31 August 1917:

My warmest congratulations at your unopposed return for Norwich, in a sense I was sorry the Condensed Milk Group had not the courage to fight, they would have been wiped out, they evidently knew that … still old Comrade you have a huge task before you, we have the Grimmest Fight before us yet, there is a seething Discontent under the service [surface], Grim and Real, Cost of Living and Profetering is the fire smouldering beneath, I move amongst it every day, and have done my bit to hold your corner up.

W.A. Harvey, BEF France, to Roberts 6 Sept 1917:

I find upon perusing our local paper viz *The Eastern Weekly Press* that you have been appointed to a most responsible office in the Government, may I on behalf of two Norwich comrades and myself offer you many congratulations from the 35th Squadron Royal Flying Corps, somewhere in France, who are 'doing their bit.' I was further pleased to read that the citizens of Norwich have still every confidence in you by returning you unopposed to the House of Commons. The more I see of the ruthlessness and wanton destruction wrought by the huns, the more firmer am I of the opinion that your action regarding the Allied cause is justified.

George Lincoln to Roberts, 13 Sept 1917:

In reference sent you from the Circuit Quarterly Meeting of the United Methodists of Norwich, I would like you to know something of the strength which was behind it, so you may appreciate it at its real value. There were from thirty to forty present, the question which never should have been raised, was sprung upon the meeting, without any notice whatever, by a few men who politically belonged to the party who were once your avowed supporters, but for some cause or other which you can better understand than some of us, have some grievance against you and the government, and took this opportunity of ventilating it. Those of us who did our best to defeat it endeavoured to point out that its object was not to help the government in dealing with this difficult question, but to embarrass it. We also claimed and I think rightly that there is not one person who is imprisoned for being a conscientious objector but for refusing the piece of National service allotted to them, under the pretence that the work they were already doing was of national importance. This claim could equally made by every man that is taken from a shoe factory or any other industrial or professional business. And we also claim that it is tantamount to saying that the thousands of lads who have left our Sunday schools and churches have no conscientious objection to war, of course they have, but like yourself have felt conscience calling them to give themselves to the work of winning this war.

Letter to Roberts from the Independent Labour Party 21 Oct 1917:

Doubtless you are aware that a vast amount of difference has existed between the local branch and yourself for some time past and the climax to such difference was made manifest a short time ago when the Local Movement repudiated your candidature at the recent bye-election at Norwich. In view of this position I am instructed to inform you that the above branch at its meeting on October 15th passed a resolution in favour of asking you to resign your membership of the branch.

Roberts replied ten days later:

while this seems to me an ungracious act, especially having regard to the fact that I have been a member of the branch for about twenty-two years, and whilst I doubt whether a majority of the branch would, if properly tested, endorse this action, still I am sufficiently democratic to recognise that those who exert and interest themselves in the affairs of the branch will prevail. Therefore I have no alternative but to bow to the decision you have conveyed.

In June 1918 the Labour party withdrew its support for the coalition but Roberts, with a few other ministers, stayed in the Coalition and left the Labour party. Roberts stood for Norwich again in the General Election of December 1918, but as a Coalition Independent rather than for Labour. His election manifesto stated: 'throughout the War I have co-operated whole-heartedly in the measures which were proved necessary for its prosecution, and which have enabled Great Britain and the Allied nations to achieve Peace through Victory.'

The *Norwich Mercury* published on 11 November 1919 a tribute to Roberts' role in the war: 'the outbreak was the point from which Roberts' meteoric rise may be watched with interest. From the first he took a definite, uncompromising, patriotic position. 'Right at the beginning,' I remember he declared to me one dark Sunday afternoon that was a fit type of the grim position of affairs in France, 'I made up my mind that my country was in the right, and being in the right, I determined to support it until peace comes and we may resume political activities again.' I regret my attitude has caused a break with erstwhile Labour friends in Norwich, but I cannot help it. I am doing what I believe to be right and I shall do it to the end.'[3]

Roberts won the 1918 election, but his political journey was not quite over. He stood again in the 1922 election, this time as an Independent. Once more the people of Norwich supported him, but in the following year he moved even further to the right and joined the Conservative Party. This was a step too far for many Norwich voters. Roberts was defeated in the 1923 general election and retired from politics. He died in 1928.

The First World War produced one of Norfolk's most famous heroines: **Edith Cavell**. She was born at Swardeston in 1865, the daughter of the Reverend Frederick Cavell who was rector there for over 40 years. In 1890 she took a nursing post in Brussels where she stayed for five years. She went back to Brussels in 1907 and was

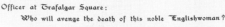

EDITH CAVELL,
Nurse–Patriot–Martyr.

THE above wreath, to the memory of EDITH CAVELL, was placed at the
Nelson Column, Trafalgar Square, London, October 21st, 1915, by the
London Society of East Anglians, and afterwards deposited at St. Mary
Magdalen Church, Swardeston, Norfolk, on the day of the great Memorial
Service, St. Paul's Cathedral. It was at Swardeston that EDITH CAVELL first
saw the light, to quote her own words, "Where she found life fresh and
beautiful, and the country so desirable and sweet." British people will
henceforth pay love and homage to the name of CAVELL, reverence, appreciation
and respect to a great and useful life, and register her for all time within
the annals of our race a great and a noble soul.

**The proceeds of the sale of these cards will be devoted to placing a
stained glass window to Edith Cavell's memory in Swardeston Church.**

Donations for the Memorial Window should be forwarded direct to the Rev. HUBERT
GREEN, The Vicarage, Swardeston, Norwich.
                                          DAILY GRAPHIC PHOTO.

110   *'Nurse – Patriot – Martyr'.*

soon in charge of a training school for nurses. In 1914 she was on a visit to her mother, who then lived in College Road in Norwich, when she heard that Germany had invaded Belgium. She returned at once to Brussels and helped soldiers of all nationalities under the Red Cross. She also helped British and allied soldiers to escape to neutral territory in Holland, from where they were able to get back to this country. She was arrested in August 1915 and held in solitary confinement. At her trial she agreed she had helped soldiers to escape and she was condemned to death. She was shot by a firing squad on 12 October 1915: she was 49 years old.

Edith Cavell was executed at dawn on 12 October. The process of reporting this fact is a fascinating contrast to the present age of instant news. Nothing was made public until the Press Bureau issued a brief statement at 10.30 pm on Friday 15 October. The *Eastern Daily Press* included the statement on the following day, but it had arrived too late for editorial comment. The statement ran:

ENGLISH LADY EXECUTED IN BRUSSELS

The Foreign Office are informed by the United States Ambassador that Miss Edith Cavell, lately head of a large Training School for Nurses at Brussels, who was arrested on the 5th August last, by the German authorities at that place, was executed on the 13th inst [sic, actually it was the 12th] after sentence of death had been passed on her.

It is understood that the charge against Miss Cavell was that she had harboured fugitives, British and French soldiers and Belgians of military age, and had assisted them to escape from Belgium in order to join the colours.

So far as the Foreign Office are aware, no charge of espionage was brought against her.

No papers were published on Sunday, but Monday's EDP included an editorial stressing Cavell's local connections, and that her widowed mother was living in College Road in Norwich.

A full report only appeared in the local press on 22 October, ten days after Edith's execution. Further reports appeared on the following day including a letter from the Rev. Gahan, British chaplain at Brussels. He saw Edith on the night before she was shot:

111 *Queen Alexandra unveils the Edith Cavell in Norwich. The Cavell Memorial Nurses' Home is in the background.*

She said: 'I have no fear or shrinking. I have seen death so often that it is not strange or fearful.' She further said: 'I thank God for this ten weeks quiet before the end. Life has always been hurried and full of difficulty. This time of rest has been a great mercy. They have all been very kind to me here. But this I would say, standing as I do in the view of God and eternity. I realise that patriotism is not enough. I must have no hatred or bitterness towards anyone.' They took Holy Communion together. The next day the German chaplain was 'with her to the end'.

On the same day, 23 October, the *EDP* published another editorial on Cavell: 'the blood of Edith Cavell cries aloud not for revenge but for justice' and concluded 'the name of Edith Cavell should prove more powerful as a recruiting symbol than any other at this moment'.

FOR
KING
AND
COUNTRY

HUMANITY

EDITH CAVELL
BRUSSELS
DAWN
OCTOBER 12ᵗʰ
1915

PHOTO BY
BASSANO, LTD.

MEMORIAL TO NURSE CAVELL.
PATRIOT AND MARTYR.

112   *Memorial to Nurse Cavell in London.*

It is hard to say if the Germans had the legal right to shoot a citizen of an enemy country in an occupied city. The English politician Duff Cooper thought so. In 1934 he said, 'If ever a woman was justly executed according to the rules of warfare Nurse Cavell was. She used her position as a nurse to get soldiers back to England. The German soldiers were perfectly entitled to do what they did.' However, the shooting was definitely a terrible mistake from the propaganda point of view. The novelist Rider Haggard noted in his *War Diaries* as early as 23 October 1915 that her name and portrait were already being used by speakers urging men to enlist and fight the Germans. Two days later he quoted an unnamed American newspaper as saying that 'Emperor William would have done better to lose an entire army corps than to butcher Miss Cavell'. In both Britain and France postcards were issued with slogans such as 'REMEMBER EDITH CAVELL'.

Publicity in England included a postcard of an officer at Trafalgar Square holding up a wreath:

Who will avenge the death of this noble Englishman? The above wreath, to the memory of EDITH CAVELL, was placed at the Nelson Column, Trafalgar Square, London, October 21st 1915, and afterwards deposited at St Mary Magdalen Church, Swardeston, Norfolk, on the day of the great Memorial Service, St Paul's Cathedral. It was at Swardeston that EDITH CAVELL first saw the light, to quote her own words, 'where she found life fresh and beautiful, and the country so desirable and sweet'. British people will henceforth pay love and homage to the name of CAVELL, reverence, appreciation and respect to a great and useful life, and register her for all time within the annals of our race a great and noble soul. The proceeds of the sale of these cards will be devoted to placing a stained glass window to Edith Cavell's memory in Swardeston church.

Almost at once, funds were started to create memorials to Edith, at parish, county and national level. The parish church of Swardeston led the way, raising money for a stained glass window. Contributions flooded in. A lady from Cheshire sent five shillings writing, 'if her death is a stimulus to recruiting, I cannot help feeling that she will be glad to have made the sacrifice'. A Mr Knight wrote of 'that noble woman

113   *Edith Cavell's grave in the Cathedral Close, Norwich.*

who made the supreme sacrifice to aid our country and its allies in the most righteous cause any nation could espouse'.

Margaret Gurney, of Keswick Hall, wrote on 16 November that she had spoken to Edith's mother: 'I found that she so much liked the idea of seating the church'; Mrs Gurney's husband offered a contribution of £20. Green must have queried this as she wrote two days later explaining that 'Mrs Cavell's preference was for a window, but she made no great point of it'. However, Mr Gurney would only give 10 guineas towards a window. In spite of this setback, a window was decided upon. The designer, Herbert Bryans of London, put forward six options, ranging from £250 down to £50. The most ambitious were designs to fill the large east and west windows of the church, the cheapest was for a 'single light south window, in which I have suggested the Figure on the Cross with a kneeling figure of Nurse Cavell & an angel at the foot of the Cross. Below is a picture showing the Good Samaritan'. The end result was very satisfactory. The most expensive option was chosen and the new glass filled the east window. The window was formally dedicated on 1 July 1917. Bryans wrote to Green on 3 July 1917: 'I hope you will go on finding something fresh in the glass. There is a sort of riddle set for you and your good parishioners in the tracery and I shall be glad to hear if anyone has found out the conundrum … I am pleased to hear that Mrs Cavell [Edith's mother] likes the window'.

The county wanted a memorial too, and there was a debate as to what form this should take. Richard Jewson supported a proposal that an appropriate memorial to Edith Cavell would be a national home for 'sick, old or convalescent nurses'. He thought there should also be a local memorial and suggested taking over the District Nurses' Home and calling it 'Cavell House'. This idea would enable the District Nursing Association – of which Jewson happened to be chairman! – 'to secure the services of an additional nurse, and thus directly benefit the suffering poor of our city, and the perpetuation in the best possible way of the memory of the martyred nurse'. He added: 'as to the construction of a statue, your correspondent, Mr W.T.F. Jarrold, probably realises by this time that his suggestion does not meet favour'.

In the event, both ideas were realised. On 12 October 1918, three years to the day after Edith's execution, Queen Alexandra visited Norwich and unveiled the Cavell memorial on Tombland. The statue shows Edith in her nurse's uniform and with a soldier hanging up a laurel wreath: it is by J.G. Gordon Munn. Originally it stood on the central roundabout, but it has since been moved to stand near the Erpingham Gate. On the same day, the Queen opened the adjacent Cavell Memorial Nurses' Home.

Edith's body was originally buried on the rifle range in Brussels where she was shot, but in 1919 she was reburied just outside Norwich Cathedral, her parents preferring this to a burial in Westminster Abbey. Norwich Cathedral archives show that her family also suggested that her tomb should be of the design adopted by the Government for fallen soldiers. This was not in fact done; Edith Cavell's grave, with its simple cross, can still be seen in the Cathedral Close. There is also a memorial statue to her in London, a short distance from Trafalgar Square.

Edith's death produced a range of reactions. Kate White had caught Edith's message well when she wrote from Folkestone in 1915: 'what sorrow this war is causing but I pray that we shall learn some of the lessons that it is meant to teach us.' The Prime Minister, Herbert Asquith, saw Edith as an example to men as well as women: 'she has taught the bravest man amongst us a supreme lesson of courage; and in the United Kingdom and throughout the Dominions of the Crown there are thousands of such women, but a year ago we did not know it.' On the Clyde a munitions factory was named the Edith Cavell Projectile Factory in her honour. What would Edith have made of that?[4]

Eight

The End

The war ended on 11 November 1918, but this was not the end of the wartime experience. The demobilisation of the soldiers took a long time and a lot of red tape. The 2nd Norfolks were welcomed back to Norwich on their return from Mesopotamia in April 1919; but the 12th Norfolks only arrived in the city for demobilisation on 31 May 1919, seven months after the end of the war.

The Artis family papers include six documents showing the process of demobilisation:

1. Artis was still in the Army in May 1919 when his father wrote to the War Office asking for his release. The reply, dated 21 May 1919 reads:

> In reply to your letter dated *25th March* applying for the release of No *1620 Pte R E Artis NCC* I am directed to inform you that all the circumstances have been carefully considered, and it has been decided that the case is not one of such extreme urgency that immediate release on compassionate grounds can be granted.
>
> I am to add that if the services of this soldier are not required for duty with the Armies of Occupation his demobilisation will be carried out under the procedures detailed in the Daily Press of the 30th January 1919, as soon as military exigencies permit.

2. The Nominal Roll (all Ranks) form dated 18 November 1919 started the actual process: Artis and three other men also of No 1, Aldershot Company, Non-Combatant Corps, were ordered to proceed from Aldershot to the Special Dispersal Unit, Hilsea Hutments, Cosham.

3. On 19 November Artis was issued with the key document in the discharge process, his Protection Certificate and Certificate of Identity (Soldier not remaining with the colours). The form bears the stamps for each payment made at the Post Office. Artis received his weekly money at South Gorleston Post Office on 27 November and on 4 and 10 December 1919: he had finally come home just over a year after the end of the war.

4. The cover and stubs of the Furlough Pay and Allowances on Demobilisation book.

5. Certificate on Demobilisation. There are four categories, three of which are struck out on each certificate. The categories are: Discharge; Transfer to Reserve; Disembodiment; Demobilisation. In this case all are struck out except Transfer to Reserve. The document gives more information on the man's army career. Artis was called up on 27 May 1916, he received no Medals or Decorations, and did not serve

☞ IF FOUND, please drop this Certificate in a Post Office letter box.   Army Form Z 11

NOTICE—"This document is Government property. It is no security whatever for debt, and any Person being in possession of it, either as a pledge or security for debt, or without lawful authority or excuse, is liable under Section 156 (9) of the Army Act to a fine of twenty pounds (£20) or imprisonment for six months, or to both fine and imprisonment."

PROTECTION CERTIFICATE AND CERTIFICATE OF IDENTITY
(SOLDIER NOT REMAINING WITH THE COLOURS)

Dispersal Unit Stamp and date of dispersal.

SPECIAL DISPERSAL UNIT — 19 Nov. 1919 — HILSEA

Surname.......... ARTIS
(Block Letters)

Christian Names ...... Robert Edmund

Regtl. No. ... 1620 ...... Rank....... Pte ....   Record Office.......... Warwick

Unit.... 1/ Warwicks .... Regt. or ... R.W.R. ....   Pay Office....... Warwick
                              Corps

I have received an advance of £2.   † Address for Pay...... St Benedicts Lane
                                                                Dereham ....

(Signature of Soldier) ...... R E Artis

The above-named soldier is granted 28 days' furlough   Theatre of War or
from the date stamped hereon pending*........3......(as far   Command
                                                          Born in the Year.....
as can be ascertained) which will date from the last day
of furlough after which date uniform will not be worn   Medical Category....
except upon occasions authorized by Army Orders.   Place of rejoining in ⎫ ... Watford
                                                          case of emergency   ⎭
   * If for Final Demobilization insert 1.   Specialist Military ⎫
       Disembodiment insert 2.   Qualification   ⎭ ... Nil
       Transfer to Reserve insert 3.

† As this is the address to which pay and discharge documents will be sent unless further notification is received, any change of address must be reported at once to the Record Office and the Pay Office as noted above, otherwise delay in settlement will occur.

R.J. Meade

This Certificate must be produced when applying for an Unemployed Sailor's and Soldier's Donation Policy or, if demanded, whenever applying for Unemployment benefit.

DISPERSAL — SPECIAL — 19 Nov. 1919 — HILSEA

Date.......... Office of Issue.......... Policy issued No. 36   A   041239

This Certificate must be produced when cashing Postal Drafts and Army Money Orders for weekly pay whilst on furlough.

The Postmaster will stamp a ring for each payment made. | P.O. Stamp to be impressed here
                                                          | when Savings Bank Book is issued.

(1)

114   *Protection Certificate and Certificate of Identity.*

Overseas on Active Service. The document concludes: he is Transferred to Army Reserve on 16 December 1919 in consequence of Demobilisation.

6. Certificate of Employment During the War:

(To be completed for, and handed to, each soldier)

A soldier is advised to send a copy rather than the original when corresponding with a prospective employer.

It is particularly important that an apprentice whose apprenticeship has been interrupted by Military Service should have recorded on this form any employment in a trade similar to his own on which he has been engaged during such Military Service.

Regtl No *1620* Rank *Private*

Surname *Artis*

Christian Names in full *Robert Edmund*

Regt *Non-Combatant Corps Unit No 1 Company, Aldershot NCC*

1. Regimental Employment
   Nature of Period
   Groundsman From July 1917 to Nov 1919

2. Trade or calling before Enlistment
   Fish Curer Group 7 Code 383

3. Courses of Instruction and Courses in Active Service Army Schools, and certificates if any
None

4. Military qualifications
None

5. Special Remarks as to qualifications, work done or skill acquired during service with the Colours. This is required as a help in finding civil employment.
None

NOTES – The object of this certificate is to assist the soldier in obtaining employment on his return to civil life. The form will be completed as soon as possible in accordance with Demobilisation Regulations.

As soon as signed and completed it will be given to the soldier concerned and will remain his property. He should receive it as early as is compatible with making the necessary references in order that he can either send it home or keep it in his possession.

One form will be issued to each man, and no duplicate can ever be issued.[1]

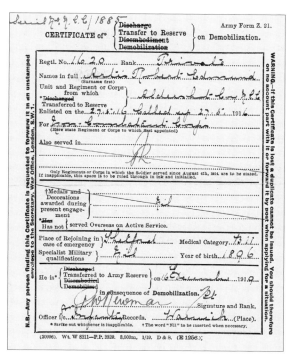

115   *Certificate on Demobilisation.*

116 *'Gassed in the above attack', drawn by a patient at Sheringham Hospital.*

The Earlham Road Cemetery in Norwich contains the grave of Second Lieutenant Ernest Bean, the son of Ada Bean of Wodehouse Street, Norwich. He died on 11 November 1918, the very day that the Armistice was declared: he was 24 years old and had served throughout the war, only to die on its last day. The inscription on his gravestone reads: 'After four years service in the Great War his end was peace.'

In fact, although the war had ended on 11 November, it continued to claim victims for months and even years to come. Philip Wodehouse, son of the 2nd Earl of Kimberley, had suffered paralysis after falling from the Town Wall in Boulogne on 25 June 1918, less than a month after his brother Edward had been killed in action. Philip was brought back to England and lingered until 6 May 1919: he is buried in Kimberley church.

A memorial in the Rosary cemetery captures a new horror of this war. It is to Walter Stock who died on 21 June 1919, eight months after the end of the war; it records that he had been 'wounded and gassed in France'. Gas had been first used by the Germans on 22 April 1915. When it was followed just a fortnight later by the sinking of the *Lusitania*, it was easy for the Allied propaganda machine to portray the Germans as barbarians. Of course the Allies soon began to use gas as a weapon themselves. The most famous victim of an Allied gas attack was Adolf Hitler, gassed near Ypres in October 1918. Like Stock, Hitler was in hospital at the time of Armistice. Unlike Stock he was to recover, with fatal consequences for the next generation in Norfolk and the whole world.

Many men continued to suffer in body and mind. In May 1919 Mr Charlesworth of Gunton Hall wrote to Colonel Gilbert about his son:

> I think if you had seen Joe when he first got home that you would have thought him looking very ill: we believe he is improving & the rest he is now having is doing him good, but he is certainly not yet what he was before his very trying experiences in Mesopotamia. And for a boy of 19 to be working hard in Bombay & then in what I believe is one of the hottest places in the world – Basra – in the hottest time of the year was enough to knock all the vitality out of him.[2]

Mrs Sinclair described her son's state in a letter written on 5 January 1920:

> He is still in hospital at the Countess of Dudley's Orthopaedic hospital at Brighton, and I am thankful to say is far before the Prince of Wales' or Epsom. The treatment was very indifferent at the latter place, in fact was time wasted.

They have come to the conclusion that the stiffened joints are due to the septic poisoning he contracted in the September and they tell him the only surprising part is that he lived through it, and not that he was left as he is. They have marked the wound in his side as equivalent to the loss of a limb but, they tell him, they don't think he will ever properly regain the use of his arms. The right elbow moves fairly free but the wrist and left elbow will only come half way; and when he had a fall at Epsom and hurt the right elbow he had to be fed again. The shoulders apparently will not move at all, although he is having thoroughly good massage and electrical treatment.[3]

So many men had suffered disabilities that newspaper articles giving medical information and advice for former soldiers were published in the local press in July and August 1921. This included:

ARTIFICIAL LIMBS

Every man who has lost a limb in the War is entitled to an artificial limb from the State, and when such has been supplied is provided with a duplicate for use when the original needs repairs or adjustments. The duplicate may, if a pensioner desires, instead of a mechanical leg, be an articulated (jointed) peg leg, which is more suitable for some vocations, such as a miner, fisherman or agricultural labourer.

A man who needs repair, adjustment, or renewal of his artificial limb or accessories, or further surgical amputated stump should report to the War Pensions Committee nearest to his home (address obtained from any Post Office).

Full provision is made by the Ministry of Pensions for the supply and maintenance of artificial limbs and any treatment of the amputated stump, and no man need suffer any inconvenience or discomfort by reason of ill-fitting artificial limbs. Complaints addressed to War Pensions Committees will receive immediate attention.

ACCESSORIES

With the first issue of an artificial leg six stump socks are supplied, and a walking stick with a rubber shoe. With first issue of an artificial arm four arm mitts are supplied, together with a hook or split hook, a brush, a Nelson knife and a pair of cotton gloves.

SPECIAL APPLIANCES – CRUTCHES

When a disabled man has been fitted with a suitable limb etc, he is usually independent of crutches; should, however, a pair be required the supply can be arranged by the War Pensions Committee. When a man's disablement is of such a nature that it cannot be rectified by an artificial limb, and he is totally dependent on his crutches, a more elaborate crutch is necessary so as to avoid crutch paralysis ...The most suitable crutch for such cases is the forearm stick crutch, supplied through War Pensions Committees.

ARTIFICIAL EYES

A pensioner requiring an artificial eye on account of his disability should apply to the War Pensions Committee, and for any renewals required. A pensioner may ordinarily be supplied with two artificial eyes per annum.

INVALID AND BATH CHAIRS, SPINAL CARRIAGES, AND TRICYCLES

Mechanical chairs and hand propelled tricycles are provided in the following cases: Paraplegia case (paralysis of the legs), a light chair for indoor use; amputation of both legs, hand propelled tricycles for outdoor use. Applications for Bath chairs and spinal carriages are considered on their merits. The man is expected to keep his chair, carriage or tricycle cleaned and oiled, and in good running order, such repairs as are necessary by fair wear and tear, or by circumstances beyond the man's control, may be carried out free of cost to the man.[4]

So many ex-soldiers suffered severe face and head injuries that new medical techniques had to be developed: 'the enormous number of casualties from the Great War led to many developments in the treatment of injuries, including the teeth, jaws and face'. A pioneer in this field was John Kohler Steel, who worked as a dentist in Norwich from 1923: he had served in the navy during the war, losing the hearing in one ear through gunfire in a destroyer.[5]

The pensions offered to disabled men were thought by many people to be a disgrace. A quarter of veterans suffered some kind of disability. The amount of pension given varied from 20 per cent to 100 per cent, according to the nature of the disability. Those who qualified for the full pension had to have suffered:

> Loss of two or more limbs, loss of an arm and an eye, loss of both hands or all fingers and thumbs, loss of both feet, loss of a hand and a foot, total loss of sight, total paralysis, lunacy, wounds or disease resulting in a man being permanently bedridden, wounds to internal organs or head involving total permanent disability, very severe facial disfigurement.

Douglas Haig himself led the discontent at the disability pension rate. In 1921 the full pension was raised to £2 a week, and £1 6s. 8d. for a widow. The extent of long-term suffering caused by the war is shown in the fact that 1,187,450 received a disability pension: no fewer than 36,400 men were so badly wounded that they qualified for the full disability pension. These were men whose war would last all their lives.

Haig lent his support to Warriors' Day, organised by the entertainment world as a tribute to ex-service men: He wrote in the programme:

> All will remember those hours when I was forced to write:
>
> With our backs to the wall, and believing in the justice of our cause, each one of us must fight to the end. The safety of our homes and the freedom of mankind depend alike upon the conduct of each one of us at this critical moment.
>
> Think what might have happened then. In those days you would not have grudged anything to the men who stood between you and disaster. And you will not withhold your help now?
>
> Many of those for whom I appeal stood with their backs to the wall on that day. They are still with their backs to the wall fighting, against terrible odds, the battle of life.
>
> At the call of their country these men flung aside every personal consideration. Their prospects were sacrificed, their careers abandoned, their homes broken up.
>
> I have heard it said the Nation has already forgotten those who fought to protect it from the horrors of defeat and the slavery that must have followed. I do not believe it.
>
> I believe that the facts have only to be published to all, to secure immediate sympathy and help.
>
> You owe a big debt to these men and their dependants, and this your opportunity to pay it.

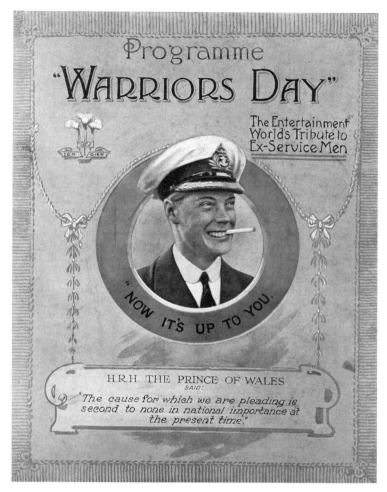

117 *'Warriors' Day' Programme.*

I ask you, not to sympathise with their misfortune and forget your duty, but to act and help them as they acted to help you in those dark and terrible days of the Great War.[6]

Even before the war ended an organisation – the Comrades of the Great War – was set up to look after the interests of ex-servicemen. The Norfolk branch was founded in 1918. Its chairman was William Boyle, MP for Mid-Norfolk. He threw all his energy into the cause, but the strain on his own health proved too much: he died on 2 October 1918. Major Ayton of the Wymondham branch of the Comrades, wrote to Boyle's widow:

These local Heroes (many wounded and broken by recent service) earnestly desired me to convey to you their grief in this sad hour, and to say how much they deplored the loss of one who had absolutely given the latter days of his life so successfully to their cause.[7]

118   *William Boyle, MP, chairman of the Norfolk branch of the Comrades of the Great War.*

The war led to much rethinking of people's status and rights. Many glaring inequalities had been brought to light, and several Acts of Parliament were passed to try to improve the state of Britain after the war. Four of the most important of these included:

1. Representation of the People Act, 1918 – extended the franchise from eight million to 21 million. Women over 30 who were ratepayers, or were married to ratepayers, were given the vote for the first time in British history. Residence qualifications for men were reduced from a year to six months, and men aged 19 and 20 on active service were allowed to vote. However conscientious objectors were disenfranchised unless they could prove they had been doing work of national importance.

2. Housing Act, 1919 – designed to enable the building of 'homes for heroes' by local councils. The plan was to build half a million homes in three years. Norwich led the way in this – the Mile Cross estate was the first major council house estate outside London. Smaller communities took part too, including the

119   *'Homes for Heroes' – Norwich led the way in its council housing programme after the war. These houses, with their large gardens for vegetable growing, are on the Mile Cross estate.*

120   *Peace Celebrations at Sporle.*

Newtown estate at Thetford, and the groups of houses at Garboldisham and East Harling built out of clay-lump, a local material which was little used by this date.[8]

3. Education Act, 1918 – raised the school leaving age from 12 to 14. It also proposed continuation classes of eight hours a week for those leaving school early, but this was never implemented. At first it was intended to introduce compulsory military drill into the school timetable but people were tired of war; it was replaced with an emphasis on physical games and exercises to improve children's health.

4. Unemployment Insurance Act, 1920 – under this Act the number of workers entitled to Unemployment Benefit rose from 2¼ million before the war to 12 million after it.

It is, of course, a matter of debate how many of these reforms would have been introduced even if there had been no war.

The role of women undoubtedly changed in the war. Many women themselves felt their lives had changed. We saw in chapter two how Ruth Hewetson felt that her work in the VAD had altered her attitudes. Her father, Canon Hewetson, replied:

121   *Ingham and the war: wounded soldiers at Ingham Old Hall Red Cross Hospital.*

I am glad I think to know that you are feeling just now the call of life. Life out in the open where you are able both to receive & to give & to become a leader in the living world that is to be. It needs just now girls that are fitted by nature & by Providence to be leaders in this new world, where quite apart from politics, but including them, women will be able to give the purest, simplest influence and give the wise influence in building up the new natural life.[9]

How many British people were killed in the First World War? This simple-sounding question has no simple answer as it depends on how exactly you define your terms. The usual figure given is about 725,000. These people were all men, and almost all young men.

John Winter reckons that out of just over six million who served, 722,785 died or were killed, making just under 12 per cent, or about one in eight of those who served. He summarises the figures:

Force	Number serving	Number killed	Percentage
Army	5,215,162	673,375	12.91
Navy	640,237	43,244	6.75
RFC/RAF	291,175	6,166	2.12

The death rate in the flying force may seem surprisingly low, but this is because the

122 *Ingham and the war: the village war memorial, soon after its erection.*

great majority in the force did not actually fly; the death rate among airmen themselves was very much higher.[10]

The total killed was 118 per thousand mobilised, 63 per thousand males aged between 15 and 49, and 16 per thousand of the entire population. Well over half a million men aged between 18 and 30 were killed between 1914 and 1918, and this had a dramatic effect on the population left behind – widows with orphans to raise alone, young single women with less likelihood of finding husbands. Of course these statistics, like all figures, can be counter-balanced with others. In the fifty years before the First World War, Britain was a country from which many more people left than arrived. Over six million Britons emigrated between 1871 and 1911. These people were also overwhelmingly young males, so that it could be argued that the loss of young men in the war was no greater then the loss of young men who were emigrating in the pre-war period.

However, for the individuals concerned, no amount of number-crunching can compensate for the loss of a generation of fathers, husbands and sons. Almost 200,000 women in Britain became widows as a result of the war, and over 350,000 children lost their fathers.

Nine

We Shall Remember Them

Henry Rider Haggard's introduction to the *Norfolk Roll of Honour* (published in 1920) points out that the roll contains almost 12,000 names. He claims that the death rate for Norfolk was probably the highest for any county. Certainly it was above the average. In the UK as a whole, one person out of every 57 was killed in the war. For Norfolk the figure is one person out of every 42. Haggard reminds us of the further cost: 'to this total must be added all the crippled; all the sick and, what is sometimes worse, all the wounded in mind.' The *Norwich Roll of Honour*, published in 1824, lists 3,544 'citizens of Norwich who fell in the Great War'. (These men are included in the Norfolk Roll of Honour, but the Norwich volume is more useful for researchers as it includes the regiment or service arm in which the man served, which the Norfolk volume does not.)[1]

123 *The anonymity of death: an unknown British Officer's grave, 1916.*

The topic of war memorials is a fascinating and rewarding one. I have taken groups of children to look at their local memorial and this is often a good way to start a teaching session on the First World War. The surnames may well include those of children known to them, or even their own family name. The number of the dead can be related to the population of the village, as given in the 1911 census, to give a sense of how great the local sacrifice was.

In a small community it may be possible to recreate the social and economic structure of the village through the 1901 census, when those who fought in the war will appear as young children. Their father's occupation, social status, family size etc can be calculated. (Detailed census returns are closed for 100 years, so it will only be possible to do this work with the 1911 census in 2012.)

One of the first things to think about is the location of the memorial. It may be in the parish church, or in its churchyard, or in a secular location – the village green, perhaps, or the market place. The second, related, consideration is its shape. Does it have a specifically Christian theme – a cross, or an image of Christ – or is it entirely secular? It will be recalled that the national Cenotaph in Whitehall is deliberately without Christian connotations. Sir Edwin Lutyens, its designer, was clear that he wanted the memorial to be for people of all faiths and of none. It could be argued that all inhabitants of a Norfolk village in the early 20th century would think of themselves as Christians: however by no means all would attend the Anglican parish church, several families thinking of themselves as 'chapel' rather than 'church'. In the towns there might be a Jewish community, and also a number of people who thought of themselves as agnostics or humanists rather than Christians. A related question is that of the inscription. Is there a general text? Is it from the Bible or is it a secular text?

Then there are the names themselves. In what order are they arranged? The arrangement has a lot to say about society in early 20th-century England. They are normally arranged in one of three ways: by military rank, by date of death, or in alphabetical order. These may be combined; for example those of a particular rank may be listed alphabetically.

Also of interest is how much further information, if any, is given about individuals on the memorial. This can include: medals won; the regiment or force in which the man served; date of death; place of death; cause of death. The place of death will most commonly be somewhere on the Western Front, but could be Salonika or the Middle East or, in the case of naval men, almost anywhere in the world. The places in which young men of the village or town died can be drawn on a map to show how the war was indeed a world-wide struggle.

One other question to ask is whether the names of any women appear on the memorial. As we have seen, no women fought in the Army, but women *were* killed in

124 *(left) Standard form of Commonwealth War Commission grave in a battlefield cemetery in France. This is the grave of Private Green of the Norfolk Regiment. (author's photo)*

125 *(right) Commonwealth War Commission grave, Earlham Road Cemetery, Norwich. This soldier died on the last day of the war, 11 November 1918. (author's photo)*

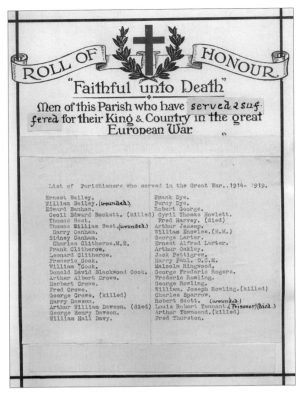

ROLL OF HONOUR

"Faithful unto Death"

Men of this Parish who have served & suffered for their King & Country in the great European War

List of Parishioners who served in the Great War..1914- 1919.

Ernest Bailey.
William Bailey.(wounded.)
Edward Banham.
Cecil Edward Beckett. (killed)
Thomas Best.
Thomas William Best.(wounded.)
Harry Canham.
Sidney Canham.
Charles Clitheroe.M.M.
Frank Clitheroe.
Leonard Clitheroe.
Frederic Cook.
William Cook.
Donald David Blackwood Cook.
Arthur Albert Crowe.
Herbert Crowe.
Fred Crowe.
George Crowe. (killed)
Harry Dawson.
Arthur William Dawson. (died)
George Henry Dawson.
William Hall Davy.

Frank Dye.
Percy Dye.
Robert George.
Cyril Thomas Howlett.
Fred Harvey. (died)
Arthur Jessop.
William Knowles.(M.M.)
George Larter.
Ernest Alfred Larter.
Arthur Oakley.
Jack Pettigrew.
Malcolm Ringwood.
George Frederic Rogers.
Frederic Rowling.
George Rowling.
William. Joseph Rowling.(killed)
Charles Sparrow.
Robert Scott. (wounded.)
Louis Robert Tennant.(Prisoner)(died.)
Arthur Townsend.(killed)
Fred Thurston.

126 *Roll of Honour, East Carleton. Originally designed to list only the dead, it has been amended to include all the villagers who served in the war.*

war-related deaths: nurses might be bombed or shelled, munitions workers or farm labourers might die in accidents at work, civilians might die in air raids. Probably, none of these people will appear on a village war memorial. The name of Edith Cavell *is* the first on the Swardeston memorial, and the memorial at Cromer includes an image of a Red Cross Nurse along with a soldier, a sailor and an airman. Red Cross nurses are also shown on a window in Swaffham church, as mentioned in chapter two. These are rare examples of the sacrifice made by women receiving official local recognition.

A monument is not the only possible form a memorial might take. Money raised might be put to a practical use, such as part or all of a Hospital (as at North Walsham) or the Norfolk Regiment War Memorial Cottages on the Norwich Ring Road. Some such memorials were put up by and for individuals rather than the community as a whole. A good example is the extension to Heacham almshouses built to commemorate two brothers, Arthur and Alfred Neville Rolfe, both killed in action. The family spent £120 on the work, and the boys' mother, Ada Neville Rolfe, made the memorial plaques in the gable ends.[2]

In addition to any memorial, there may be individual plaques to those killed in action overseas, or, occasionally, actual graves. During the war it was decided not to bring back the bodies of the dead but to bury them close to where they fell, on or near the battlefields, dressing stations or hospitals where they died. To preserve equality in death, the graves were given a standard form of headstone, the text of which was thought up by Rudyard Kipling, who himself lost his son on the Western Front. For reasons stated above this is not a cross but a plain stone. It is not uncommon to find this standard headstone in English cemeteries and churchyards. These may be of servicemen who died in training accidents, or of wounded men who have come home to die.

A few churches have Rolls of Honour that list not only those who died in the war but also all those who served. These are obviously of great value in assessing the impact of the war on the community: it is a great shame there are not more of these.

To illustrate in detail exactly how the process of creating a local memorial worked, I am taking five local examples: a plaque to an individual at Burston, a memorial

MR. AND MRS.
GARNHAM
AND THEIR
SOLDIER SON.

127   *Mr and Mrs Garnham and their soldier son.*

plaque at Billingford near Diss, a street memorial at Wighton, a churchyard memorial at Cromer, and the town memorial at Great Yarmouth.

Burston

A memorial tablet in Burston Church reads: 'In Memory of Herbert Garnham, Sgt 9th Norfolks, Killed in Action in France, Sept 15th 1916, aged 25 years. 'Thy Will Be Done.' Erected by his uncle R.B. Ford.' This is a common enough memorial, slightly unusual in being put up by an uncle rather than by parents. One might think that the parents had predeceased their son but that would be wrong in this case. Herbert's father was very much alive, and totally opposed to the setting up of the memorial plaque.

The dispute originated in the Burston School strike, described in chapter five. As a keen supporter of the Higdons, Henry Garnham objected strongly to his son being honoured in the church of the great enemy of the school, the Rev. Eland. It was this strong feeling that led him into violent action.

In July 1917 he was brought before the Diss magistrates charged with damaging a tablet put up in Burston church to his own son. Daisy Garnham, Herbert's sister, was charged with assisting, and Thomas Higdon and Charles Garnham were charged with assault in connection with the affair.

Henry had tried to get the tablet removed in the correct legal manner, by application to the Norwich Consistory Court. The Chancellor of the court decided that the tablet could remain he was then (he claimed) assaulted verbally by the Garnhams and Higdon. Garnham and Daisy finally took matters into their own hands. They went into the church and Garnham 'with a large hammer struck the tablet a

128 *Tablet to Herbert Garnham, erected by his uncle not his parents.*

number of hard blows and cracked it as well as indented it in several places. It was impossible to repair it'.

In his defence Garnham said that 'he thought that the tablet was erected out of spiteful feeling' and added 'I'll suffer death as my son has done before allowing the tablet to remain'. He was sentenced to one month in prison. Higdon offered to pay £20 to keep Garnham out of gaol: this was refused.

The Norfolk Roll of Honour has eight names for Burston, including Herbert Garnham and also George Durbidge junior, the son of the man of the same name referred to several times in this book. Herbert Garnham's body was never found: his name is on the Thiepval Memorial to the missing.[3]

Billingford Near Diss

The story of Billingford's memorial is told in records maintained by the rector at the time, the Reverend James Dewing:

> At a meeting held at Billingford Rectory on Jan 22nd 1919, it was decided to put up a memorial tablet in the Church in memory of those from this parish, fallen in the war. It was suggested that, if the date of the death was omitted, the names on the tablet should be put in alphabetical order, by heading the tablet 'The Great European War, 1914-1918(?). Subscriptions to the amount of £26 were promised; & it was hoped to raise £50. Texts were thought of: 'Greater love hath no man than this that a man lay down his life for his friends'; 'Make them to be remembered with thy saints in glory everlasting'.
>
> At a second meeting, held at the Rectory May 27th 1919, letters from subscribers were read together with a list of subscriptions. It was decided to have a small committee of five, viz Mr Blofield, Mr Fox, Mrs Race, Mrs Nunn & myself. Designs were submitted, & it was thought advisable to obtain the best tablet possible, whether from a London firm or a local one. It was proposed that the names should be placed in order of date of death, should it not entail too much cost as regards lettering, otherwise in alphabetical order. It was arranged that a collection should be made in the Parish on behalf of the Fund. There were three suggestions as to texts: 'Be thou faithful unto death, & I will give thee a crown of life'; 'Honour to whom honour is due'; 'Greater love hath no man than this that a man lay down his life for his friends'.

At a Committee meeting held on August 1919, at the Rectory, it was unanimously agreed to erect a marble tablet on the north wall of the nave of the church, and the design submitted by Messrs Wippell & Co, Ltd, was approved and accepted. It was also recommended to put a new organ in the church in place of the organ now in use, with the surplus money.

Dewing wrote to Leonard Bolingbroke, 26 March 1920: 'I herewith enclose the design of organ which we propose to place in the Church as a part of our war Memorial. There will be a small brass fixed on the same, with suitable inscription: the inscription suggested is: "This Organ and Memorial Tablet are dedicated to the Glory of God and in Memory of the Heroes of this Parish who gave their lives in the Great War".'

The vicar took his role seriously, compiling notes about the eight men whose names were to appear on the memorial:

Arthur Nunn, RN officers' steward, first class. Killed in action off Lowestoft, on *HMS Conquest*, 25 April 1916, aged 22. Nunn was born in Billingford 25 April 1894, and enlisted on 15 July 1913. He was buried at sea.

John Lewis Whiting, private, 2nd Norfolks, died at Bombay on 9 May 1917, of wounds received in action in Mesopotamia, aged 22. Whiting was born in Whitechapel, London, 12 October 1895. He enlisted on 11 November 1914. He was wounded twice, on 21 and 23 February 1917 while in action in Mesopotamia. He is buried in Bombay.

Herbert Race, corporal in the 9th Norfolks. Killed in action in France on 1 April 1917, aged 23. Race was born at Billingford on 9 May 1894. He enlisted on 11 November 1914. He is buried at Philosophe near Vermelles.

129   *Gordon Flowerdew, V.C.*

Walter Race, bombardier in the Royal Field Artillery. Killed in action in France on 11 August 1917, aged 33. Race was born at Billingford on Christmas Day 1884. He was a professional soldier, having enlisted on 25 February 1903. He was killed during the Third Battle of Ypres, and is buried at Dickebusche.

Allan Fox, private in the 8th Norfolks and winner of the Military Medal, killed in action in France on 21 March 1918, aged 22. Fox was born at Billingford on 28 July 1895. He too enlisted in November 1914. He won the Military Medal for 'gallant conduct and devotion to duty in the field, near Poelcappelle' on 22 October 1917.

Gordon Muriel Flowerdew, born at Billingford 22 January 1885. He emigrated to Canada in search of work. When war broke out in August 1914 he immediately enlisted as a private in Strathcona's Horse. He won the Victoria Cross on 30 March 1918 at Bois de Morieul. The citation tells the story: 'For most conspicuous bravery and dash when in command of a squadron detailed for special service of a very important nature. On reaching the first objective, Lieut. Flowerdew saw two lines of the enemy, each about 60 strong, with machine guns in the centre and flanks, one line being about 200 yards behind the other. Realising the critical nature of the operation, and how much depended upon it, Lieut. Flowerdew ordered a troop under Lieut. Harvey, VC, to dismount and carry out a special movement, while he led the remaining three troops to the charge. The squadron (less one troop) passed over both lines, killing many of the enemy with the sword, and wheeling about galloped at them again. Although the squadron had thus lost about 70% of its numbers killed and wounded from rifle and machine gun fire directed on it from the front and both flanks, the enemy broke and retired. The survivors of the squadron then established themselves in a position where they were joined, after much hand-to-hand fighting, by Lieut. Harvey's party. Lieut. Flowerdew was dangerously wounded through both thighs during the operation, but continued to cheer on his men. There can be no doubt that this officer's great valour was the prime factor in the capture of the position'. Flowerdew died of his wounds on 31 March: he is buried at Namps au Val.

Charles William Thrower, lance-corporal in the Suffolk Yeomanry, killed in action in France on 18 September 1918, aged just 20. Thrower was born at Scole on 15 December 1898. He enlisted into the 15th Suffolk Regiment on 2 June 1915. He is buried in France.

George Frederick Punt, private in the Duke of Cornwall's Light Infantry, died at 15th Clearing Station on 6 October 1918 of wounds received while in action in France. Punt was born in Shelfanger on 13 January 1898. He enlisted on 22 February 1916. He is buried near Houchin in France.

Clearly, these notes raise questions. What exactly was meant by 'of Billingford?' Flowerdew, although born in Billingford, had emigrated several years earlier – would he have been included had it not been for the kudos of his Victoria Cross, and the fact that his relatives were generous contributors to the memorial, as the list of subscribers demonstrates? On the other hand, some of the names are of men not born in Billingford: what connection did Whiting and Thrower have with the village? Are they also commemorated on memorials erected at their places of birth?

SUBSCRIBERS

Mr and Mrs Blofield	10 guineas
Mrs Flowerdew	10 guineas
Miss Flowerdew	10 guineas
Myself and wife	7 pounds
Mr George Wilson	5 pounds
Mrs White	3 pounds
Mr Alan White	2 guineas
Miss Mary F White	1 pound
Miss White	10 shillings
Mr Race	1 pound, promised
Mrs Race	1 pound, promised
Mr Christopher Race	1 pound, promised
Mr Sidney Race	10 shillings
Mr and Mrs Nunn	1 pound, promised
Mr Fox	1 pound, promised
Mr J Batley	1 pound, promised
Mrs Stringer	1 pound, promised
Mrs Punt	1 pound, promised
Miss Annie Redgrove	1 pound
Miss Elsie Harvey	10 shillings
Mr Eric Crawford	1 pound
Dr Symonds	1 guinea
Mr Dawson	1 guinea

Several of these people were obviously related to the dead, and others were probably relations or friends. It is perhaps surprising how few people were needed to create a local memorial, something, which must have been a very personal act to each of them.[4]

Wighton

Robert Claxton, a local builder, chaired the Committee at Wighton. He may well have had a personal interest: the names on the memorial include that of William George Claxton, killed in France on 29 September 1915. It was decided to have a free-standing memorial and a design for it was prepared by London architects Kennard and Kennard.

Claxton put the work out to tender and received four estimates in May 1919:

From Edward Case, Lynn	£75
From J.R.E. Beaver, Burnham	£110
From F.J. Holman, Lynn	£100
John Daymond & Sons, London	£115

Not surprisingly Case was given the commission: by October he was ready to prepare the foundations. The committee was helped by a generous offer from Lord Leicester: 'I understand you wish to have permission to erect this memorial at the

commencement of Kirk Street, opposite the Malthouse Yard, and I shall be very pleased to give the site of it to the village.'

The final bill from Case was submitted, appropriately, on Armistice Day in 1919. It was for £80 5s. in total: £75 for the Portland Stone Memorial, £4 12s. 6d. for the letters for the names, and 12s. 6d. 'extra on drilling holes in base, shaft & cross & supplying brass dowels for same as ordered'. This was satisfactory to the Committee and the bill was promptly paid on 16 November.

In 1921, it was decided to put a wrought iron railing around the memorial. Bayliss, Jones and Bayliss of Wolverhampton were approached and estimated this would cost £40. Claxton could not accept this: 'I certainly expected your price to be about £30 which would have been accepted, as from the old price in the Catalogue … In the circumstances I am afraid I cannot do business with you, & must negotiate elsewhere, as this is only a Village Memorial & as you will

130   *Proposed War Memorial, Wighton.*

appreciate Funds are not in abundance.' The firm gave in, offering a rather simpler form of railing for £33 10s. Claxton accepted this but asked the firm to make the charge for timber packing to protect the rails in transit as low as possible; 'the balance of the Subscriptions is only sufficient to meet the cost of the railings & in the circumstances I have agreed to erect these railings free of cost'. In fact they did not charge for the timber at all, as the final account for the Memorial Fund shows:

Receits [*sic*]

Mr Emmerson's Collection	3	10	2
Mr Downing's Collection	10	17	9
Lord Leicester	20	0	0
Mr R Claxton	5	0	0
Captain Wright	5	5	0
The Vicar	5	0	0
The School Box	1	1	0
Mr Hudson	10	0	0
Mr Miles Blomfield	25	0	0
Mr Albert Blomfield	5	0	0
Mr H B Green	20	0	0
Three small donations per Vicar		12	6
Mr R Tuck	1	0	0
Mr F Wright	5	0	0
	117	6	5

Payments

1919, Nov 15, E J Case	80	5	0
1921, Dec 15, R Claxton	33	10	0
Balance in hand	3	11	5
	117	6	5

June 1st 1922, Walter Harcourt, Treasurer

Thus, a large free-standing memorial with railings had been set up for a little under £120.[5]

Cromer

Cromer had a population of 4,073 in 1911: it lost 70 men in the war. The Committee here decided upon a monument set within the churchyard. A design was chosen and an appeal for money made in July 1919:

Dear Sir or Madam, The raising of a Local Memorial in honour of the men who have given up their lives in the service of their country during the Great War has been practically universal. The form of Memorial has naturally varied, and in Cromer, after full discussion of various proposals, the Public Meeting decided in favour of

A CHURCHYARD CROSS

To be erected in the open space on the south side of the chancel of the Parish Church.
The Cross has been designed by Mr W D Caroe, MA, FSA, Westminster. The design is founded on the best traditional forms, an imposing stepped base from

which rises a lofty stem surmounted by a cross head containing 'The Great Sacrifice' in a canopied niche. The stem bears a figure of St George. The base will contain figures of a typical Sailor, Soldier, and Red Cross Nurse. The inscription and the names of those men who have fallen in the War will be inscribed on the two topmost risers of the base, so that the types of service may be handed on for all time, and the Cross, while keeping in perpetual remembrance the names of those whose self-sacrifice has rendered possible that Victory in which we all rejoice, will also remind us of others amongst us who served in the War, but whose lives have been mercifully preserved.

The estimated cost is between £600 and £700, and the Executive Committee confidently appeal to the whole Parish for its generous support.

They feel that everyone – as a tribute of affection to those who have fallen, as a mark of gratitude for those who have been spared, as a humble acknowledgement of the mercy of Providence by which our parish has escaped devastation from the sea and air, and in grateful recognition of the Victory which has crowned our arms – will consider it a privilege to contribute so far as their means allow towards the cost of the Memorial, and they earnestly desire that every household may be represented on the list of subscribers.

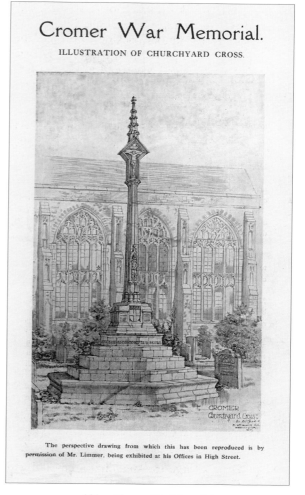

Cromer War Memorial.
ILLUSTRATION OF CHURCHYARD CROSS.

The perspective drawing from which this has been reproduced is by permission of Mr. Limmer, being exhibited at his Offices in High Street.

131 *Cromer War Memorial.*

It was not the cost that caused problems in this case but the design. 'The Great Sacrifice' referred to is an image of Christ on the Cross, and some townspeople felt this was not appropriate – it was the vicar who was to be its chief opponent. A series of meetings was held in the town, beginning even before the formal appeal was launched:

1919, Jan 13. The Cromer Urban District Council passed a resolution that a Public Meeting be called to consider the question of a War Memorial.

Jan 23. First Public Meeting held when various suggestions were made and referred to a Committee for consideration.

132   *'The War to end War'? Cromer memorial among the ruins caused by Second World War bombs.*

June 4. Second Public Meting convened by public notice, copies being also sent to all relatives of men who had fallen in the War, when a resolution was unanimously passed in favour of the erection of a Memorial Cross in the Churchyard and a design submitted by Mr W.D. Caroe of Westminster showing a Cross with Crucifix at the head of the shaft was approved with none dissentient.

June 27. The Executive Committee met the Architect to discuss details, when the Rev E.M. Davys stated that objections were entertained by himself and others to the Crucifix. The Architect informed the Committee that in another instance in which he was connected a robed figure of the saviour in the act of blessing had been substituted for the Crucifix, but the Committee were of opinion that as the Crucifix formed an integral part of the design approved by the Public Meeting it was not competent for them to alter it.

Sept 18. At a Vestry Meeting then held, the proposal and design were approved by 39 votes to 28.

Certified copy of the Minutes of the Vestry Meeting of Cromer held on 18 September 1919:

A special Meeting of the Vestry was held on Thursday, September 18th 1919 to consider the plan for a Memorial Cross to be erected in the Churchyard to the memory of those who had fallen in the War. As there was an attendance of about a hundred people (more or less) the Meeting was adjourned to the Parish Hall.

After the Vicar had opened the meeting with prayer, Mr J.K. Frost, Clerk to the Cromer Urban District Council, stated that the design submitted had been passed at a Public Meeting held on June 4th and had subsequently been approved at a meeting of the War Memorial Committee which had been called to meet the architect, Mr W.D. Caroe, and that the Committee with Mr Caroe had then proceeded to the Churchyard and selected a site near to the railings facing Bond Street.

Mr H. Rust then moved that 'The Plans ... which together with a description thereof have now been laid before this meeting, be approved, and that the Vicar and Churchwardens be requested to apply to the Consistory Court for a Faculty authorising the carrying out of this work'.

Mr H.C. Dent, MRCS, seconded the proposal.

The Vicar (the Rev E.M. Davys) stated that he approved of the design with the exception of the Crucifix near the head of the shaft. This he opposed most strenuously, as he had done at the Public Meeting and in Committee, not only on his own behalf but on that of many of those who had lost relatives, and of very many of the parishioners. He read several letters including two from parents definitely refusing their sons' names to be placed on a memorial which contained a Crucifix. He urged the Vestry to adopt as a War Memorial some other design which would give pain to none, and which all could heartily join in subscribing towards.

Mr F.H. Barclay suggested that a design of Christ standing in front of the Cross with Hands uplifted in Blessing (as suggested by the architect) to take the place of a Crucifix, be adopted. Mr Hansell also spoke in support of this suggestion, stating that although he considered that a Crucifix would be helpful rather than harmful, yet that the suggestion seemed to be a ray of hope for unanimity.

The Vicar then asked the mover of the resolution if he was prepared to alter it so that it should embody this suggestion, but Messrs Rust and Dent stated that they felt unable to do so. A considerable number of parishioners who were present but who were not payers of Poor Rate were then asked to stand apart while a division was taken, and the resolution was then put to payers of poor rate and carried by 39 to 28 votes.

1919 17th October. Third Public Meeting held, convened 'to consider a suggested alteration in the form of the Churchyard Cross'. The Meeting was a large and representative one. The alternative design, showing a robed figure in the act of blessing in place of the Crucifix, was submitted to the Meeting and the following proposition made and seconded:

'That in the hope of securing unanimity with regard to the Memorial to the Men of Cromer who have fallen in the war this Meeting adopts the alternative scheme.'

After full discussion the proposition was put to the Meeting when 30 (at the outside) voted for it and a very large number against it and the Chairman declared the Motion defeated by an overwhelming majority.

Davys was resigned to defeat. His final act was to register a protest with the Bishop's court on 30 October: 'I wish to formally oppose the granting of a faculty for the execution of the War Memorial churchyard according to the design submitted, E M Davys.' The memorial, with its Crucifix, still stands in Cromer churchyard. As we have seen, it is unusual in that it includes a figure of a Red Cross nurse on the base. This is on the north side, facing the church: unfortunately it is difficult to make out because of the decay of the stone over the years.[6]

133   *Proposed War Memorial for Great Yarmouth.*

Great Yarmouth

As a large town that had made a great sacrifice in the war, Yarmouth naturally had grander ideas for its war memorial than the smaller towns and villages of Norfolk. They commissioned Sir Edwin Lutyens himself to design a monument for them. However, the cost was a worry. By February 1920, £3,000 had been raised and a further £1,500 promised. The Committee approved the model prepared by Lutyens, but wrote to inform him that they did not think the total they would raise would be more than £5,000. By the following spring the fund had reached £3,763, with a further £858 promised, but this was not nearly enough. The Committee had obtained six estimates from builders for the Lutyens design: the lowest was £7,750 and the highest £10,267. They reluctantly decided to abandon the project, and instead asked local architect F.R.B. Haward to design a memorial for them – he agreed to do so and said that he would take no payment, other than out-of-pocket expenses.

At the same time, the Committee were drawing up the names to go on the Memorial. They are in strict alphabetical order of surname, with initials only of forenames, and with no indication of the arm in which they served. There is a draft list in the Norfolk Record Office giving more details of the 773 men who came from Yarmouth itself. (Unfortunately no such lists survive of the men from Southtown and Gorleston.) The list gives a powerful impression of the wide range of forces in which the men of Yarmouth served in the Great War.

Of the 773 names, 239 were in the Norfolk Regiment. Not surprisingly for such an important port, the navy was well represented: 130 were in the Royal Navy or the Royal Naval Reserve, and five in the Trinity Service, including four men killed on the Corton lightship disaster described in chapter four. Just five of the names are of men from the Royal Air Force or Royal Flying Corps. The other names come from

134 *Prince Henry unveils the Yarmouth Memorial as actually built.*

an incredibly wide field, including over 60 different regiments in the British Army, and from the Australian, Canadian, South African and New Zealand Forces. There are no women's names, and those civilians killed in Yarmouth by enemy action – such as Samuel Smith and Martha Taylor – are not included. Perhaps this was regretted later: the nearby Second World War memorial specifically states that it *does* include such people.[7]

'War tourism', or the desire to visit the sites where relatives had fought and died, had begun even before the war was over. Within 18 months, Cook's were involved in organising tours. Judith Ferrier of Hemsby was 17 in 1920 and staying in Paris:

19 May 1920 – We got up early, that is to say the party which was going to do 'Cooks Tour Arras-Lens, Vimy Ridge'. We went slowly through the Town [Arras] which is very ruined in parts. We then came out in to a long road without <u>a tree</u>

135   *The Norwich War Memorial on Guildhall Hill. Chamberlin's the clothing manufacturers can be seen behind. The memorial has since been moved to a 'memorial garden' in front of City Hall.*

136   *'The Cross of Sacrifice', designed by the architect Reginald Blomfield. It can be found in war cemeteries across the world: this example is in the Earlham Road cemetery in Norwich.*

to be seen either side of the road as far as one could see was dry looking grass. All shell holes. I think the elevation was high but, it was more or less flat, Nell & I agreed that it might have been the marshes in good old Norfolk … Well St Catherine's was pointed out to us, that is to say, a heep of bricks & dust, it is <u>absolutely</u> true to say thair [*sic*] was not <u>one</u> brick left on another. We went on till we got to Neuville St Vaast, where we stoped & went over a 'dugout' made by the Germans when they occupied Lens from 14 to 17. It was dug out of a chork [*sic*] cliff 17 feet below the ground & to hold 2000, two Thousand !!!!! I would never have believed such a thing we then looked at a 'Canadian Cemitry' of which I took a photo.

We then went on over 'Vimy Ridge' passing a Cross put up to the Canadian Artillery of which I have a photo given me. We arrived at Lens having passed lots of 'Pill Boxes' & also ruins … we left Lens about 3.30 & motered back to Vimy

137 *'From Vimy Ridge'. Photographs taken in 1920 by Yarmouth schoolgirl and 'war tourist' Judith Ferrier.*

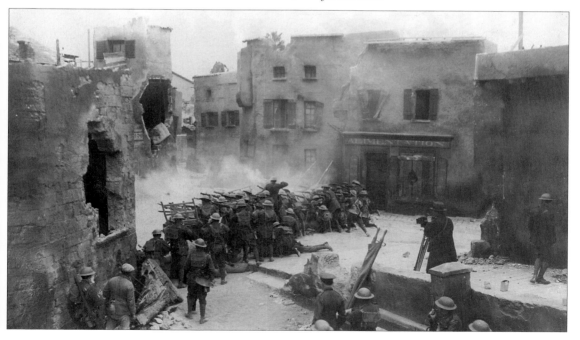

138 *The Last Stand 1918: a still from the film* The Roses of Picardy, *based on* The Spanish Farm *by Norwich writer R.H. Mottram.*

Ridge where we got out & walked up the very steep rise to the summit – it was very hard going as it was riddled with shell holes & barb wire with a good many very live shells about of which we had to take great care … After this it began to rain very hard & as the hill was chalk it became very slipery, the grass was very green here & long & the birds were singing, it seemed hard to believe that it had cost us so much to win. It was taken by the ANZACs on April 19 [19]17. At the top we examined two concret gun implacements made by the Germans….We started to decened & the rain stoped & the sun came out. We stoped half way down to look at a German 'Howitzer' of which I took a photo.

We looked for souveners. We wer not alowed to take any shells as so many actcydens [*sic*] had occored from shells still being alive. I found an old German all bashed in & very durty which I gave to Nell who wanted it very much, as I did not see how I was to get it home & contented myself with an emty rifil bulet which our guide agreed was quite safe as it had no top We arrived at Paris at 9.30 pm & got back to the house at 10.30, having had a day of from 7.30 am to 10.30 pm, which I enjoyed very much & thank Daddy & Mother very much for.[8]

As the years passed, many books were published describing people's experiences in the war. One of the best was a novel by a Norfolk man – *The Spanish Farm*, by Ralph Mottram. It was also made into a film, *The Roses of Picardy*. It is still one of the most vivid evocations of life during the war on the Western Front.

Ten

Epilogue

A month after the war ended, Corporal George Durbidge succumbed to his wounds at the Military Hospital in Etaples, France, dying on 15 December 1918: he was just 21 years old. His father survived the war and returned to Burston. However, war service and the loss of his son were too much for this volatile character: he became increasingly drunk and violent towards his surviving family. On 21 February 1920 he threatened his wife Harriet with a gun: she fled with her youngest daughter to another daughter's house in London, leaving George alone with his two surviving sons. On 20 March, George's son Hector turned up at Diss Police Station without coat or boots: he said simply 'I have killed my father'. He was detained and the police went to the cottage in Burston where they found George dead in his chair. A discharged service rifle was found in the garden. Hector's brother, Frank, said that he had a heard a quarrel and a shot. On being charged, Hector said 'I don't care as long as I have saved my mother'.

The name of George Durbidge, like that of Colonel Robson mentioned at the beginning of this book, appears on no war memorial. Both could, however, be considered as indirect victims of a war whose effect on Norfolk was so profound that, almost a century later, it has not yet been fully understood.

'Welcome Home' Dinner

On 29 October 1919 the Norwich Church of England Young Men's Society held a 'Welcome Home' Dinner at the Criterion Café. The programme for the dinner included the names of all their members who had served, including those who did not come back. This must serve as a 'sample' roll of honour, celebrating the sacrifice made by men of Norfolk in the First World War. (Italics indicate that, so far as is known, the member was killed or has died.)[9]

TO OUR SERVICE MEMBERS

MENU

SOUP

THICK OX TAIL

FISH

BOILED COD AND PARSLEY SAUCE

FILLETS OF PLAICE

JOINTS

ROAST BEEF ROAST MUTTON

BOILED SALT BEEF

VEGETABLES IN SEASON

SWEETS

CABINET PUDDING FRUIT AND CUSTARD

CHEESE   CELERY

Abel W A
Abel H
Abbott R
Alexander J W
Arnold A L
Ashurst C L
Auston E
Ayers F W

Bacon A E W
Bacon H F
Back H A W
Bagshaw E
Barney H
Bailey L
Balls O K
Barton W F
Basher W
Balhatchet F J
Beaver R
Bennett H R
Bell N A W
Bell C W
Betts E
Bishop H R
Block R V
Bond E C

Boston Geoffrey
Bowhill A H
Brett C
Brett J W
Bransby R W
Brownham K A
Buck C H
Bullen L
Bunn R
Burton E G
Butler C H
Bunn R W C
Burrows H W

Cadge B J
Campling R
Campling S R
Cannell Wm
Carter H W
Carter B T
Case G E
Cattermole A H
Chamberlin G L
Chapman E T
Clarke R A M
Clare R G
Clifton C

Cocks J W
Cohen A
Cole C J
Cole W
Cook D S
Cousins T E
Crook G G
Crotch J A
Cubitt B B
Cutler D

Daplyn W G
Daniels L M
Daniels R A
Davies J F
Davis L
Daynes C W
Denny G D
Denmark A G
Dennington W
Dixon J A
Doe S J
Doggett W A
Dorman E J
Dunham W
Dunton S G
Durrant B H
Durrant S F
Durrant P R
Dye A S

Eastwood W W R
Edwards H
Elleston -
Ellison G
Enright P A
Everitt J B
Everitt E W
Evison C T
Ewing J H

Finch P
Fildes H
Frost B J

Garnham B

Garnham C J
Gaymer E J
Gaymer W D
Gearch R E
George P F
George W T
Gedge H
Gifford H B
Gibson A
Glover M H
Goffin H G
Golden h A
Gostling G F
Goulder R C
Goulder J L
Green V F
Grice E J
Grimswade H M
Green Dr A

Harman G D
Hansell W E
Hardy A E
Harrison J
Harrison G
Hale F W
Hale T H
Hale F J
Harrowven B
Hase A G
Hastings S R
Haward F
Hawes A
Hemnell R J
Hindle C
Hindle Jack
Hide W J
Hide W J
Holmes H
Holt S W
Hook H J B
Hornigold W G
Hill S G
Hubbard H
Hubbard J J
Hunt W J

Ives W S
Ives C M V

Jackson L E
Jarvis W
Jarrold W
Jeary P L
Johnson C H

Keefe C H
King E
Kirby C E
Kirby F A
Kenny D S
King K J A
Knivett W

Lain C W
Lain A E
Langham H
Larking R C
Larking C G
Lawrence J H
Leeds F E
Leeds S A
Little K J
Lockett G J W
Lovatt L M

Mackenzie —
Mansfield P R
Martin W H
Mason C E
Mattock T
Matthewson Dr
May R
Mays G R
Manning A J
Melton G G
Mills H W
Mitchell H
Mitchell O F
Moll R C
Money B E
Morgan Dr B
Moore B C

Moore E W
Moore R A
Morris R H
Morris D G
Morse C J
Muirhead R C
Murrell J S

Neave J A
Nevett R B
Neville R H A
Norton C
Nunn F
Nunn E G

Owens Dr J H

Padgett A J B
Palmer L S
Palmer J L
Parfrement H W
Parker M G
Paston E A
Parker E H
Paul W S
Paul D H
Pearson H R
Pegg S
Pegg G
Perfitt L W
Peacock S G
Pearse F L
Phillippo A V
Pick S G
Pillow H MS
Phipps P H
Pilch R G
Pilch W F
Poll C H
Polly R H
Porrett G L
Potter A
Pye H

Quinton —

Ramsey R J
Ralph H E
Ransome C T
Reeve C F
Revell R S
Rigby T E
Riley F C
Roberts H
Rose W J
Royal C
Rout S
Rudd H
Rudd B H
Ryall J H

Sale E W
Sampson A J
Savage W H
Savage A C
Sawford A D C
Saunders F W
Sayer W G
Scarles E H
Scott W G
Sewell E S
Sidney J A
Smith W H E
Sparls T W
Smith E
Smith F
Smith W H
Staniforth L H
Starling G
Starling W L
Stannard D F
Stevens G S
Stevenson G H
Stewart R E
Stockings E C
Stone R W
Stubbs A

Talbot C A
Talbot P H
Taylor A E
Tennant W L
Thackery W
Thayne H
Thompson J W
Thrower J H
Thurgar R W
Tillett A W
Tillott J H
Treglown G B
Trollope A C
Tuddenham —
Tyrrell H E

Utting K G
Utting O K

Wakelin D A
Walsh L W
Ward H B
Walpole A R
Westgate S W G
Websdale G R
Weyer S W
Wharton L
White H J
Whittle A G
Wigg R
Wilson G W
Winfield R A
Winter A C
Wire R B
Wisken J E
Winter S S
Williamson W W
Wood, Henry
Wood A F
Wood R G
Woodhouse J C
Worrell G H
Wright R T

Further Reading

Abbot, Patrick, *The British Airship at War* (1989)

Anon, *The Leaf and the Tree – the story of Boulton and Paul 1897-1947* (1947)

Bird, Christopher, *Silent Sentinels: the story of Norfolk's fixed defences during the twentieth century* (1999)

Braithwaite, David, *Savage of King's Lynn, Inventor of machines and merry-go-rounds* (1975)

Carew, Tim, *The Royal Norfolk Regiment* (1991 edition)

Clayton, Eric G., *The First 100 Years of Telephones Viewed from Norwich* (1980)

Edwards, Bertram, *The Burston School Strike* (1974)

Gurney-Read, Joyce, *Trades and Industries of Norwich* (1988)

Kinsey, Gordon, *Pulham Pigs: the history of an airship station* (1988)

Lane, Michael R., *The Story of the St Nicholas Works: a History of Charles Burell and Sons Ltd* (1994)

Richards, George, *Lasting Impressions – the History of a Norwich Dental Practice* (1993)

Stokes, Sir Wilfred, *A short history of the East Anglian Munitions Committee 1914-1918* (nd)

Wightman, Clare, *More than Munitions – Women, Work and the Engineering Industries 1900-50* (1999)

Zamoyska, Betka, *The Burston Rebellion* (1985)

Notes

1. To Go for a Soldier – or not?, pp.1-26

1. *Eastern Daily Press* (hereafter *EDP*), 8 August 1914.
2. NRO, MC 2165/1/16.
3. *EDP*, 14, 31 August 1914.
4. *EDP*, 1 September 1914.
5. *Norwich Mercury* (hereafter *NM*), 12 August 1914.
6. *Carrow Works Magazine*, vol.VIII, no.1, October 1914, p.10.
7. *EDP*, 6 January 1915.
8. Davage, Mike, *Canary Citizens* (1994), *passim*.
9. NRO, MC 166/114/1.
10. NRO, MC/257/1.
11. Simkins, Peter, *Kitchener's Army – the Raising of the New Armies 1914-6* (1988), p.207.
12. NRO, MC 156/3.
13. Mansfield, p.28.
14. NRO, MC/257/1.
15. *EDP*, 16 November 1914.
16. NRO, MC 2165/2/36.
17. NRO, MC 166/37/19.
18. Simkins, *op. cit.*, p.302.
19. NRO, MC 651/9.
20. *EDP*, 12 July 1916, *NM*, 2 June 1917.
21. *EDP*, 6 January 1916.
22. NRO, MC 156/25.
23. NRO, N/TC 1/58.
24. *EDP*, 14 April, 5 May, 9 Aug 1916.
25. *NM*, 1 July 1916; *Eastern Evening News* (hereafter *EN*) 9, 12 June 1916.
26. *NM*, 15 July 1916.
27. NRO, N/TC 28/31.
28. *EN*, 19 June 1916.
29. *EN*, 20 June 1916.
30. NRO, MC 1623.
31. Pearce, Cyril, *Comrades in Conscience* (2001), pp.181, 182.
32. *NM*, 5 July 1916.
33. *EDP*, 9 May 1916.
34. *EDP*, 1 August 1916.
35. Pearce, p.203; Wasley, Gerald, *Devon in the Great War* (2000), p.109.
36. NRO, C/ED 16/9; *NM*, 9 June 1917.
37. *EDP*, 12 December 1933.
38. *NM*, 24 November 1919.
39. *EDP*, 29, 31 March 1956; Meeres, F., *George and Dorothy* (forthcoming).

2. The Face of Battle, pp.27-62

1. Carew, Tim, *The Royal Norfolk Regiment* (1991 edition).
2. *EDP*, 3 September 1914.
3. *EDP*, 27 October 1914.
4. *Carrow Works Magazine*, vol.VIII, no.3 (April, 1915), p.89.
5. *NM*, 15 May, 7 July 1915.
6. NRO, UPC 150/55.
7. NRO, C/ED 67/6.
8. NRO, MC 643/5/18.
9. NRO, MC 947/1.
10. NRO, MC 789/1.
11. *EDP*, 6 January 1916.
12. NRO, MOT 111.
13. NRO, MC 651/16.
14. NRO, BUL 16/73.
15. *Carrow Works Magazine*, vol.XI, no.2 (January 1918), p.52.
16. *Ibid.*, p.53.
17. NRO, MC 81/31.
18. NRO, NEV 7/71.
19. NRO, MC 818/3.
20. *Carrow Works Magazine*, vol.XI, no.3 (April 1918), p.80.
21. NRO, MC 81/32/2.
22. NRO, MC 156/8.
23. NRO, MOT 111.
24. NRO, MC 117/3.

25. *Carrow Works Magazine*, vol.IX, no.2, January 1916, p.51.
26. *Ibid.*, p.53.
27. *Ibid.*, p.53.
28. NRO, PD 190/104.
29. Acle Branch, British Legion: *Not Just Names in Stone* (2003).
30. NRO, MC 643/5/7.
31. NRO, UPC 188.
32. NRO, COR 3/1/4.
33. Narborough Aircraft Research Group: The Great Government Aerodrome (2000).
34. NRO, MC 166/37/4.
35. *NM*, 26 May 1917.
36. NRO, MC 2254/129.
37. NRO, MC 2254/134.
38. NRO, COR 3/1/4.
39. *NM*, 13 January 1917.
40. NRO, PD 85/94.
41. *NM*, 9 June 1917; *EDP*, 21 September 1917.
42. NRO, MC 510/1.

3. The Healing Game: Nursing Work at the Front, pp.63-85
1. *EDP*, 10 May 1915.
2. *NM*, 15 May 1915.
3. NRO, MC 947/1.
4. *EDP*, 27 September 1917.
5. NRO, UPC 188.
6. NRO, MC 634/81-4.
7. NRO, MC 166/113/20.
8. *EDP*, 1 April 1918.
9. *Carrow Works Magazine,* vol.IX, no.1 (October 1915), pp.12-13.
10. NRO, MC 2165/1/17; MC 2165/2/32.
11. NRO, MC 31/69/1.
12. NRO, NNH 64.
13. NRO, SAH 340.
14. *EN*, 28 June 1916.
15. *Carrow Works Magazine*, vol.VIII, no.4 (July 1915), p.141.
16. *NM*, 19 May 1917.
17. *EDP*, 27 October 1914.
18. Gliddon, Gerard, *The Aristocracy and the Great War* (2002), p.260.
19. Bujak, P., *Attleborough, The Evolution of a Town* (1990), p.31.
20. NRO, UPC 188.
21. NRO, BR 209/13.
22. NRO, MC 84/204.
23. Knight, C.E., *The Auxiliary Hospitals of the British Red Cross Society and St John Ambulance in Norfolk 1914-1919* (1989).

24. NRO, MC 117/3.
25. NRO, MC 643/16.
26. NRO, MC 510/1.
27. NRO, MC 643/16.
28. NRO, MC 166/114/1.
29. Hales, Jane, *A Tale of the Norfolk Red Cross* (1970), p.12; Crease, C.M. and Carpenter, S.C., *Before Your Time – Medical Matters* (1997), p.13.

4. The Home Front: War Comes to Norfolk, pp.86-100
1. NRO, UPC 62.
2. Hedges, Boon, Meeres, *Yarmouth is an Antient Town* (2001), p.71.
3. NRO, MC 561/122.
4. NRO, PD 374/83.
5. NRO, UPC 188.
6. Fiddian, Val, ed., *Salthouse, the Story of a Norfolk Village* (2003), p.90.
7. Rutledge, Paul, ed., 'William Harbet's Diary', in *Yarmouth Archaaeology* (1989), p.49.
8. *EDP*, 22 January 1915.
9. NRO, Y/TC 90/.
10. NRO, UPC 188.
11. *NM*, 5 February 1916.
12. NRO, MC 1933/12.
13. *NM*, 29 April 1916.
14. NRO, MC 81/26/405.
15. NRO, MS 21382.
16. NRO, MC 266/1.
17. NRO, MC 2165/1/17; MC 2165/2/26.
18. *EN*, 22 June 1916.
19. Larn, R. and B., *Shipwreck Index of the British Isles, vol.3: the East Coast of England* (1997), Norfolk chapter.
20. *EN*, 1 May 1916.
21. NRO, UPC 188.

5. The Home Front: Living and Working on the Farm, pp.101-134
1. *NM*, 12 August 1914.
2. *NM*, 8 January 1916.
3. NRO, PD 445/24.
4. *EN*, 6 May 1916.
5. *EDP*, 25 July 1917.
6. NRO, C/C 10/16.
7. *NM*, 24 January 1917.
8. NRO, C/C 10/17.
9. Gurney-Read, Joyce, *Trades and Industries of Norwich* (1988), pp.43, 68.
10. Wightman, Clare, *More Than Munitions – Women, Work and the engineering Industries* (1999), pp.47-62.

11. NRO, N/TC 1/58.
12. *NM*, 24 January 1917.
13. For example, Braybon, Gail and Summerfield, *Penny Out of the Cage: Women's Experiences in the World Wars* (1987). Despite this minor quibble, I strongly recommend this book.
14. *EDP*, 10 September 1917.
15. Lane, Michael, *The Story of the St Nicholas Works – a History of Charles Burrell and Sons Ltd* (1994), p.275.
16. HANSARD, 15 August 1916.
17. Clayton, Eric, *The First 100 Years of Telephones Viewed from Norwich* (1980), p.63.
18. Gourvish, T., *Norfolk Beers From English Barley: the story of Steward and Patteson 1793-1963* (1987).
19. *NM*, 14 October 1916.
20. *NM*, 23 September 1916.
21. *NM*, 6 January 1917.
22. *NM*, 12 August 1914.
23. *NM*, 15 August 1914.
24. NRO, MC 2043/37/1 – *Holt, Melton Constable and Wells Post* (hereafter *HP*), 15 December 1916.
25. *EDP*, 20 September 1917.
26. *EDP*, 10 January 1918.
27. *EDP*, 21 September 1917.
28. NC, 21 December 1917.
29. *NM*, 28 October 1917.
30. NC, 6 July 1917.
31. *Carrow Works Magazine*, vol.VIII, no.1, October 1914, p.20.
32. *NM*, 13, 20 January 1917; NRO, N/TC 1/58.
33. NRO, MC 156/9.
34. *NM*, 12 May 1917.
35. *NM*, 23 May 1917.
36. *EDP*, 5 April 1918.
37. NRO, MC 630/31.
38. *EDP*, 9 February 1918.
39. Rutledge, Paul, *op. cit.*
40. NRO, MOT 111.
41. *EDP*, 18 February 1918.
42. *EDP*, 21 February 1918.
43. Winter, J.M., *The Great War and the British People* (1985), p.157.
44. *NM*, 14 July 1915.
45. NRO, N/TC 1/58.
46. NRO, MC 31/69/1.
47. NRO, MC 156/3.
48. *EDP*, 6 January 1915.
49. *EDP*, 9 March 1916.
50. *NM*, 23 August 1916.
51. *EDP*, 30 January 1918.
52. NRO, MC 2043/38/1, *HP*, 22 June 1916.
53. *NM*, 12 May 1915.
54. *Diss Express*, 30 October 1914.
55. Crease and Carpenter, *op. cit.* p.14.
56. NRO, HEN 43; MC 655.
57. NRO, MC 156/8; *EDP*, 7 March 1917.
58. NRO, D/ED 23/11.
59. *EDP*, 8 May 1915.
60. *EDP*, 1 April 1918.
61. NRO, PD 238/124.

6. I Spy Strangers, pp.135-144

1. *EDP*, 2 September 1914.
2. *Carrow Works Magazine*, vol.VII, no.2 (January 1915), p.66.
3. *EDP*, 19 July 1916.
4. *East Anglian Magazine*, January 1958.
5. *NM*, 12 August 1914.
6. *EDP*, 16 November 1914.
7. *EDP*, 6 January 1915.
8. *NM*, 20 January 1917.
9. *EDP*, 3 September 1917.
10. NRO, MC 643/4/14; *EDP*, 19 May 1915.
11. *EDP*, 5 February 1916.
12. *EDP*, 7 and 9 March 1916.
13. NRO, C/C 10/15, 16.
14. NC 6 July 1917; *EDP*, 27 July 1917.
15. NRO, MC 2043/38/1; *HP*, 22 June 1917.
16. NRO, PD 108/41.

7. Four Case Studies, pp.145-166

1. Public Record Office, soldiers' papers, regimental diary.
2. NRO, MC 643 – the Hewetson family letters and papers.
3. NRO, MC 655 – the papers of George Roberts; *NM*, 11 November 1919; Meeres, Frank, *George and Dorothy* (forthcoming).
4. NRO, PD 199/33; MC 1105/1; DCN 24/12; *EDP* October 1915-March 1916; *The Times*, 3 November 1915.

8. The End, pp.167-177

1. NRO, MC 1623/1.
2. NRO, MC 651/19.
3. NRO, MC 643/13/21.
4. NRO, MC 156/8; *EDP*, 16 August 1921.
5. Richards, G., *Lasting Impressions – the History of a Norwich Dental Practice* (1993).
6. NRO, MC 2019/27.
7. NRO, MC 497/3.
8. Pevsner, N. and Wilson, B., *The Buildings of*

England – Norwich and North East Norfolk
(1997).
9. NRO, MC 643/17/42.
10. Winter, *op. cit.*, p.73.

9. We Shall Remember Them, pp.178-194
1. Norfolk Roll of Honour; Norwich Roll of
Honour; NRO, DCN 147/1 is a list of the
fallen arranged by parish, drawn up for the
Cathedral Book of Remembrance.

2. *EDP*, 20 September 2003.
3. NRO, MC 31/14/21; NC 13 July 1917.
4. NRO, DN/CON 123, Billingford; PD 514/
53.
5. NRO, PD 553/34.
6. NRO, DN/CON 123, Cromer.
7. NRO, Y/TC 90/47.
8. NRO, MC 578/10.
9. NRO, MC 457/2.

Index

Figures in **bold** refer to illustration page numbers.